RAC

FARMHOUSE
ACCOMMODATION
GREAT BRITAIN & IRELAND

Sliders Farm, Uckfield

Published by RAC Publishing, RAC House,
Bartlett Street, South Croydon, CR2 6XW

© RAC Motoring Services Ltd 1994

ISBN 0 86211 306 7

A CIP catalogue record for this book is available from
the British Library

Design by Chuck Goodwin
Farmhouse Fare by Susannah Perry
Photographs by David Burton
Cartography by RAC Publishing
Data management by West One Publishing
Printed and bound in Spain by Grafo S.A, Bilbao
Cover picture Hyning Cottages, Kendal

Advertising Managers:
West One Publishing,
104 New Bond Street, London W1Y 9LG
Tel: 0171-493 4769

Contents

DIRECTORY OF FARMS
Arranged alphabetically in county order

About this guide

In this book, you will find details of nearly 2,000 farms throughout Great Britain and Ireland where visitors are welcomed, either for a stay in the farmhouse or on a self-catering basis.

The arrangement of farms by county should help you find one in your chosen holiday area. Within each county, farms are divided into those offering bed and breakfast (often with an evening meal as well) and those with converted farm buildings and cottages for self-catering holidays.The farms are arranged alphabetically by place; some, of course are in isolated areas, so are listed under the nearest town. The entry will give a clear indication of how to find the farm.

The maps at the back of the guide show the location of all the farms listed, and the index of farms lists them under their nearest towns, for easy reference.

CHOOSING YOUR FARM

The type of farm and the part of the country you choose to visit will depend on the holiday you have in mind. A farm is the perfect base from which to take part in a wide variety of outdoor activities, and this may well affect your decision We hope we have provided all the information you need to choose your holiday, but if you are unsure about anything at all, check with the farm before you book.

Ginger Tamworth pigs at Park Farm

BOOKING

As a general rule, it is necessary to book your farm break, even out of peak season. When you book, check whether you need to arrive at any specific time, and what the arrangements are concerning meals, to avoid any confusion once you are there. A deposit is usually payable in advance, which will be deducted from the total bill, and you should confirm when and how payment should be made.

CANCELLATIONS

Should you, for any reason, cancel, fail to take up the accommodation or leave earlier than planned, your deposit may be forfeited, and an additional payment may be demanded if the accommodation cannot be re-let for the booked period.

COMPLAINTS

Should you have any cause for complaint at any farm featured in this guide, speak to the owners as soon as the problem arises. This gives them a opportunity to put it right and you the chance to enjoy your stay. However, if you are still dissatisfied after making your complaint, write to us at the address below.

While we cannot take responsibility for the way in which farmhouses are run, we can ensure that we include in our guide only those farms that maintain proper standards.

Farmhouse Accommodation,
RAC Motoring,
PO Box 100,
Bartlett Street, South Croydon,
Surrey CR2 6XW.

RURAL ATTRACTIONS

You will find some ideas of places to visit with a farming theme listed at the end of each county section.

EXPLANATION OF AN ENTRY

The farms are listed alphabetically by country, county and town. Within each county, all those establishments offering bed and breakfast appear before the self-catering listings.

SAMPLE ENTRY
(fictitious)

---

❶ BENTLEY   4 A2 **❷**

❸ Cordys Farm   Long Lane, Bentley   RAC
01394-123456   Jane Doe **❹**

❺ This attractive Victorian farmhouse sits within 600 acres of undulating arable and pasture land. Recently renovated to accommodate every modern comfort, from en-suite facilities to a covered swimming pool, the house has lost none of its charm and character. There are ground floor rooms suitable for the disabled. Pony trekking, fishing, sailing near by. From the A234, take the Bentley–Chisholm road south. The farm is clearly signposted.

❻ Open Mar – Nov
❽ 4 bedrs (1 twin sh/wc; 2 double ba/wc; 1 family) 1ba, 1wc ☎ (4) ⓬ 🏠 ⋔ ♛♛♛
£ B&B dy £15-20, wk £90-£125, EM £8.50,
❿ HB wk from £140, ☎ rates.

---

❶ The towns and villages are listed in alphabetical order within each county.

❷ The map references for each town refer to the map page and square in the map section at the end of the book. Use the directions in the text for guidance only. Farms are often in isolated positions some distance from the nearest town or village, so always request detailed directions from the farms when booking.

❸ The establishment's name, address and telephone number are given in full. The telephone numbers include the new codes incorporating an additional digit after the first zero. These have been in use since August 1994, and the old codes will no longer be functional after April 1995. When telephoning Ireland from the UK, remember to prefix the listed number with the country code – 010 353 – plus the relevant county code.

❹ The name of the owner/proprietor is given where appropriate.

❺ Descriptions of farms vary in length; they are to give readers an idea of the style of the farms and should in no way be taken as comprehensive. They will generally indicate the facilities, local attractions and directions to the farm.

❻ Opening details: Many establishments are open all year, some close for short periods, i.e. Christmas. Where an establishment indicates the months in which it is open, these are inclusive.

❼ RAC
RAC appointed farmhouses have been inspected and are members of the RAC Hotel Appointments Scheme.

❽ Accommodation
The number of bedrooms is given, followed by details of en-suite and shared facilities.

❾ Symbols
A full explanation of the symbols used in the guide is provided on page 6 and on the inside front cover.

☎   Children welcome; where restrictions exist, the minimum age appears in brackets.

⓬ In the owners' opinions, farms with this symbol are suitable for disabled guests. However, to ensure every particular requirement is met, it is advisable to check before booking.

🏠 Some establishments are happy to provide pack lunches and/or afternoon tea on request.

⋔ Dogs may be restricted to certain areas; it is always advisable to check before booking.

✗ No smoking throughout the farmhouse. Where this symbol does not appear, smoking may be restricted to certain areas; it is always advisable to check before booking.

♛ ⚑ Farms registered with the English, Welsh or Scottish Tourist Boards are listed with their crown rating if offering bed and breakfast accommodation, or with a key rating if offering self-catering accommodation. In Ireland, some farmhouses are registered with the Borde Failte, and this is shown in full.

🔟 Prices

B&B If an establishment only indicates one price, this should be taken as the minimum price per person. If a range of prices appears, these denote the minimum and maximum price per person, unless otherwise stated, and are based on low and high season, single and sharing, and the quality of the accommodation. Some establishments also provide weekly rates (WR), and weekly rates with evening meal – WR/D.

D Average prices for evening meals are listed where applicable.

Self catering These prices are weekly rates for the accommodation, regardless of the size of the party.

The prices quoted here are forecasts made by the owners of what they expect to charge in 1995. As they have to be set well in advance, there may be changes, and it is advisable to check with the owner before booking.

SYMBOLS

	ENGLISH	FRANÇAIS	DEUTSCH
♣RAC	RAC inspected farm	chambres à la ferme classement RAC	Bauernhaus mit RAC-Klassifizierung
♿	facilities for the disabled	aménagements pour handicapés	Einrichtungen für Behinderte
�	children welcome (minimum age)	enfants bienvenus (âge minimum)	Kinder wilkommen (mindestalter)
🐕	dogs permitted by arrangement	chiens admis	Hunde erlaubt
🚭	no smoking anywhere in farmhouse	défense de fumer	Nicht rauchen
🍱	packed lunch and/or afternoon tea available	possibilité de déjeuner à emporter ou thé de cinq heures	Lunch-Paket und/oder Abendbrot erhältlich
👑	Tourist Board rating – bed and breakfast	classement tourisme – chambre et petit déjeuner	Tourismus Kategorie – Übernachtung mit Frühstück
🍴	Tourist Board rating – self-catering	classement tourisme – facilités pour cuisiner	Tourismus Kategorie – für Selbstversorger
B&B	bed and breakfast per person per day	chambre et petit déjeuner par personne par jour	Übernachtung mit Frühstück pro Person pro Tag
WR	weekly rate	prix par semaine	Wochengebühr
D	evening meal	dîner	Abendessen
WR/D	bed, breakfast and evening meal per person per week	prix demi-pension par personne par semaine	Halbpension pro Person pro Woche
sh	shower	douche	Dusche
cc	credit cards	cartes de crédit	Kreditkarten
☕	light refreshments (places to visit)		
✕	restaurant (places to visit)		
🛍	shop (places to visit)		

Farmhouse Fare

Park Farm, Earsham, near Bungay in Suffolk

Bobbie Watchorn and her husband, Simon, live at Park Farm in Earsham, just outside Bungay in Suffolk, with their children, William, Jim and Alice. While Simon farms the 589 acres of arable land, Bobbie is busy with farmhouse visitors, a business which is renowned for warm hospitality and superb food.

The handsome redbrick farmhouse, built in 1870, is set among green fields with woods behind. There is a traditional country garden on one side and flocks of ducks, turkeys and chickens on the other. Inside, the farmhouse is pretty, fresh and very comfortable; the atmosphere welcoming and informal. Family members do not hide away, but go about their daily business in an unobtrusive way, which leaves the guests at their ease.

Bobbie Watchorn is a farmhouse cook in the best possible tradition. She takes the finest ingredients, wherever possible from the farm or the garden, and cooks them in ways that combine tradition with imagination, so that the flavours and textures are enjoyed to the full. There is nothing pretentious or fussy about her cooking, but neither is it in any way dull; in short, it represents the best of British home cooking and is very much what people come to the country to enjoy.

The kitchen, which looks out onto the garden, is spacious and attractive. Mrs Watchorn designed it herself when she and Simon came to Park Farm five years ago. Knowing that she would be using it for her business, she consulted the Environmental Health officer before employing a local firm of kitchen fitters. She is justifiably very happy with the result which is both eminently practical and unmistakably 'country'. Mrs Watchorn uses the lovely old Aga for most of her cooking, but is in no sense shy of modern technology and has a electric cooker and a microwave which she uses when the occasion demands. The kitchen is decorated with playful farmyard themes : the clock is in the shape of a pig and the egg basket is a white china duck.

Both dinner and breakfast are served in the light and airy dining room, with its sweeping views of the Waveney valley. The decor reflects the same combination of tradition and innovation that is so successful in Mrs Watchorn's food: over the fireplace there is a beautiful 17th-century map of the farm lands, a traditional English dinner service is displayed on an old-fashioned Welsh dresser, while the walls and floor are decorated with delightful stencilled floral patterns, designed by Mrs Watchorn herself. Helped by girls from the village Mrs Watchorn

Bobbie Watchorn in the dining room

serves dinner in a friendly yet undistracting way, with the aim of fostering a sense of warm conviviality among the guests. The atmosphere is homely and comfortable, as if you were having a dinner party with friends rather than going to a restaurant. The arrangements for breakfast are intended to be as relaxed and informal as possible; guests are invited to serve themselves to cereals, including home-made muesli, while Mrs Watchorn prepares traditional English breakfasts to order.

For £12 per person, guests are served a three-course evening meal including coffee, chocolates and a glass of wine. Mrs Watchorn agrees the dinner menu with her guests beforehand and plans what she cooks to suit their preferences. She is very careful to ensure that the guests are able to relax and enjoy the meal, so she avoids anything that requires precise timing, such as a soufflé or elaborate restaurant-style dishes. Instead she chooses roasts, casseroles and pies, which are more adaptable as well as being thoroughly delicious. The puddings are lavish and indulgent, just the way you want them. The quality of her food won her a rare 10 out of 10 from the English Tourist Board, while it is clear from the visitors' book that her personal style of entertaining is a winning formula : "wonderful hospitality", "excellent in every way" – the verdict is unanimous.

Mrs Watchorn is an entirely self-taught cook. In addition to great flair, she has a natural understanding of what makes for good food, combined with the competence and down-to-earth practicality you would expect of someone who lives and works on a farm. The results are stunning. She combines her ingredients with confidence and imagination, imparting an original touch to traditional themes. Starters include Seafood Pudding, a kind of savory bread and butter pudding made with prawns and fish (see recipe below) and a warm salad of fresh garden vegetables with bacon and a walnut oil dressing. For her main courses she often uses duck, chicken or pork from the farm. She might bake a duck whole in a Chinese-style plum sauce or perhaps casserole it with green peppercorns and white wine. Her puddings are irresistible: a raspberry fudge pie made with a sweet hazelnut pastry, a toffee filling and fresh raspberry and cream topping. Crow's Nest Pie is a meringue nest filled with chocolate and coffee mousse topped with toasted hazelnuts and delicate quills of caraque (shaved) chocolate.

Listening to Mrs Watchorn describe her food, it is clear that she pays meticulous attention to the quality of her ingredients. Wherever possible, she uses produce from her farm and garden. She is proud to use meat from the animals reared on the farm and does not shy away from telling the guests where the meat comes from; indeed she and Simon consider that informing their guests about

Some of the food which won Bobbie Watchorn highest praise from the English Tourist Board

Bobbie and daughter Alice, feeding the turkeys and hens

farming techniques is an important part of their job. It is clear for all to see that the animals are in the peak of health and kept in ideal conditions, fully free-range with fields to roam in as well as shelter, with a full and varied diet.

She has chosen to rear traditional breeds such as Norfolk Black turkeys, Aylesbury ducks and Buff Orpington chickens because of the quality of their meat and eggs, and not for their fancy plumage. Both duck eggs and turkey eggs are richer than hens eggs as well as being larger. In her recipes Mrs Watchorn uses three duck or turkey eggs to every four size-3 hen's eggs. Becuase the birds are raised in such ideal conditions and the eggs used are so fresh, the yolks are bright yellow and the flavour superb.

The pork from the Watchorns' Ginger Tamworth pigs has an exceptional flavour and produces superb crackling. The finest back meat is cured by Mr Jerry (who, incidentally, counts Delia Smith among his customers) in nearby Peasenhall, to make bacon of incomparable quality. The sausages for breakfast are also made from the farm's Ginger Tamworth meat by the local butcher who adds the bare minimum of seasonings to produce a fabulous, meaty flavour and texture. Mrs

Watchorn likes to cook seasonal ingredients and makes full use of the produce from her beautiful walled kitchen garden. In the summer, in addition to raspberries, strawberries and blackcurrants, she also grows figs and even melons which she combines with grapes to make a light and refreshing starter dressed with home-made raspberry vinegar and fresh mint. She produces a wonderful selection of vegetables, including runner beans, courgettes and carrots, which she either steams or stir-fries to retain maximum flavour and goodness. She also has an enviable collection of herbs – from the familiar parsley, bay and thyme to more unusual borage, tarragon and chervil – all of which she uses with typical confidence to subtle effect. In the autumn she picks blackberries from the hedgerows and gathers wild mushrooms, such as horse mushrooms and puffballs, from the fields, although she is always careful to consult the guests before including them in any dish.

She is also a skilled and careful shopper, who has built up a good relationship with local suppliers, such as the fishmongers in Bungay and Norwich markets as well as with her local supermarket who supply goods of the excellent quality that she demands. She will go to great lengths to get the ingredients she wants: the best bread she knows is from Baines Bakery in Uppingham in Rutland where she used to live, so whenever she visits, she will bring back 50 or 60 loaves and freeze them so that her guests can enjoy it too. She offers the delicious dry white wine from the Rookery Farm Vineyard, which is on the Earsham Estate, no more than a few miles away.

Friends also supply ingredients, such as delicious, fully ripe tomatoes, while her home-smoked trout, which she marinades overnight in herbs, brown sugar and salt before smoking over applewood chips, is made from the freshest fish caught locally by friends.

To cook successfully for farmhouse visitors is a demanding and skilled job. Mrs Watchorn draws on her many talents and the resources available to her with great imagination and versatility. She exudes an air of confident practicality and displays great sensitivity to the needs of her guests. There is a real sense that she loves what she is doing that comes through not only in the quality of her cooking but also in the way she welcomes her guests. Nothing could be more appealing in a farmhouse cook.

Seafood Pudding

This is a starter that combines ingredients from the farm, such as the herbs and eggs, with seafood from the nearby Suffolk coast. Mrs Watchorn emphasises that it is a very adaptable dish: for example, you could use ham and leeks in place of the seafood.

The quantities given are for six.

Seafood mixture

1/4 pint mayonnaise

1 small stalk celery chopped fine

1 tablespoon finely chopped onion

3 tablespoons finely chopped herbs – ideally parsley, tarragon, chervil and chives

3/4 – 1 lb mixed seafood cooked – prawns, mussels, crabsticks and squid (flaked cooked white fish, such as cod or haddock, can be used to replace some of the seafood)

3 tablespoons grated parmesan

Pudding

Plenty of white bread, crusts removed and medium sliced

butter

4 eggs (size 3)

9 fl oz milk

9 fl oz single cream

salt

3-5 shakes Tabasco sauce, according to taste

6 oz grated cheddar (not too strong)

One large oven-proof service dish or six individual ones

If possible, start well before serving time to allow the bread to absorb the cream and egg mixture as much as possible.

For the seafood mixture:
Mix all the ingredients together in a large bowl so that the pieces of seafood are evenly coated by the mayonnaise.

For the pudding:
Butter the bread and use half of it to line the serving dish, buttered side down. Fill with seafood mixture and cover with the rest of the slices of bread, buttered side up.

Beat the eggs, milk and cream together, season lightly with salt (remembering that the cheese is salty) and a few drops of Tabasco, according to your taste. Pour this mixture over the puddings, making sure that all the bread slices are properly soaked. If possible, leave the puddings to stand for an hour or so at this point so that the bread soaks up as much as possible of the egg mixture. Sprinkle the cheddar cheese over the top and bake in a medium oven (Gas mark 4/350° F/180°C) for 30-45 minutes until the puddings are puffed and golden .

Serve immediately.

RAC

Advice for foreign visitors
LE GUIDE DU VISITEUR

Climat
Vous savez probablement que le climat anglais est peu fiable et constitue bien souvent un sujet de conversation privilégié pour les britanniques. Les conditions climatiques peuvent varier considérablement d'un jour à l'autre, et il n'est pas rare de voir un soleil éclatant, la pluie, le brouillard et des rafales de vent se succéder au cours d'une même semaine. Tout ce que vous pouvez faire est vous y préparer. Ne vous aventurez jamais de l'autre côté de la Manche sans au moins un chaud pull-over et un imperméable.

Lois réglementant la vente d'alcool
Les pubs sont autorisés à servir de l'alcool de 11 à 23 heures du lundi au samedi, et de 12 à 14 heures 30 et de 19 à 22 heures 30 le dimanche. Bien qu'ils puissent rester ouverts toute la journée pendant le week-end, de nombreux pubs des villages et des petites villes choisissent de fermer l'après-midi. Si vous comptez vous rendre dans un pub bien précis, il est recommandé de vous informer au préalable de ses heures d'ouverture.

Banques
La plupart des grosses agences des principales banques sont ouvertes de 9 heures 30 à 17 heures du lundi au vendredi, et jusqu'à midi le samedi. Les heures d'ouverture des petites agences sont susceptibles d'être plus limitées.

Argent
Avec des coupures de £5, £10 et £20 aujourd'hui toutes de la même taille, l'argent britannique peut parfois susciter une certaine confusion. La clé est la couleur. Retenez donc que les billets de £5 sont bleus, ceux de £10 bruns et ceux de £20 violets. De nombreux vendeurs ont pour instruction de vérifier de temps à autre, voire toujours, que les billets qui leur sont donnés ne sont pas faux. Ne vous sentez pas offensé si cela vous arrive, c'est pratique courante dans tout le pays.

Cartes de crédit
Toutes les principales cartes de crédit sont largement acceptées par les magasins, les stations-service, les hôtels, les restaurants, les théâtres, les cinémas et autres lieux d'intérêt. Vous pouvez également utiliser les guichets automatiques situés à l'extérieur des banques et des grands supermarchés pour retirer de l'argent avec votre carte de crédit.

Poste
Les bureaux de poste sont ouverts de 9 à 17 heures du lundi au vendredi et jusqu'à 12 heures 30 le samedi. Des distributeurs de timbres sont installés à l'extérieur des bureaux de poste, mais exigent bien souvent la monnaie exacte. Vous pouvez également acheter des carnets de quatre ou dix timbres chez la plupart des marchands de journaux.

Magasins
Heures d'ouverture: les magasins sont généralement ouverts de 9 à 17 heures du lundi au samedi. Un jour par semaine peut être réservé à une nocturne, les magasins restant alors ouverts jusqu'à 20 ou 21 heures. Ce n'est toutefois pas là une règle universelle et la situation peut même varier selon la période de l'année. Les magasins de certaines petites villes ont gardé l'habitude de fermer un jour l'après-midi.

Marchés
les marchés ont généralement lieu une ou deux fois par semaine dans la plupart des villes, habituellement le samedi et un autre jour de la semaine. En plus de produits frais, les échoppes peuvent vendre des vêtements, des jouets, des livres, des plantes et de nombreux autres articles.

En cas d'urgence
Si vous devez contacter les services d'urgence, formez le 999 et demandez le service désiré, police, service incendie ou ambulance. Les appels au 999 sont gratuits.

Téléphones
Nos célèbres cabines téléphoniques rouges existent toujours dans certaines régions, mais beaucoup ont été remplacées par des cabines transparentes plus modernes, mais moins typiques. Les téléphones publics acceptent la

plupart des pièces, mais si vous envisagez d'appeler l'étranger, il est préférable d'acheter une carte téléphonique BT verte, disponible chez les marchands de journaux. Vous trouverez des appareils à carte près des téléphones publics à pièces.

Autres appareils publics, les téléphones Mercurycard sont caractérisés par leurs cabines bleu vif. Ils acceptent la plupart des cartes de crédit ou les Mercurycard disponibles dans les principaux bureaux de poste, chez les grands marchands de journaux ou dans des machines situées à proximité de certains téléphones à carte Mercury.

Animaux

N'emmenez aucun animal en vacance en Grande-Bretagne. Les animaux doivent en effet passer plusieurs mois en quarantaine pour éviter l'introduction de la rage dans le pays. Pour emmener un animal, vous devez avoir une licence d'importation, qui peut être obtenue six semaines à l'avance auprès du Ministère de l'Agriculture, de la Pêche et de l'Alimentation — Ministry of Agriculture, Fisheries and Food, Hook Rise South, Tolworth, Surbiton, Surrey KT6 7NF, téléphone 0181-330 4411.

Emporter un animal au Royaume-Uni sans licence est une violation de la loi. Tout animal importé illégalement est susceptible d'être supprimé.

Drogues

Le Royaume-Uni impose des peines sévères contre le trafic de drogue. Veillez à ce que votre bagage soit toujours sous surveillance et ne passez jamais un bagage ou des paquets à la douane pour quelqu'un d'autre.

Automobile

Conduite à gauche

Gardez votre gauche, même en présence de deux ou trois voies, sauf si des panneaux et des marquages routiers indiquent autre chose. Lors des dépassements, reprenez la voie de gauche dès que possible. Ces règles s'appliquent à toutes les routes, y compris aux autoroutes.

Limitations de vitesse

La vitesse maximale sur les autoroutes et les routes à quatre voies est de 110 km/h ou 95 km/h pour les véhicules tractant une remorque ou une caravane. Dans les agglomérations, la vitesse est limitée à 50 km/h pour tous les véhicules.

Routes à une voie

Certaines routes ne sont assez larges que pour un véhicule. Elles sont susceptibles de comprendre des aires de croisement spéciales. Lorsqu'un véhicule se dirige vers vous, arrêtez-vous dans une aire de croisement sur votre gauche ou attendez en face d'une aire de croisement sur votre droite. Chaque fois que vous le pouvez, cédez le passage aux véhicules qui montent. Ne stationnez pas dans les aires de croisement.

Passages pour piétons

Les passages pour piétons sont identifiés par des marquages noirs et blancs et par des poteaux avec des signaux lumineux clignotants oranges. Vous devez vous arrêter si des piétons traversent ou attendent au passage pour piétons. Ne stationnez pas ou ne dépassez pas sur les passages pour piétons, y compris dans la zone marquée d'une ligne en zigzag.

Stationnement

Vous ne devez pas stationner aux endroits où le stationnement est interdit par des lignes jaunes sur le bord de la route. Les périodes d'interdiction de stationner sont indiquées par des panneaux à proximité du trottoir ou à l'entrée d'une zone de stationnement contrôlée. Utilisez toujours un emplacement de stationnement autorisé.

Vous ne devez pas stationner dans un emplacement réservé à des usagers particuliers, tels que les détendeurs d'un insigne orange ou les riverains, sauf si vous êtes autorisé à le faire.

Utilisation de l'avertisseur

Vous ne devez pas utiliser votre avertisseur :
● entre 23 heures 30 et 7 heures dans une agglomération
● lorsque votre véhicule est à l'arrêt, sauf si un véhicule en mouvement représente un danger

Ceintures de sécurité

Vous devez porter une ceinture de sécurité si elle est disponible.

Si vous avez le moindre doute en ce qui concerne le code de la route britannique, vous pouvez vous en procurer un exemplaire publié par HMSO (Her Majesty's Stationery Office), chez la plupart des marchands de journaux, pour 99p.

FÜHRER FÜR BESUCHER

Wetter

Das englische Wetter ist bekanntlich unzuverlässig und ist als Gesprächsthema bei den Einheimischen sehr beliebt. Die Witterungsverhältnisse können von Tag zu Tag au·erordentlich veränderlich sein, und es ist durchaus nicht ungewöhnlich, im Laufe derselben Woche strahlenden Sonnenschein, Regen, Nebel und böigen Wind anzutreffen. Deshalb sollten Sie gewappnet sein und sich nicht ohne mindestens einen warmen Pullover und einen Regenmantel über den Kanal wagen!

Ausschankzeiten

Gaststätten sind während der folgenden Zeiten für den Ausschank alkoholischer Getränke konzessioniert: 11.00 bis 23.00 Uhr an Wochentagen, 12.00 bis 14.30 und 19.00 bis 22.30 Uhr an Sonn- und Feiertagen. Obwohl sie während der Woche den ganzen Tag über geöffnet haben dürfen, ziehen viele Gastwirtschaften in Dörfern und Kleinstädten vor, nachmittags zu schließen. Wenn Sie ein bestimmtes Lokal besuchen möchten, erkundigen Sie sich also am besten vorher nach den öffnungszeiten.

Banken

Die meisten grî·eren Zweigstellen der Großbanken haben montags bis freitags von 9.30 bis 17.00 Uhr und samstags von 9.30 bis 12.00 Uhr geöffnet. Bei kleineren Zweigstellen sind die öffnungszeiten u.U. etwas kürzer bemessen.

Geld

Da die £5-, £10- und £20-Scheine jetzt alle dieselbe Größe haben, ist englisches Geld möglicherweise etwas verwirrend. Das Wichtige ist die Farbe: £5-Scheine sind blau, £10-Scheine sind braun, und £20-Scheine sind lila. In vielen Geschäften ist das Verkaufspersonal angewiesen, einige oder auch alle Banknoten auf Fälschungen zu prüfen. Fühlen Sie sich dadurch bitte nicht beleidigt – diese Art überprüfung ist überall in Großbritannien ganz normal.

Kreditkarten

Alle fährenden Kreditkarten werden weithin in Läden, Tankstellen, Hotels, Restaurants, Theatern, Kinos usw akzeptiert. Außerdem können Sie mit Ihrer Kreditkarte Bargeld an den Geldautomaten erhalten, die außen an Banken und größeren Supermärkten angebracht sind.

Post

Postämter haben montags bis freitags von 9.00 bis 17.00 Uhr und samstags von 9.00 bis 12.30 Uhr geîffnet. Sie können Briefmarken auch an Postamtautomaten ziehen, die aber kein Wechselgeld geben. Außerdem verkaufen die meisten Zeitungshändler Heftchen mit vier bzw zehn Briefmarken.

Einkaufen

Ladenöffnungszeiten: Geschäfte haben allgemein montags bis samstags von 9.00 bis 17.00 geöffnet. Unter Umständen bleiben die Läden an einem Tag in der Woche bis 20.00 oder 21.00 Uhr offen ('late night shopping'), doch dies ist keineswegs überall der Fall und kann auch von der Jahreszeit abhängen. In manchen kleineren Städten haben die Geschäfte noch an einem Tag in der Woche nachmittags geschlossen.

Straßenmärkte: In den meisten Städten wird ein- bis zweimal wöchentlich, gewöhnlich am Samstag und einem anderen Wochentag, Markt abgehalten. Neben frischem Obst und Gemüse werden dort Kleidung, Spielzeug, Bücher, Pflanzen und viele andere Waren angeboten.

In Notfällen

Die Notrufnummer ist 999. Wenn sich die Zentrale meldet, müssen Sie angeben, welchen Hilfsdienst Sie benîtigen: Police (Polizei), Fire (Feuerwehr) oder Ambulance (Krankenwagen). 999-Anrufe sind kostenlos.

Telefonzellen

Unsere berühmten roten Telefonhäuschen sind zwar in manchen Gegenden noch zu sehen, haben aber zum großen Teil modernen, weniger charakteristischen, durchsichtigen Zellen weichen müssen. öffentliche Fernsprecher nehmen die meisten Münzen an, doch wenn Sie Auslandsgespräche führen wollen, kaufen Sie am besten eine grüne BT Phonecard bei einem Zeitungshändler. Auf Telefonkarten ausgelegte Zellen stehen meist neben den Münzfernsprechern.

Alternative öffentliche Fernsprecher sind die leuchtend blauen Mercurycard-Zellen, in denen Sie die meisten Kreditkarten oder aber eine Mercurycard benutzen können. Diese speziellen Telefonkarten sind in Postämtern und führenden Zeitungshandlungen erhältlich; bei manchen Mercurycard-Telefonzellen kann man die Karten auch aus Verkaufsautomaten ziehen.

Tiere

Nehmen Sie kein Haustier mit in den Urlaub nach Großbritannien, da alle Tiere mehrere Monate in Quarantäne gehalten werden, um zu verhindern, da· Tollwut ins Land eingeschleppt wird. Um ein Tier mitbringen zu können, müssen Sie eine Einfuhrerlaubnis haben, die mindestens sechs Wochen im voraus beim Ministry of Agriculture, Fisheries and Food, Hook Rise South, Tolworth, Surbiton, Surrey KT6 7NF, Telefon: 0181-330 4411, zu beantragen ist. Wenn Sie ein Tier ohne diese Erlaubnis nach Großbritannien einführen, machen Sie sich strafbar und müssen außerdem damit rechnen, daß das Tier getötet wird.

Drogen

In Gro·britannien wird der Drogenschmuggel schwer bestraft. Lassen Sie Ihr Gepäck nicht unbeaufsichtigt stehen und bringen Sie nie Gepäckstücke oder Pakete für jemand anderen durch den Zoll.

AUTOFAHREN

Links fahren

Fahren Sie auch auf Straßen mit zwei oder mehr Spuren auf der linken Seite, sofern Verkehrszeichen und Straßenmarkierungen nichts anderes vorschreiben. Wechseln Sie nach dem überholen wieder in die linke Spur, sobald es gefahrlos möglich ist. Dies gilt für alle Staßen einschließlich Autobahnen.

Geschwindigkeitsbegrenzungen

Die Geschwindigkeitsbegrenzung für Personenwagen auf Autobahnen und zwei-spurigen Fahrbahnen ist 113 km/h (70 m/h) bzw. 96 km/h (60 m/h) für Pkw mit Anhänger oder Wohnwagen. Bei einspuriger Fahrbahn ist die Geschwindigkeit für Personenwagen auf 96 km/h und für Pkw mit Anhänger oder Wohnwagen auf 80 km/h (50 m/h) begrenzt. In geschlossenen Ortschaften gilt für alle Personenwagen eine Geschwindigkeits-begrenzung von 48 km/h (30 m/h).

Einspurige Straßen

Manche Straßen sind nur breit genug für ein einziges Fahrzeug. An solchen Straßen gibt es oft spezielle Ausweichstellen. Fahren Sie in eine Ausweichstelle auf der linken Seite oder halten Sie gegenüber einer Ausweichstelle auf der rechten, wenn Sie ein Fahrzeug auf sich zukommen sehen. Lassen Sie bergauf-fahrenden Fahrzeugen nach Möglichkeit die Vorfahrt. Parken Sie nie in Ausweichstellen.

Fußgängerüberwege

Zebrastreifen sind durch schwarze und weiße Straßenmarkierungen und Pfähle mit blink-enden orangefarbenen Signalleuchten gekennzeichnet. Sie müssen halten, wenn sich Fußgänger auf dem überweg befinden oder am Zebrastreifen warten. An Fußgängeräberwegen einschließlich des mit einer Zickzacklinie markierten Bereichs dürfen Sie nicht parken oder überholen.

Parken

Sie dürfen nicht parken, wo Beschränkungen durch gelbe Linien am Fahrbahnrand angezeigt sind. Während welcher Zeiten das Parkverbot besteht, ist auf Schildern am Bordstein bzw am Anfang der Sperrzone angegeben. Benutzen Sie möglichst einen zugelassenen Parkplatz. Sie dürfen nicht auf einem Platz parken, der für bestimmte Benutzer wie Anwohner oder Behinderte mit orangefarbener Plakette reserviert ist, sofern Sie nicht dazu befugt sind.

Hupen

Hupen ist nicht gestattet:
● zwischen 23.30 und 7.00 Uhr in geschlossenen Ortschaften
● wenn das Fahrzeug steht, es sei denn, ein fahrendes Auto stellte eine Bedrohung dar

Sicherheitsgurte

Sie müssen angeschnallt fahren, wenn Ihr Fahrzeug mit Sicherheitsgurten ausgerüstet ist.

Falls Sie irgendwelche Zweifel über die in Großbritannien geltenden Verkehrsregeln haben, können Sie in einer Buchhandlung für 99p ein Exemplar der Straßenverkehrsordnung 'Highway Code' kaufen, die von Her Majesty's Stationery Office (HMSO) herausgegeben wird.

Useful addresses

BRITISH TOURIST AUTHORITY

Tourist Information Centres are located in cities and towns throughout Great Britain with information on places of interest for tourists. These Information Centres are indicated by distinctive 'i' signs placed in their vicinity. The addresses of the National and Regional Tourist Boards are as follows.

English Tourist Board
Head Office: Thames Tower, Black's Road, Hammersmith, London W6 9EL
(written enquiries only)

Scottish Tourist Board
Head Office: 23 Ravelston Terrace, Edinburgh EH4 3EU
Tel: 0131-332 2433
(written and telephone enquiries only)

Wales Tourist Board
Head Office: Brunel House, 2 Fitzalan Road, Cardiff CF2 1UY
Tel: 01222-499909

Northern Ireland Tourist Board
Head Office: St Anne's Court, North Street, Belfast BT1 1ND
Tel: 01232-231221

LONDON OFFICE: 11 Berkeley Street, London W1X 5AD
Tel: 0171-493 0601

Irish Tourist Board (Bord Failte)
Head Office: Baggot St. Bridge, Dublin 2
Tel (00 3531) 2844768

LONDON OFFICE: 150 New Bond Street, London W1Y 0AQ
Tel: 0171-493 3201

Channel Islands
STATES OF GUERNSEY TOURIST COMMITTEE
PO Box 23, White Rock, St Peter Port, Guernsey
Tel: 01481-723552

STATES OF JERSEY TOURISM COMMITTEE
Liberation Square, St Helier, Jersey
Tel: 01534-78000

NATIONAL PARKS

The most beautiful, spectacular and dramatic expanses of country in England and Wales have been given the status of National Parks under the National Parks and Access to the Countryside Act, 1949, in recognition of their national importance. Ten National Parks were established during the 1950s: Brecon Beacons, Exmoor, Dartmoor, Lake District, Northumberland, North York Moors, Peak District, Pembrokeshire Coast, Snowdonia and the Yorkshire Dales. In addition, the Norfolk and Suffolk Broads (The Broads), were established in 1989. Although not a National Park by name, it has equal status to the Parks. The New Forest is also considered by many to be of comparable quality to a National Park and legislation that will provide it with similar protection is currently being drafted.

The essence of each of these areas is in the striking quality and remoteness of much of their scenery, the harmony between activity and nature that they display and the opportunities they offer for suitable forms of recreation. National Parks are 'national' in the vital sense that they are of special value to the whole nation. But designation of an area as a National Park does not affect the ownership of the land. It does not remove from local communities the right to live their own lives, nor does it give the public any right of access.

The 1949 Act also created Areas of Outstanding Natural Beauty. The landscape in these areas is no less beautiful but the opportunities for extensive outdoor recreation are lacking. The following 39 Areas of Outstanding Natural Beauty have been designated:
Anglesey; Arnside and Silverdale; Blackdown Hills; Cannock Chase; Chichester Harbour; Chilterns; Clwydian Range; Cornwall; Cotswolds; Cranborne Chase & West Wiltshire Downs; Dedham Vale; Dorset; East Devon; East Hampshire; Forest of Bowland; Gower Peninsula; High Weald; Howardian Hills; Isles of Scilly; Isle of Wight; Kent Downs; Lincolnshire Wolds Lleyn; Malvern Hills; Mendip Hills; Norfolk Coast; North Devon; North Pennines; Northumberland Coast; North Wessex Downs; Quantock Hills; Shropshire Hills; South Devon; South Hampshire Coast; Suffolk Coast and Heaths; Surrey Hills; Sussex Hills; Sussex Downs; Solwy Coast, Wye Valley.

Although there are no National Parks or Areas of outstanding Natural Beauty in Scotland, there are 40 National Scenic Areas (NSAs), designated in 1980 under the 1972 Town and Country Planning (Scotland) Act, which are given a measure of protection through special development control procedures. Protection of the NSAs is the duty of Scottish Natural Heritage (formed from the merger of the Countryside Commission for Scotland and the Nature Conservancy Council for Scotland in 1992).

Countryside Commission
John Dower House, Crescent Place, Cheltenham, Gloucestershire GL50 3RA
Tel: 01242-521381

The Countryside Council for Wales
Plas Penrhos, Fford Penrhos, Bangor, Gwynedd, LL57 2LQ
Tel: 01248-370444

FOREST PARKS

The Forestry Commission
231 Corstorphine Road, Edinburgh, EH12 7AT
Tel: 0131-334 3303

The Forestry Commission is one of Britain's largest providers of tourist and recreation facilities, attracting over 50 million day-visitors every year and encouraging the public to enjoy the publicly-owned forests in its care through its freedom to roam policy. It also provides for many activities including walking, picnics, mountain biking, orienteering, skiing, field sports, water sports and nature study.

THE NATIONAL TRUST

The National Trust is an independent charity responsible for the preservation of many historic houses, industrial monuments, formal and romantic gardens, nature reserves, open countryside and hundred of miles of Britain's coastline.
Details of the various National Trust activities can be obtained from:

The National Trust
36 Queen Anne's Gate, London SW1H 9AS
Tel: 0171-222 9251

The National Trust, North Wales Office
Trinity Square, Llandudno, Gwynedd LL30 2DE
Tel: 01492-860123

The National Trust, South Wales Office
The King's Head, Bridge Street, Llandeilo, Dyfed SA19 6BB Tel: 01558-822800

The National Trust, Northern Ireland
Rowallane House, Saintfield, Ballynahinch, Co. Down BT24 7LH Tel: 01238-510721

The National Trust for Scotland
5 Charlotte Square, Edinburgh, EH2 4DU
Tel: 0131-226 5922

ENGLISH HERITAGE

Over 350 ancient monuments, buildings and other sites are looked after by English Heritage (formerly known as the Historic Buildings and Monuments Commission). Further details can be obtained from:

English Heritage
Fortress House, 23 Savile Row, London W1X 1AB   Tel: 0171-973 3000

THE COUNTRY CODE

- Enjoy the countryside and respect its life and work
- Guard against all risk of fire
- Keep your dogs under close control
- Keep to the public paths across farmland
- Use gates and stiles to cross fences, hedges and walls
- Leave livestock, crops and machinery alone
- Take your litter home
- Help to keep all water clean
- Protect wildlife, plants and trees
- Take special care on country roads
- Make no unnecessary noise

ENGLAND

AVON

BATH 3F1

Poplar Farm Stanton Prior, Bath BA2
9HX 01761 470382   Mr. Hardwick

Open all year
3 bedrs (1 twin ba/wc; 2 double ba/wc) 1
ba, 2 wc ❦ *Listed-Commended*
£dB&B £30-£40, child rates.

BLAGDON 3E1

Aldwick Court Farm Blagdon, nr
Bristol, BS18 7RF 01934 862305

Open all year
✂

BRISTOL 3E1

Model Farm Norton Hawkfield,
Pensford, Bristol BS18 4HA 01275 832144
Margaret Hussell

A 200 year old farmhouse on a beef and
arable farm. Quietly situated and nestling
under the Dundry Hill. 2 miles off the A37.

Open all year
2 bedrs (1 double; 1 family) 1 ba ❦ 🏠
♨♨
£B&B £18, child rates.

Pool Farm Wick, Bristol BS15 5RL
0117 9372284   Mrs. Wilmott

Open Jan-Dec

2 bedrs (1 twin; 1 family) 1 ba ❦
£B&B £15-£18, child rates.

CHEW MAGNA 3E1

Woodbarn Farm Denny Lane, Chew
Magna BS18 8S2 01275 332599
Mrs. Hasell

Woodbarn Farm stands on the outskirts of the
village of Chew Magna, south of Bristol. This
working mixed farm is only 5 minutes from
the peace and beauty of Chew Valley Lake.
An ideal location for trout-fishing and
birdwatching.

Open Mar-Dec (closed Xmas)
2 bedrs (1 double ba/wc; 1 family sh/wc)
❦(3) ✂ *Listed*
£B&B £17.

CHEWTON MENDIP 3E1

Franklyn's Farm nr Bath, Chewton
Mendip BA3 4NB 01761 241372   Betty
Clothier

Open all year
❦ 🏠 ✂

Pantiles Bathway, Chewton Mendip BA3
4ND 01761 241519   Mr. Hellard

Open all year

PENSFORD 3E1

Valley Farm Sandy Lane, Stanton Drew,
Bristol BS18 4EL 01275 332723 Mrs. Keel

80 acre farm situated in an old village. Good
position for sightseeing, walking and fishing.
Friendly welcome assured. TV in all rooms,
tea & coffee facilities. Close to Bath, Bristol,
Wales and Cheddar.

Open all year
3 bedrs (1 twin ba/wc; 1 double sh/wc; 1
family) 1 ba
£dB&B £30-£36.

TEMPLE CLOUD 3E1

Temple Bridge Farm Temple Cloud, Bristol BS18 5AA 01761 452377Mrs. Wyatt

A 17th century, white farmhouse with old beams, log fires, and a large garden. Central heating, large parking area. Take A4 Bristol Rd from Bath, at roundabout take A39/Wells, 8 miles junction with A37 turn R, farm is ½ mile on R.

Open Jan-Dec
2 family bedrs; 1 ba ☎(2) ♟ ♨*Commended*
£B&B £16-£17, child rates.

SELF CATERING

BRISTOL 3E1

Cleve Hill Farm Ubley, Bristol BS18 6PG 01761 462410 Mrs. Perry

Stone built cottages forming part of farmhouse range. Working dairy farm. Visitors welcome to explore, but please follow 'Country Code' i.e. close gates etc.

Cider House has 2 bedrooms + sofa bed sleeping 6 with washer/dryer and iron. Belters End has 1 bedroom + sofa bed sleeping 5. Facilities for both include elec. cooker, kettle, TV, water heater, parking. A368 E from Ubley through Compton Martin R at 1st crossroads, follow road up hill & straight over Mendip top.

2 units; 3 bedrs ☎ ♟
£Wk £70-£200

PLACES TO VISIT

BATH

Norwood Rare Breeds Survival Farm Bath Road, Norton St Philip, Nr Bath 01373-834356
The only organically certified/approved rare breeds centre in the country. See, touch and feel many rare breeds. Young stock being born all through the season. Farm walk through organically managed farmland.
Location: B3110 from Bath, S to Norton St Philip
Open: 24 Mar-24 Sep, daily 10.30am-18.00pm.
Entrance: adult £3 child £2
OAP/concessions £2.50 WC ♿ ✗ ♌

Rode Bird Gardens
Rode, Nr Bath 01373-830326
Hundreds of exotic birds can be seen in 17 acres of beautiful woodland and flower gardens including a Clematis collection and an ornamental lake.
Location: off the A36 at Woolverton, 10 miles south of Bath.Open all year daily, summer 1000-1800, winter 1000-dusk.
Entrance (1995) Adult £4.10 child £2.10
OAP/concessions £3.60. WC ♿ ✗ ♌

BEDFORDSHIRE

PULLOXHILL 4C1

Pond Farm 7 High Street, Pulloxhill MK45 5HA 01525 712316 Mrs. Tookey

Open all year
3 bedrs (1 twin; 1 double; 1 family) 1 ba, 1 wc ☎ *Listed*
£B&B £14, child rates.

SANDY 4C1

Gransden Lodge Farm Little Gransden, Sandy SG19 3EB 01767 677365 W. M. Cox

A spacious farmhouse on a 860 acre arable farm. All bedrooms contain a colour television, and tea & coffee making facilities. Farmhouse is centrally heated throughout the year. From the A603 go onto the B1046. The farm is located between the villages of Langstone and Little Gransden.

Open all year
3 bedrs (1 twin; 2 family inc 1 ba/wc, 1 sh/wc) 2 ba, 2 wc ☎ ⊞ ♟ ♨♨
£B&B £14-£18, WR £100-£110, child rates.

Highfield Farm Tempsford Road, Sandy SG19 2AQ 01767 682332 Mrs. Codd

Open all year
12 bedrs (4 twin inc 3 ba/wc; 2 double
sh/wc; 1 family sh/wc; 4 single inc 1
ba/wc, 3 sh/wc) 1 ba, 1 wc ♋ 🏠 🐓 ♛♛
Highly commended
£B&B £16-£25, WR £112-£175, child rates.

STAGSDEN   4C1

Firs Farm Bedford MK43 8TB
01234 822344   Mrs. Hutcheon

Open all year
3 bedrs (1 twin; 2 double inc 1 sh/wc) ♋
♛♛
£B&B £15-£20, WR £105-£140, child rates.

PLACES TO VISIT

BROMHAM

Bromham Mill
Bromham 01234-824330
A working watermill with milling
demonstrations on the last Sunday of
each month. Exhibitions on agriculture,
milling and the waterways. On sale: high
quality craft work and art jewellery.
Location: signposted from A428 Bedford-
Northampton road.
Open: Apr -Sept, Wed-Fri 1030-1630, Sat,
Sun & Bank Hols 1130-1800
Entrance: adult 70p,
child/OAP/concessions 35p WC ♿

SANDY

The Lodge RSPB Nature Reserve
Sandy SG19 2DL
01767-682242
106 acres of mixed woodland, heath and
grassland with a man-made lake.
Location: Entrance off B1042 Sandy-
Cambridge road.
Open: Reserve - 0900-2100; Shop - Mon-
Fri 0900-1700, Sat/Sun 1000-1700.
Entrance: adult £2, child £0.50p,
OAP/concessions £1. WC ♿ 🦽

BERKSHIRE

LAMBOURN   4B2

Lodge Down Lambourn Woodlands, Nr
Newbury, Lambourn RG16 7BJ
01672 540304   Mr. Cook

Country house with luxury accommodation
including en suite bathrooms. Set in lovely
grounds (tennis court and swimming pool in
season). 70 acres of fields and woods with
views of the downs and gallops. Baydon Rd out
of Lambourn. Lodge Down is 1ml from Baydon
on right hand side, 300 metres down drive.

Open Jan-Dec
3 bedrs (1 twin ba; 1 double ba/wc, sh/wc;
1 family inc sh/wc) ♋ 🏠 ♛♛ *Commended*
£B&B £20, WR £140, child rates.

MAIDENHEAD   4C2

Moor Farm Holyport, Maidenhead SL6
2HY 01628 33761   Mrs. Reynolds

Open all year
3 bedrs (2 twin inc 1 ba/wc, 1 sh/wc; 1
double sh/wc) ♋ ⚕ ♛♛ *Highly
Commended*
£dB&B £30-£45.

NEWBURY   4B3

Manor Farm Brimpton, Newbury RG7
4SQ 01734 713166   Mrs. Bowden

Open all year
2 bedrs (1 twin; 1 double) 1 ba, 1 wc
£B&B £20-£40.

READING 4B2

Boot Farm Southend Road, Bradfield,
Reading RG7 6EJ 01734 744298
Mrs. Dawes

Open Jan-Dec
4 bedrs (1 twin; 2 double inc 1 sh/wc; 1
single) 2 ba ☎(8) ⌂ ♨♨ *Highly
Commended*
£B&B £16-£20.

SELF CATERING

MAIDENHEAD 4C2

Moor Farm Holyport, Maidenhead SL6
2HY 01628 33761   Mrs. Reynolds

For full farm description see B&B Entry.
Accommodation in attractively converted
barns and Georgian stable block. M4 junction
8/9 is 1ml from farm. Take A308 & at next
roundabout the A330 to Holyport, farm ½ mile
on right.

☎ ⁇⁇⁇ *Highly Commended* 4 units; 7 bedrs
£Wk £200-£400

BUCKINGHAMSHIRE

AYLESBURY 4C2

New Farm Oxford Road, Oakley,
Aylesbury HP18 9UR 01844 237360
Mrs. Pickford

Open except Christmas & New Year
3 bedrs (1 twin; 2 double) 1 ba, 1 wc ☎(6)
Listed Commended

LONG CRENDON 4B2

Foxhill Farmhouse Kingsey,
Aylesbury, Long Crendon HP17 8LZ
01844 291650   Mrs. Hooper

Open Feb-Nov
3 bedrs (2 twin/wc 1 sh; 1 double/sh) 1 ba,
1 wc ☎(5) ✂ *Listed*
£B&B £19-£22, WR £133-£154.

MARLOW 4C2

Monkton Farm Little Marlow, Marlow
SL7 3RF 01494 521082   Mr. Kimber

Open Jan-Dec
3 bedrs (1 twin; 1 family; 1 single) 1 ba, 2
wc ☎(5) ✂ *Listed Commended*
£B&B £18-£20, child rates.

MILTON KEYNES 4C1

Spinney Lodge Farm Forest Road,
Hanslope, Milton Keynes 01908 510267
C. Payne

Open all year
2 bedrs; (1 twin sh/wc; 1 double sh/wc) 1
ba, 1 sh 1 wc ☎(12) ⌂ ✂ ♨♨♨

WINSLOW 4C1

Foxhole Farm Little Horwood Road,
Winslow MK18 3JW 01296 714550
Mrs. Bates

This well-appointed, fine modern farmhouse
is set in 70 acres of pasture and woodland.
Foxhole Farm stands between the A421 and
the A413 S of Milton Keynes.

Open Jan-Dec
3 bedrs (1 twin; 1 double; 1 single) 1 ba, 2
wc *Registered*
£B&B £17-£20.

SELF CATERING

OLNEY 4C1

The Old Stone Barn Home Farm,

Warrington, Olney MK46 4HN
01234 711655   Mr. Pibworth

Home Farm is an arable farm situated 2 miles
north of Olney on the A509. Accommodation
is offered in 2 stone barns converted into 6
units with 1-3 bedrooms, sleeping 2-6. Ground
floor unit, cot, highchair available. Use of
swimming pool and garden inc.

Take A509 towards Wellingborough for 2
miles. On reaching Warrington, Home Farm is
located on your right.

& ⅏ ⋔ ♙♙♙ cc Ac Vi
£Wk £140-£280

PLACES TO VISIT

BEACONSFIELD

Bekonscot Model Village
Warwick Road, Beaconsfield HP9 2PL
01494-672919
The oldest model village in the world,
portraying rural England in the 1930s, it
covers one and half acres with
landscaped gardens, miniature houses,
castles, shops, churches and railway
stations with a fine Gauge One model
railway 400 metres long. Play area and
picnic facilities. On sale: souvenirs.
Location: signposted from M40.
Open: 12th Feb - October daily, 1000-1700.
Entrance: adult £3, child £1.50,
OAP/concessions £2. WC ▙ & ✗

CAMBRIDGESHIRE

CAMBRIDGE   9D4

Manor Farm Landbeach, Cambridge
CB4 4EA 01223 860165   Mrs. Hatley

Located in the village of Landbeach, 3 miles
north of Cambridge, Manor Farm is a 620-acre
mixed beef, sheep and arable farm. The
Grade II listed, Georgian house stands in an
enclosed, walled garden. Separate guest
lounge and dining room.

Open all year except Xmas
3 bedrs (1 twin ba/wc; 1 double sh/wc; 1
family sh/wc)
⅏(5) ⋔ ♨♨ *Commended*

The Willows 102 High Street,
Landbeach, Cambridge CB4 4DT
01223 860332   Mrs. Wyatt

Open all year
3 bedrs (1 twin; 1 double; 1 family) 1 ba, 2
wc ⅏ ⋔ ⅄ ♨♨
£B&B £15-£16, child rates.

ELY   9D3

Hill House Farm 9 Main Street,
Coveney, Ely CB6 2DJ 01353 778369
H. E. Nix

Fine Victorian farmhouse on an arable farm 3
miles west of Ely. Enjoy high quality
accommodation and food. Access from A142
or A10.

Open Jan-Dec
3 bedrs (inc 1 twin sh/wc; 1 double sh/wc)
⅏(5) ⅄ ♨♨ *Highly Commended*
£B&B £18-£20, child rates.

Spinney Abbey Wicken, Ely CB7 5XQ
01353 720971   Valerie Fuller

This spacious listed farm house was rebuilt from the former priory in 1775. It stands in a large garden with tennis court on our dairy farm which borders the National Trust Nature Reserve 'Wicken Fen'. All rooms with tea and coffee making facilities. Leave A10 at Stretham roundabout, 3 ½ miles B & B sign on right.

Open Jan-Dec
3 bedrs (1 twin ba/wc; 2 double inc 1 ba/wc, 1 sh/wc) ☻(5) ♨♨ *Commended*
£B&B £18-£19.

HUNTINGDON   8C4

Molesworth Lodge Farm Molesworth, Huntingdon PE18 0PJ 01832 710309
Mrs. Page

Open all year
2 bedrs (1 twin; 1 family) 1 ba, 1 wc ☻
Listed

SELF CATERING

ELY   9D3

Hill House Farm 9 Main Street, Coveney, Ely CB6 2DJ 01353 778369   H. E. Nix

For full farm description see B&B Entry. A luxury converted farm building overlooking the fens to Ely Cathedral. Access from A142 or A10.

1 unit; 3 bedrs; sleeps 6 ☻(5) ♔♔♔♔ *Highly Commended*

PLACES TO VISIT

SACREWELL

Sacrewell Farm & Country Centre Sacrewell PE8 6HJ 01780-782222
See small animals, birds and fish and a working 18th century watermill. Huge collection of farm and domestic animals and bygone crafts. Farm, nature and general interest trails. Maze. Trampolines and toys for children. Suitable for school parties, birthdays and adult groups. On sale: honey, PYO fruit.
Location: off A47, 8 miles west of Peterborough.
Open: daily.
Entrance: adult £3.00 child £1.00
OAP/concession £2.00. WC ৬ ♔ ✕ ঌ

CHESHIRE

ALTRINCHAM   10C4

Ash Farm Guest House Park Lane, Little Bollington, Altrincham WA14 4JJ
Highly Acclaimed   RAC
01619 299290   David Taylor

Open all year

CONGLETON   7E1

Pedley House Farm Pedley Lane, Timbersbrook, Congleton CW12 3QD
01260 273650   Mrs. Gilman

Open all year
1 bedrs (1 family) 1 ba, 1 wc ☻
£child rates.

Yew Tree Farm North Rode, Congleton CW12 2PF 01260 223569 Mrs. Sheila Kidd

If you are looking for that quiet away from it all holiday, then our farm is the answer. Just 20 minutes from the M6, it is easily accessible, yet it has a peaceful setting in wooded parkland. Guests are invited to look around the farm. Take the A536 heading towards Macclesfield, after about 3 mls turn right at the sign post for North Rode, turn left.

Open all year
3 bedrs (2 twin; 1 double sh/wc) 1 ba, 1 wc ⌘ 🏠 *Listed*
£B&B £15-£17, D £10, WR £105-£119, WR/D £175-£189, child rates.

HYDE 10C4

Needhams Farm Uplands Road, Werneth Low, Hyde SK14 3AQ ⛨
01613 684610 Charlotte Walsh

A warm welcome awaits all visitors to this small working farm just off the A560, 5 miles northeast of Stockport.The house is 16th-century, with beams in most rooms. Ideally situated for Manchester, Stockport, Glossop and Manchester Airport.

Open all year

6 bedrs (1 twin 3 double inc 2sh/wc, 1wc; 1 family sh/wc; 1 single sh/wc)
⌘ 🏠 ♖ 🏆🏆🏆 *Commended*Acclaimed
cc Ac Vi

Shire Cottage Farmhouse Benches Lane, Chisworth, Hyde SK14 6RY 01457 866536 Mr. Sidebottom

Mixed hill farm with sheep and beef cattle. Peaceful location with magnificent views. A626 towards Glossop via Marple. Benches Lane is opposite Woodleys Restaurant, Shire Cottage Farmhouse is 4th on right.

Open all year
4 bedrs (1 twin sh/wc; 1 twin, 1 double sh/wc; 1 single) 1 ba, 2 wc ⌘ 🏆🏆
£B&B £15-£18, WR £90-£115, child rates.

MACCLESFIELD 7E1

Golden Cross Farm Siddington, Nr Macclesfield, SK11 9JP 01260 224358 Hazel Rush

Closed Xmas and New Year
4 bedrs (2 double; 2 single) 2 ba, 2 wc ⌘
🍴 🏆🏆

Lower Harebarrow Farm Over Alderley, Macclesfield SK10 4SW 01625 829882 Mrs. Leggott

Open all year

Oldhams Hollow Farm Manchester Road, Tytherington, Macclesfield SK10 2JW 01625 424128 Mrs. Buxton

Dairy and sheep farm with a 16th Century farm house with a wealth of oak beams.

Open Jan-Dec
3 bedrs (1 twin; 2 double) ⌘ 🏠 ♖ 🏆 *Listed*
£B&B £16-£17, D £9, WR £112-£175, child rates.

MARTON 7E1

Sandpit Farm Messuage Lane, Marton, Macclesfield SK11 9HS 01260 224254 Mrs. Kennerley

Cherished oak-beamed farmhouse on grass/arable land. Quiet location one mile from village with easy access to motorways and 14 miles from Manchester Airport. Leave Congleton on Manchester Rd A34. Morton village look for Davenport Arms L. Next L into Bruce Ln, next junction R.

Open Jan-Dec
3 bedrs (2 twin inc 1 sh/wc; 1 double sh/wc) 1 ba, 1 wc ⛱ 🐂 ♨♨
£B&B £14-£20, child rates.

MIDDLEWICH 7E1

Forge Mill Farm Warmingham, Middlewich CW10 0HQ 01270 77204 Mrs. Moss

Open Jan-Dec
2 bedrs (1 twin; 1 double) 1 ba, 1 wc ⛱ ♨♨
£B&B £15, WR £105.

NANTWICH 7E1

Lea Farm Wrinehill Road, Wybunbury, Nantwich CW5 7NS 01270 841429 Mrs. Callwood

Lea Farm lies off the A500 towards Nantwich from M6 Jn 16. The charming farmhouse is set in landscaped gardens where peacocks roam on a 150-acre dairy farm. Good home cooking. Pool/snooker table and fishing. From the village of Wynbury, go to the church tower, turn down Wrinehill Rd. The B&B is 1 ½ miles.

Open all year
3 bedrs (1 twin; 1 double sh/wc; 1 family sh/wc) 1 ba, 1 wc ⛱ 🏠 🐂 ♨♨
£B&B £14-£16, D £7.50-£8, WR £100-£110, child rates.

Little Heath Farm Audlem, Crewe, Nantwich CW3-0HE 01270 811324 Mrs. Bennion

Old working dairy farm which features a beamed dining room and a lounge with a large open fire and television. Bedrooms are spacious and tastefully decorated, with tea making facilities provided. Take A529 from Nantwich. At the '30mph' sign turn right, farm is then to your right.

Open Apr-Nov
3 bedrs (1 twin; 2 double inc 1 sh/wc) 1 ba, 2 wc ⛱ 🏠 ♨♨♨ *Commended*
£B&B £13.50-£18, D £8.50, WR £95-£112, WR/D £154-£170, child rates.

Stoke Grange Farm Chester Road, Nantwich CW5 7NS 01270 625523 Mrs. West

Open all year
3 bedrs (2 twin sh/wc; 1 double) 1 ba, 1 wc ⛱ ♨♨♨ *Commended*
£B&B £17.50-£20, child rates.

NORTHWICH 7E1

Beechwood House 206 Wallerscote Rd, Weaverham, Northwich CW8 3LZ 01606 852123 Mrs. Kuypers

Open Jan-Nov
3 bedrs (1 twin sh/wc; 2 single) 1 ba, 1 wc ⛱ ⊁ ♨♨ *Listed*
£B&B £13.75-£17.50, D £5-£7.50, WR £96-£120, WR/D £145-£169, child rates.

SELF CATERING

HYDE 10C4

Needhams Farm Uplands Road, Werneth Low, Hyde SK14 3AQ ⚓️RAC 01613 684610 Charlotte Walsh

For full farm description see B&B Entry Modern 2-bedroom bungalow adjoining farmhouse. Sleeps 6. ⛺ 🐴 ✗ *Commended* cc Ac Vi

Shire Cottage Farmhouse Benches Lane, Chisworth, Hyde SK14 6RY 01457 866536 Mr. Sidebottom

For full farm description see B&B Entry. A626 towards Glossop via Marple. Benches Lane is opposite Woodleys Restaurant, Shire Cottage Farmhouse is 4th on right.

1 unit; 2 bedrs ♿ ⛺
£Wk £175-£300

NANTWICH 7E1

Stoke Grange Farm Chester Road, Nantwich CW5 7NS 01270 625525 Mrs. West

For full farm description see B&B Entry. From Nantwich take the A51 north-bound towards Chester.

2 units; 4 bedrs ⛺ ♚♚♚ *Commended*
£Wk £150-£350

STOCKPORT 10C4

Shaw Farm New Mills, Stockport SK12 4QE 01614 271841 Mrs. Burgess

Open all year
1 unit; 2 bedrs ⛺ 🐴 ✗ ♚♚♚ *Commended*

CLEVELAND

STOKESLEY 11D2

Dromonby Hall Farm Busby Lane, Kirkby, Stokesley TS9 7AP 01642 712312 Mrs. Weighell

160 acre working farm, arable with sheep and horses.

Open Jan-Dec
3 bedrs (2 twin, 1 double) 1 ba, 2 wc ⛺ ♿
🚽 ✗ 🍺
£B&B £15-£20, WR £90-£105, child rates.

CORNWALL

BODMIN 2B3

Mennabroom Warleggan, Bodmin PL30 4HE 01208 82272 Mrs. Miller

Reputedly the oldest house on Bodmin Moor, this medieval, Cornish farmhouse is full of character with oak beams and granite

fireplaces. Set on a working farm with a beef suckler herd. Here you can enjoy good home cooking.

Open Apr-Sept
3 double bedrs inc 1sh/wc; 1 ba, 1 wc
⛺(10) *Highly Commended*

Treffry Farm Lanivet, Bodmin PL30 5AF
01208 74405   Mrs. Smith

Lovely 18th Century, listed, Georgian farmhouse on dairy farm. Also delightful cottages. Take B3268 from Bodmin towards Lostwithiel, after 2½ mls turn R at mini roundabout, farm 300 yds down lane on R.

Open Easter-Oct
3 bedrs (2 twin sh/wc; 1 double) 1 ba ☎(6)
🏠 ♨♨ *Highly Commended*
£B&B £18.50, D £9, WR £122, WR/D £182, child rates.

BUDE   2B3

Darzle Farm Woodford, Morwenstowe, Bude EX23 9HY 01288 331222
Mrs. Cholwill

40 acre beef farm with chickens.

Open Jan-Dec
4 bedrs (1 double sh/wc; 3 family ba/wc) 1 ba, 1 wc ☎ 🏠 🐎 ♨♨♨ *Approved*
£B&B £15-£18, D £6-£8, WR £95-£105, WR/D £140-£150, child rates.

Lower Northcott Farm Poughill, Bude EX23 7EL 01288 352350   Mrs. Trewinn

Georgian farmhouse on a 400 acre arable and dairy farm with outstanding views of the Heritage coastline. From Bude town centre take Poughill Rd, at Poughill village PO turn L (signposted Northcott Farm), farm is R down lane.

Open Jan-Dec
5 bedrs (1 twin sh/wc; 1 double ba/wc; 3 family inc 1 ba/wc) 1 ba ☎ 🏠 🐎 ♨♨
Approved
£B&B £15, D £6, WR £105, WR/D £140, child rates.

Tackbeare Farm Marhamchurch, Bude EX23 0HH 01288 381264 Cynthia Cholwill

16th century manor house on 240 acre dairy/beef farm, just 5 miles from Bude. Children welcome, large garden with swings and playroom. Take A39 southwards for 2 miles, turn L, following signs to Titson Trough village. Farm 1 mile on L.

Open all year
5 bedrs (1 twin; 1 double ba/wc; 2 family inc 1 ba/wc; 1 single) 2 ba, 2 wc ☎ 🐎
£B&B £15-£16, D £6-£7, WR £91-£98, WR/D £130-£147, child rates.

CAMBORNE 2A4

Cargenwen Farm Blackrock, Praze-an-
Beeble, Camborne TR14 9PD
01209 831442 Mrs. Peerless

Cargenwen Farm is comfortable, fully
modernised and quiet. Set on a south west
facing hillside the house has extensive country
views from all bedrooms. Good traditional
homemade meals are provided using fresh
home produce.

Open except Xmas and New Year
3 bedrs (1 twin sh/wc; 2 double sh/wc) 1
ba ☎ ⚡
£B&B £16, D £8.

HAYLE 2A4

Rosehill Farm Leedstown, Hayle TR27
6DH 01736 850315 Mrs. Christophers

Open Jan-Nov
2 bedrs (1 twin; 1 double) 1 ba ☎ 🛏 🐕 ☕
£B&B £12-£15, WR £84, child rates.

Treglisson Hayle TR27 5JT
01736 753141 Mr. Runnalls

A former mine captain's home, built in the
1780's. Treglisson farmhouse sits on a working
arable farm of some 130 acres, including 1½
acres of grass. Take B3301 in an easterly
direction. Turn right at double mini-
roundabout, Treglisson approx 1 mile on left.

Open Dec-Oct
5 bedrs (1 twin sh/wc; 2 double sh/wc; 2
family ba/wc) ☎ ☕☕ *Highly Commended*
£B&B £17.63-£23.50, child rates.

HELSTON 2A4

Higher Trevurvas Farm Ashton,

Helston TR13 9TZ 01736 763613
Mr. Jenkin

Beef and sheep farm with all home comforts
and traditional farmhouse cooking. A394
Helston to Penzance road, sign at end of lane,
after village of Ashton.

Open all year
4 bedrs (1 twin ba/wc; 3 double sh/wc)
☕☕
£B&B £16.50-£18.50, D £10-£12, WR
£115.50-£129.50, WR/D £185.50-£213.50.

Little Pengwedna Farm Helston TR13
0BA 01736 850649 Mrs. White

This Cornish granite farmhouse is located on a
working farm with pedigree Charolais show
cattle, situated 4 miles outside Helston. The
house is beautifully furnished to provide a
comfortable and relaxing home from home
atmosphere.

Open all year
3 bedrs (1 twin; 2 double sh/wc 1 ba; 2
wc) ☎ 🐕 ☕ *Commended*

Longstone Farm Trenear, Helston TR13
0BA 01326 572483 Mrs. Lawrance

Longstone is a working dairy farm deep in
peaceful countryside 4 miles north of Helston.

The modernised farmhouse has a TV lounge, sun room and ground floor bedrooms. Good farmhouse fare. Poldark Mine 3 miles. Flambards, Leisure Centre 4 miles. B3297 from Helston towards Redruth for about 2 miles. Turn left to Coverack Bridges, take next right, then left.

Open March -November
5 bedrs (1 twin; 2 double inc 1 sh/wc; 2 family inc 1 sh/wc) 2 ba, 2 wc ☒ ♀ ☙☙
Approved
£B&B £14-£18, D £8, WR £95-£110, WR/D £130-£150, child rates.

Polgarth Farm Crowntown, Helston
TR13 0AA 01326 572115   Mrs. Dale

Open Jan-Nov
3 bedrs (3 twin inc 2 ba/wc) 1 ba, 1 wc ☒
♀ *Approved*

LAUNCESTON   2C3

Hurdon Farm Launceston PL15 9LS ⓇⒶⒸ
01566 772955   M. Smith

Hurdon Farm is on a 400 acre mixed working farm with a gracious, 18th Century, stone farmhouse which is a listed building of architectural interest. 1 miles from A30 bypass.

Open May-Nov
6 bedrs (1 twin; 2 double; 2 family ba/wc; 1 single) 1 ba, 1 wc ☒ ⚭ ⚹ ☙☙
£B&B £14-£18, D £9, WR £84-£105, WR/D £138-£159, child rates.

Trethorne Leisure Farm Kennards House, Launceston PL15 8QE
01566 86324   Mrs. Davey

A 140 acre working dairy farm with cows, ducks and pony. Staying in the farmhouse you can enjoy home-cooked food in a relaxed

atmosphere. Golf course on the farm and a licensed restaurant separate to the farmhouse. 3 miles south of Launceston on A30.

Open Jan-Dec
6 bedrs (1 twin sh/wc; 2 double sh/wc; 3 family sh/wc) 1 ba, 2 wc ☒ ⚼ ♀
£B&B £15-£16, D £8.50-£9, WR £105, WR/D £164.50-£166, child rates.

LISKEARD   2B3

Tregondale Farm Menheniot, Liskeard
PL14 3RG 01579 342407   S. R. P. Rowe

A characteristic farmhouse on a 180 acre mixed farm where animals are naturally reared in the peace of the countryside, amidst wildlife, flowers and country walks. The farmhouse is beautifully set with rural views surrounded by a walled garden. A38 off dual carriageway for Menheniot, go through village. L at junction, then R at entrance sign.

Open Jan-Dec
3 bedrs (1 twin ba/sh/wc; 2 double inc 1 ba/sh/wc) 1 ba, 1 wc ☒ ⚹ ☙☙ *Highly Commended*
£B&B £16-£18, D £8.50-£9, WR £112-£122.50, WR/D £168-£178, child rates.

Tresulgan Farm Nr Menheniot, Liskeard
PL14 3PU 01503 4268   Mrs. Elford

Tresulgan is a 140-acre dairy farm situated on the A38, 4 miles east of Liskeard. The 17th century farmhouse is very comfortable and provides good home cooking. Every care is taken to make your stay a memorable one. Beaches 4-6 miles.

Open except Xmas
3 bedrs (1 twin sh/wc; 1 double sh/wc; 1 family sh/wc) ☒ ♀ ⚹ ☙☙ *Highly Commended*

Trewint Farm Menheniot, Liskeard
PL14 3RE   RAC
01579 347155   M. E. Rowe

Situated less than 2 miles off the A38 in peaceful rural surroundings, 4 miles from the old market town of Liskeard, this 200-acre working farm has attractive valley walks, pedigree South Devon cattle, sheep, pigs, a pony for children and a play area. A38 from Plymouth to Liskeard, 4 miles Trevelfoot roundabout. R to Menheniot, ½ mile, R beside White Hart pub, 1st L.

Open Jan-Dec
3 bedrs (inc 1 double sh/wc; 1 family sh/wc) ☎ 🐾
£B&B £14-£18, D £21-£25, WR £98-£126, WR/D £147-£175, child rates.

LOOE   2B4

Bucklawren Farm St Martins, Looe
PL13 1NZ   RAC
01503 240738   Mrs. Henley

Bucklawren is a 500-acre dairy and arable farm off the B3253, 3 miles east of the picturesque fishing village of Looe. In this large spacious farmhouse, set in glorious countryside with beautiful sea views, you can enjoy farmhouse cooking. From Looe take B3253 to Plymouth, after 1 ½ miles turn R to Monkey Sanctuary, after 1 mile turn R to Bucklawren.

Open Mar-Nov
5 bedrs (1 twin ba/wc; 1 double sh/wc; 3 family sh/wc) 1 ba, 1 wc ☎ 🐾 ⚘ 🐾🐾🐾
Commended
cc Ac Vi
£B&B £16-£19, D £9, WR £112-£126, WR/D £164-£175, child rates.

Coombe Farm *Highly Acclaimed*
Widegates, Looe PL13 1QN   RAC
01503 240223   Mrs. Low

On the B3253 between Hessenford and Looe stands this lovely country house furnished with antiques. Although no longer attached to a working farm the house is set in 10 acres of lawns, meadows, and ponds with superb views down a wooded valley to the sea.

Open Mar-Oct
10 bedrs (3 twin sh/wc; 3 double sh/wc; 4 family sh/wc) ☎(5) 🐾 🐾🐾 ⚘ 🐾🐾🐾
Highly Commended

MEVAGISSEY   2B4

Treleaven Farmhouse Mevagissey,
PL26 6KZ, 01726 842413   RAC

Open All year
6 bedrs (6 en suite; 1 ba) ☎ *Listed*

NEWQUAY   2A3

Degembris Farmhouse *Acclaimed*
St Newlyn East, Newquay TR8 5HY   RAC
01872 510555   Mrs. Woodley

Open All year except Xmas
5 bedrs (1 twin; 1 double; 2 family ba/wc; 1 single) ☎ 🐾 🐾🐾🐾 *Commended*
£B&B £16-£18, D £8.50, child rates.

Manuels Farm Quintrell Downs,
Newquay TR8 4NY 01637 873577
Mrs. Wilson

Open all year
3 bedrs (2 double: 1 family sh/wc) 2 ba
2wc ⚘ 🐾🐾🐾 *Highly Commended*

PENZANCE   2A4

Kenegie Home Farm Gulval, Penzance
TR20 8YN 01736 60355   E. I. J. Osborne

This modern granite farmhouse has a panoramic view over Mount's Bay. All rooms have TV and tea/coffee facilities. B3311 St Ives Road

Open all year
3 bedrs (1 twin; 1 double; 1 family) 1 ba, 2 wc ☎
£child rates.

Menwidden Farm Ludgvan, Penzance
01736 740415   Mrs. Blewett

Mrs. Blewett provides good farm cooking,
including homemade rolls and cream, in a
friendly atmosphere at this small working
dairy farm. Cot and high chair provided. A30,
4 miles north of Penzance (Turn off at
Crowlas crossroads).

Open all year
6 bedrs (1 twin; 3 double; 2 family) 2 ba, 2
wc ☂ ♀ *Listed Commended*
  cc AmEx £child rates.

Rose Farm Chyanhal, Buryas Bridge,
Penzance TR19 6AN 01736 731808
Mrs. Lally

Open all year
4 bedrs (3 double sh/wc; 1 family sh/wc)
☂ 💥💥
£B&B £17.50-£19, WR £122.50-£133, child
rates.

SALTASH   2C4

Burcombe Farm St Dominick, Saltash
PL12 6SH 01579 50217   Mrs. Batten

Open Apr-Oct
3 bedrs (2 twin ba/wc; 1 double ba/wc) 1
ba, 1 wc 💥💥
Approved

ST AUSTELL   2B4

Poltarrow Farm St Mewan, St Austell
PL26 7DR 01726 67111   Mrs. Judith
Nancarrow

45 acre mixed working farm with a charming
old farmhouse. In a quiet yet central location.
Comfortable accommodation with good food.
Take A390 to Truro approx 1 mile, turn right
at school keep on driving for ¼ mile, entrance
on left.

Open all year
5 bedrs (1 twin ba/wc; 3 double inc 2
sh/wc; 1 family ba/wc) ☂ 💥💥 *Highly
Commended* cc Ac Vi
£B&B £18-£20, D £10, WR £125-£140,
WR/D £195-£210, child rates.

ST JUST-IN-ROSELAND   2B4

Commerrans Farm Nr Truro, St Just-
in-Roseland TR2 5JJ 01872 580270
Wendy Symons

We welcome you to stay with us on our small
farm, situated in a corner of the Roseland
Peninsula which is of outstanding beauty.
Surrounded by farmland it provides a rural and
tranquil setting, ideal for those who want to get
away from it all. Take A3078 to village of St
Just-in-Roseland, turn R onto B3289. Follow
road 1½ miles, turn L, follow signs to farm.

Open Easter-Nov
3 bedrs (1 twin 2 double) 2 ba, 2 wc ☂ ♀
£B&B £14.50-£15, D £7, child rates.

TREGASWITH

Tregaswith Farmhouse Tregaswith,
Newquay TR8 4HY 01637 881181   J. Elsom

Open except Xmas
3 bedrs (2 double inc 1 ba/wc, 1 sh/wc)
☂ ⊞ ♀ *Highly Commended*

TRURO   2B4

Arallas Ladock, Truro TR2 4NP
01872 510379   Mrs. Holt

Turn south of the A30 Bodmin-Redruth road
at Sumercourt to reach Arallas, an elegant
farmhouse formerly used as a gentleman's
sporting retreat. It is in a truly peaceful rural
area with good walks through 400 acres of
woodland and superb views.

Open Mar-Nov
3 bedrs (1 twin sh/wc; 2 double inc 1
ba/wc, 1 sh/wc) ☂ 💥💥💥 *Commended*
£B&B £16-£19.50, D £9-£12, WR £105-£119,
child rates.

Carvean Farm Probus, Truro
TR2 4HY   ♙ RAC
01872 520243   Mrs. Roberts

Open Jan-Dec
5 bedrs (5 twin inc 1 ba/wc, 2 sh/wc) ⛌ ⌂
⅟ cc Vi
£B&B £16.50-£19.50, D £12, child rates.

Lambourne Castle Farm Penhallow,
Truro TR4 9LQ 01872 572365
Mrs. Hawkey

Open Mar-Oct
4 bedrs (1 twin; 1 double; 2 family) 1 ba, 1
wc ⛌(3) ⅟ ⚘
£B&B £12-£14, D £5-£6, WR £82-£95, WR/D
£115-£125, child rates.

Nanteague Farm Guest House
Marazanvose, Zelah, Truro TR4 9DH   ♙ RAC
01872 540351   Mrs. George

On the A30 north of Truro, 2 miles from
Zelah, Nanteague can give you a real
country holiday with everything on your
doorstep. We can arrange clay pigeon
shooting, gliding, flying, diving, sailing
and horse riding. Set in 130 acres of
farmland.

Open Easter-Oct
5 bedrs (1 twin; 1 double sh/wc; 3 family
sh/wc) 1 ba ⛌ ⌂ ⚘⚘⚘ *Highly
Commended*
  cc Ac AmEx Vi

Pengelly Farm St Erme, Truro TR4 9BG
01872 510245   Mrs. Hicks

Open Jan-Dec
5 bedrs (2 double inc 1 sh/wc; 3 family inc
1 ba/wc) 1 ba ⛌ ⛏ ⚘
£B&B £13-£17.50, WR £90-£122.50, child
rates.

Treberrick Farm Tregony, Truro TR2
5SP 01872 530247   Margaret Retallack

Open Apr-Oct
3 bedrs (1 twin; 2 double) 2 ba
£B&B £13.50-£15, D £7-£8.

Trenestrall Farm Ruan High Lanes,
Truro TR2 5LX 01872 501259 Mrs. Palmer

Mixed, family-run farm with a 200 year old
stone farmhouse. Follow A3078 to Ruan High
Lanes, turn R in village signpost Philleigh &

King Harry Ferry. Farm 2nd on R approx. 1
mile.

Open Feb-Nov
3 bedrs (2 twin; 1 double) ⛌ ⛏
£B&B £13-£14, child rates.

WADEBRIDGE   2B3

Tregellist Farm *Acclaimed* Tregellist, St
Kew, Bodmin, Wadebridge PL30 3HG ♙ RAC
01208 880537   Mrs Cleave

Open all year
3 bedrs; (inc 3 ba/wc) 1 ba ⛌
£B&B £18-£34.

Trevorrick Farm St Issey, Wadebridge
PL27 7QH 01841 540574   Mr. Mealing

Open Jan-Dec
3 bedrs (1 twin; 2 double inc 1 ba/wc) 1
ba, 1 wc ⛌ ⛏*Highly Commended*
£B&B £15-£18.50, WR £90-£129.50, child
rates.

WHEDDON CROSS   3D2

Cutthorne Farm Luckwell Bridge,
Wheddon Cross TA24 7EW 0164 383255
Mrs. Durbin

25 acre sheep farm in the centre of Exmoor.
Quiet and secluded with ensuite bathrooms
and four-poster bedrooms. Log fires and
candlelit dinners. A39 to Dunster. A396 to
Wheddon Cross. B3224 to Luckwell Bridge.

Open Mar-Nov
3 bedrs (1 twin ba/wc; 2 double ba/wc) ⛌
⌂ ⛏ ⚘⚘
£B&B £19.50-£25, D £10.50, WR £136-£189,
WR/D £210-£245, child rates.

SELF CATERING

BODMIN   2B3

Treffry Farm Lanivet, Bodmin PL30 5AF
01208 74405   Mrs. Smith

For full farm description see B&B Entry. Take
B3268 from Bodmin towards Lostwithiel, after
2 1/2mls turn R at mini roundabout, farm 300
yds down lane on R.

🐂(6) ♙♙♙ *Highly Commended*
£Wk £85-£520

FALMOUTH   2A4

Boskensoe Mawnan Smith, Falmouth
TR11 5JP 01326 250257   Mrs. Matthews

An attractive granite farmhouse with two
bungalows standing on a mixed, working,
family farm. Part of the farmhouse is available
for self-catering from April to October. The
bungalows are open all year. 3 units; each
unit sleeps 8.

🐂 ⅍

LAUNCESTON   2C3

Wheatley Farm Maxworthy, Launceston
PL15 8LY   RAC
01566 781232   Mr. Griffin

🐂 ⅍ ♙♙♙ *Highly Commended*

LISKEARD   2B3

Tregondale Farm Menheniot, Liskeard
PL14 3RG 01579 342407   S. R. P. Rowe

For full farm description see B&B Entry. A38
off dual carriageway for Menheniot, go
through village. L at junction, then R at
entrance sign.

🐂 ⅍ ♙♙♙ *Highly Commended*
£Wk £75-£375

LOOE   2B4

Bucklawren Farm St Martins, Looe
PL13 1NZ   RAC
01503 240738   Mrs. Henly

For full farm description see B&B Entry.
From Looe take B3253 to Plymouth, after
1 ½ miles turn R to Monkey Sanctuary,

after 1 mile turn R to Bucklawren.

🐂 ⅍ ♙♙♙ *Commended* cc Ac Vi
£Wk £100-£400

PORT ISAAC   2B3

Trevathan Farm St Endillion, Port Isaac
PL29 3TT 01208 880248   Mrs. Symons

🐂 🐂 ⅍ ♙♙♙♙
£Wk £120-£840

ST AUSTELL   2B4

Poltarrow Farm St Mewan, St Austell
PL26 7DR 01726 67111   Mrs. J
Nancarrow

For full farm description see B&B Entry. Take
A390 to Truro approx 1 mile, turn right at
school keep on driving for ¼ mile, entrance on
left.

🐂 ♙♙♙♙ *Commended* cc Ac Vi
£Wk £150-£425

TRURO   2B4

Hendra Farm Rose, Truro TR4 9PS
01872 572273   Janet Symons

🐂 🐂 ⅍
£Wk £150-£390

Pengelly Farm St Erme, Truro TR4 9BG
01872 510245   Mrs. Hicks

🐂 🐂
£Wk £125-£150

WADEBRIDGE   2B3

Trevorrick Farm St Issey, Wadebridge
PL27 7QH 01841 540574   Mr. Mealing

Turn to A389 Padstow, centre of St Issdey turn
R to Burgols, L at end follow Trevorrick signs.

5 units; 9 bedrs sleep 2-5 ♿ 🐂 🐂 *Highly
Commended*
£Wk £120-£560

**All towns listed in this guide
are shown on the maps
at the back.**

CUMBRIA

ALSTON 10B1

Bridge End Farm Alston CA9 3BJ
01434 381261 Mr. Walton

18th century farmhouse where guests have own lounge with colour TV and open fire. All rooms centrally heated. On the A686 Alston - Penrith road. First turn off on the left-hand side at junction of Leadgate and turn off.

Open all year
2 bedrs (1 twin; 1 double sh/wc)
£B&B £14.50-£16.50, D £8.50, WR £91-£105, WR/D £131-£145, child rates.

AMBLESIDE 10B2

Fell Foot Farm Little Langdale, Ambleside LA22 9PE 01539 437294
Mrs. Harryman

Open Apr-Nov
3 bedrs (2 twin; 1 double) (9)
£B&B £15-£18, D £9, WR £98, WR/D £146, child rates.

Tock How Farm High Wray, Ambleside
01539 436481 P. Benson

A working dairy, beef and sheep farm once owned by Beatrix Potter, it now belongs to the National Trust. There are wonderful views from all the spacious, well-equipped bedrooms. In the farmyard there are peacocks, chickens and ducks.

Open all year
3 bedrs (2 double; 1 family) 1 ba, 2 wc
£B&B £14.

APPLEBY 10B2

Meadow Ing Farm Crakenthorpe, Appleby CA16 6AE 01768 352543
Mrs. Dent

Open All year except Xmas.
3 bedrs (1 twin sh/wc; 2 double inc 1 ba/wc) 2 ba
£B&B £16-£18, D £8.50, child rates.

Asby Grange Great Asby, Appleby
CA16 6HF 01768 352881 Mrs. Hayton

Asby Grange is a 17th century farm house on a working 350 acre hill farm with beef cattle and sheep in a beautiful quiet part of the Eden Valley near Appleby.

Open Apr-Oct
2 bedrs (2 double) 1 ba, 1 wc *Listed*
£B&B £13-£15, WR £84-£90, child rates.

BRAMPTON 10B1

High Nook Farm Low Row, Brampton
CA8 2LU 01697 746273 Mrs. Forster

Open May-Oct
2 bedrs (1 double; 1 family) 1 ba, 1 wc
£B&B £11-£12, WR £75, child rates.

For a full explanation of a farm entry, see page 5.

High Rigg Warton, Brampton CA8 2AZ
01697 72117 M. Mounsey

The farm is 2 miles northwest of Brampton and has panoramic views of the Pennines. Lanercost Abbey 3 miles. Golf courses, pony trekking, swimming within 5 miles.

Open all year
3 bedrs (1 twin; 1 double; 1 family) 1 ba, 2 wc ⌖ 🏠 *Approved*

Howard House Farm Gilsland, Carlisle
CA6 7AN 01697 747285 E. Woodmass

Open Jan-Dec
3 bedrs (1 twin; 1 double sh/wc; 1 family) ⌖(2) 🐾🐾 *Commended*
£B&B £16-£19, D £9, WR £110-£125, WR/D £165, child rates.

CALDBECK 10B1

Friar Hall Wigton, Caldbeck CA7 8DS
01697 478633 Mrs. Coulthard

Open Mar-Nov
3 bedrs (2 twin; 1 family) 2 ba, 2 wc ⌖ 🐕*Listed*
£B&B £16-£17, child rates.

CARLISLE 10B1

Bessiestown Farm *Highly Acclaimed*
Nr Longtown, Catlowdy CA6 5QP RAC
01228 577219 Mrs. Sisson

Open all year
5 bedrs (2 twin inc 1 sh/wc; 2 double; 1 family) 1 wc ⌖ 🐾🐾🐾*Highly Commended*

Craigburn Farm Catlowdy, Penton,
Carlisle CA6 5QP 01228 577214
Mr. Lawson

A family-run, working farm with a pets' corner and rare breeds of animals. Lovely, cosy bedrooms some four poster, friendly atmosphere and good cooking. M6 Carlisle, leave at junction 44, A7 to Longtown, R at Bush Hotel for Penton, 6 mls to Bridge Inn, R for Catlowdy, R.

Open Jan-Dec
6 bedrs (1 twin sh/wc; 3 double ba/wc; 2 family inc 1 ba/wc, 1 sh/wc) 4 wc ⌖ 🏠 🐕 🐾🐾🐾 cc Vi £B&B £19-£20, D £10-£12, WR £112.40-£112, WR/D £162.40-£179.20, child rates.

Green View Lodges & Well Cottage
Green View, Welston, nr Dalston, Carlisle CA5 7ES 01697 476230 Mr. Ivinson

Every home comfort provided for a relaxing country holiday. Tiny picturesque hamlet, unspoilt views over rolling pastures to the Caldbeck Dells 3 miles away. Take B5299 for 9 miles to Welton.

Open Jan-Dec
⌖ ♿ 🐕 ⚥ 🐾🐾🐾🐾
cc Vi

Holmhead Farm Hadrian's Wall, Greenhead-in-Northumberland, Carlisle CA6 7HY 01697 747402   Mrs. Staff

Stone farmhouse surrounded by fields and footpaths. Bordered by a stream. Built with stones from Hadrian's Wall which runs underneath the house. Take B6318 to A69, go east 3 miles.

Open all year
4 bedrs (inc 2 twin sh/wc) 🐎 ਠ 🏤 ☕☕☕
cc Vi
£B&B £21.50-£22.50, D £16-£17, WR £129-£135, WR/D £241-£254.

How End Farm Thursby, Carlisle CA5 6PX 01697 342487   Margaret Swainson

200 acre dairy farm with large farmhouse dated 1764. Original beams, lovely curved staircase, superb views to the Lakeland Fells. On A595 west from Carlisle, approx 7 miles to roundabout, site is ½ mile beyond roundabout on left.

Open Jan-Dec
2 bedrs (1 twin; 1 family) 2 ba, 2 wc 🐎 ਸ
£B&B £14-£15, child rates.

Streethead Farm Ivegill, Carlisle CA4 0NG 01697 473327   Mrs. Wilson

Open Mar-Oct
2 bedrs (1 double; 1 family) 1 ba 🐎(7) 🏤
Listed
cc Ac Vi

All towns listed in this guide are shown on the maps at the back.

Wallsend Guesthouse The Old Rectory, Bowness on Solway, Carlisle CA5 5AF 01697 351055   Ken Simpson

Open all year

CARTMELL FELL   10B2

Lightwood Farmhouse Cartmell Fell LA11 6NP 01539 531454   Mr. Cervetti

Lightwood is a 17th century farm house retaining original oak beams and staircase. It has a 2 acre landscaped garden with streams running through. Comfort and hospitality are our speciality. From Kendal follow road for Underbarrow Crossthwaite - Bowland Bridge to Masons Arms pub, farm ½ mile up road.

Open all year
9 bedrs (4 twin inc 1 ba/wc, 2 sh/wc; 2 double ba/wc; 2 family inc 1 ba/wc, 1 sh/wc) 1 ba, 1 wc 🐎 ☕☕ cc Ac Vi
£B&B £18.50-£25, WR £126-£154, child rates.

COCKERMOUTH   10A1

Bent Ash Farm Eaglesfield, Cockermouth CA13 0SF 01900 822387 Mrs. Clark

---

Open Mar-Nov
3 bedrs (1 twin sh/wc; 2 double inc 1
ba/wc, 1 sh/wc) ⌧
£B&B £16.50-£17, D £8.

Birk Bank Farm Brandlingill,
Cockermouth CA13 0RB 01900 822326
Mrs. Chester

Traditional Lakeland farm with beef cattle
and sheep situated in peaceful
surroundings. Bed time drink with
homemade biscuits included. Guests
lounge with TV. A5086 from Cockermouth
turn L at school, then R for Bradlingill,
sign for farm on L past post box.

Open Mar-Oct
3 bedrs; 1 ba, 2 wc ⌧(5)
£B&B £14-£16, D £8-£9, WR £95-£98, WR/D
£145-£150, child rates.

Brook Farm Loweswater, Cockermouth
CA13 0RP 01900 85606   Mrs. Hayton

Open May-Oct.
2 bedrs (1 twin, 1 double) 1 ba, 1 wc
⌧ ⌧ ⌧ ⌧ ⌧ *Commended*

Crag End Farm Rogerscale,
Cockermouth CA13 0RG 01900 85658
Mrs. Steel

Open all year
3 bedrs (1 twin; 1 double; 1 family ba/wc)
⌧ *Listed*
£B&B £15, D £9, child rates.

High Stanger Farm Cockermouth CA13
9TS 01900 823875   Mrs. Hewitson

A warm welcome awaits you at this 17th-
century farmhouse with attractive low ceilings,
oak beams and open fires. Cot, highchair and
babysitting available. High Stanger is a
working Cumbrian sheep farm set in the
beautiful Lorton Vale, south of Cockermouth
From town centre take B5292, 2 miles out of
town, turn right at the cross roads, 150 yds,
then L, farm on R.

Open all year
2 bedrs (1 twin; 1 double) 1 ba, 2 wc ⌧ ⌧
⌧ *Listed*

Jenkin Farm Embleton, Cockermouth
CA13 9TN 01768 776387   Mrs. Teasdale

Family-run, working, hill farm in a beautiful
quiet part of the Lake District. Tourist Board
inspected 18th Century stone farm house.
Sorry no pets.

Open Jan-Dec
2 bedrs (1 twin; 1 double) 1 ba ⌧
£B&B £15-£18.

Stanger Farm Cockermouth CA13 9TS
01900 824222   C. A. Heslop

Open all year
2 bedrs (1 twin; 1 double) ⌧ ⌧ ⌧
£B&B £14-£15.50, D £8, WR £100, child
rates.

GOSFORTH   10A2

Church Stile Farm Nether Wasdale,
Gosforth CA20 1ET 01946 726252
Mrs. Knight

Set in the pretty and tiny village of Nether
Wasdale our lovely traditional Cumbrian
house, has been carefully renovated to give

the best of 20th century comfort. A real family run hill farm. Sheep and small dairy herd. A595 to Gosforth, follow signs for Nether Wasdale.

Open Jan- Nov
3 bedrs (1 double ba/wc; 1 family ba/wc; single sh/wc) ☙ ⌂
£B&B £16.50-£21, WR £105-£138.

GREAT LANGDALE 10B2

Bayesbrown Farm Great Langdale, Ambleside LA22 9JZ 01539 437300
Mrs. Jackie Rowand

Open all year
3 bedrs (1 twin; 1 double; 1 family) 1 ba, 1 wc ☙ ⌂ ♞
£B&B £16, D £8, WR £106, WR/D £160, child rates.

Stool End Farm Great Langdale, Ambleside LA22 9JZ 01966 7615
Mrs. Jean Rowand

Open all year
2 bedrs; (1 double, 1 family) 1 ba, 1 wc ☙
£B&B £15, child rates.

KENDAL 10B2

Benson Hall Farm Kendal
01539 721419   Mrs. Ladds

Open May-Oct
4 bedrs (1 twin; 2 family; 1 single) 1 ba, 2 wc ☙
£B&B £12, WR £77, child rates.

Cragg Farm New Hutton, Kendal
01539 721760   Mrs. Knowles

Cragg Farm is a 260-acre dairy & sheep farm, situated in beautiful countryside, convenient

for both the Lake District & Yorkshire Dales, only 3 miles from M6, jn 37. The 17th-century farmhouse offers excellent modern facilities. Take A684 to Sedbergh out of Kendal, go for 3 miles, L at Docker signpost, go 1ml, turn L, farm is 1st on R.

Open Mar-Oct
3 bedrs (1 double; 1 family; 1 single) 1 ba, 1 wc
£B&B £14-£15, child rates.

Garnett House Farm *Acclaimed*
Burneside, Kendal LA9 5SF   RAC
01539 724542   Mrs. Beaty

Open Jan-Dec
4 bedrs (1 twin; 1 double; 2 family sh/wc) 2 ba, 2 wc ☙ ♨ ♨
£B&B £13, D £7, WR £91, child rates.

Gateside Farm *Acclaimed* Windermere
Road, Kendal LA9 5SE   RAC
01539 722036   June Ellis

16th Century dairy and sheep farm offering friendly and comfortable accommodation, good home cooking, ideal place for touring the Lakes. 2 miles from Kendal towards Windermere on A591, large white farmhouse on right.

Open Jan-Dec
5 bedrs (inc 1 twin; 3 double inc 2 sh/wc) 2 ba, 2 wc
£B&B £15.50-£18.50, D £7.50-£7.75, child rates.

Hollowgate Farm Selside, Kendal LA8 9LG 01539 823258   Mrs. Knowles

Open all year
2 bedrs (2 double) 1 ba, 1 wc ☙ ⌂ ♞

Low Barns Farm Docker, Kendal LA8
0DB 01539 824217   Mrs. Knowles

Open Mar-Oct
2 bedrs (2 family) 1 ba, 1 wc ☻ 🏠 🐕

Murthwaite Farm Longsleddale, Kendal
LA8 9BA 01539 823634   Mrs. Waine

Open Mar-Nov
3 bedrs (1 twin; 2 double) 2 ba, 2 wc ☻ 🏠
Listed

Myers Farm Docker, Grayrigg, Kendal
LA8 0DF 01539 824610   Mrs. Knowles

Open Mar-Nov
3 bedrs (1 double; 1 family; single) 1 ba,
1 wc ☻ 🏠

Newalls Farmhouse Skelsmergh,
Kendal LA9 6NU 01539 723202
Mrs. Taylor

Large, modernised farmhouse on a 600 acre
dairy farm with visitors private entrance into
large garden and patio. A6 Shap Road 300
yards from main road.

Open Apr-Oct
2 bedrs (1 double; 1 family) 1 ba, 1 wc ☻
Listed
£B&B £13-£14, WR £91-£98, child rates.

Tranthwaite Hall Underbarrow, Kendal
LA8 8HG 01539 568285 Mrs. Swindlehurst

This dairy/sheep farm has an idyllic setting.
Beautiful old world farmhouse dates back to
the 11th Century with magnificent oak beams
& doors. Attractive accommodation with
comfortable furnishings. Many good pubs and
inns nearby. Exit 36 from M6, A6 to Kendal, L
at Town Hall traffic lights (All Hallows Ln)
follow rd 3 mls, R into signposted lane.

Open Jan-Dec
2 bedrs (1 twin; 1 double sh/wc) 1 ba, 1
wc ☻ *Listed*
£B&B £16-£19, child rates.

KESWICK   10B2

Bassenthwaite Hall Farm
Bassenthwaite, Keswick 01768 776393
Mrs. Trafford

Beef and sheep farm with a few pigs and hens.
17th century farmhouse and cottages ideally
situated by pretty stream. A real storybook
setting. Well cared for homely property. From
Keswick take A591 at the roundabout on
outskirts of Keswick, for approx 6 miles. Then
R at Black & White house.

Open all year
2 bedrs (1 twin; 1 family) 2 ba, 2 wc ☻(8) 🐕
£B&B £14-£18, WR £90-£125, child rates.

Lonscale Farm Threlkeld, Keswick
CA12 4TB 01768 779603   Mr. Scrimgeour

Open May-Oct
2 bedrs (1 double; 1 family) 1 ba, 1 wc ☻
Member
£B&B £15, child rates.

Stybeck Farm Thirlmere, Threlkeld,
Keswick CA12 4TN 01768 773232
Mrs. Jean Hodgson

Open Jan-Dec
3 bedrs (1 twin; 2 double inc 1 sh/wc) 2
ba, 1 wc ☻ 🏠 ✂ *Listed*
£B&B £14-£17, D £10-£12, child rates.

KIRKBY LONSDALE   10B2

Barnfield Farm Tunstall, Nr Kirkby
Lonsdale, LA6 2QP 01524 274284
Mrs. Stephenson

Open Jan-Dec
2 bedrs (1 double; 1 family) 1 ba, 2 wc 🛏
🏠 ⅄ *Listed*
£B&B £14-£15, child rates.

Tossbeck Farm Middleton, Kirkby
Lonsdale LA6 2LZ 01524 276214
Mrs. Bainbridge

The farmhouse is a 17th century, listed
building featuring oak panelling and
mullioned windows. The farm is a 110 acre
mixed stock farm (sheep and cows). Take A65
towards Skipton, A683 towards Sedburgh
passing large house on R in Middleton, next R
for farm.

Open Easter-Nov
2 bedrs (1 double; 1 family) 1 ba, 1 wc 🛏
🐕 ⅄
£B&B £12-£14, WR £80-£88, child rates.

KIRKBY STEPHEN   10C2

Aughill House Farm *Highly Acclaimed*
Brough, Kirkby Stephen, CA17 4DX
017683 41305   Mrs. Atkinson

3 bedrs (1 twin sh/wc; 2 double ens ba/wc)
⅄ 🌸🌸 *Highly Commended*
£dB&B £38-£40

LONGTOWN   13E4

New Pallyards Country Farmhouse
Hethersgill, Longtown, Carlisle CA5 6PX RAC
01228 577308   Mrs. Elwen

Meadow View stands on New Pallyards Farm,
a 65-acre working farm supporting ponies,
sheep and beef cattle. Its location, northeast
of Carlisle and 6 miles east of Longtown (A7),
is 9 miles from M6. Hadrian's Wall, woodland
walks and fishing are nearby.

Open all year
6 bedrs (2 twin sh/wc 1 ba/wc; 2 double 1
sh/wc, 1 ba/wc; 2 family 1 sh/wc, 1 ba/wc)
1 ba, 1 wc 🛏 🏠 🐕 ⅄ 🌸🌸🌸 *Commended*
cc Ac Vi £B&B £18.80, D £11, WR £110,
WR/D £170-£155.

PENRITH   10B1

Bridge End Farm Kirkby Thore, Penrith
CA10 1UZ 01768 352543   Mrs. Dent

Open all year
⅄

Highgate Farm Penrith CA11 0SE
01768 483339   Mr. Smith

Open mid Feb-mid Dec
⅄

Meaburn Hill Farm Maulds Meaburn,
Penrith CA10 3HN 01931 715205 Mr. Tuer

16th century Cumbrian longhouse with view
of village green and river valley. This 200 acre
sheep/beef farm enjoys extensive footpaths
that offer views of Eden Valley & the
Pennines. Leave M6 at Jn 39. Take B6260 to
Appleby. After 7m. turn left for Maulds
Meaburn, farm is in the village.

Open Easter-Nov.
4 bedrs (1 twin sh/wc; 2 double inc 1
ba/wc, 1 sh/wc; 1 single) 🛏 ⅄ 🌸🌸🌸
£B&B £19-£23, D £12-£13.

Tymparon Hall Newbiggin, Stainton,
Penrith CA11 0HS   RAC
01768 483236   M. Taylor

Enjoy the comforts of a typical Cumbrian
home whilst staying at this 150-acre sheep
farm which has a large garden and spacious
rooms. Good home cooking. Cots available.

Open all year
3 bedrs (1 twin; 1 double; 1 family sh/wc)
2 ba, 1 wc 🛏 🏠 ⅄ *Listed Approved*
£B&B £16.50-£20, D £8.50-£10, WR £110-
£125, WR/D £180-£165, child rates.

WIGTON 10A1

Howbeck Lodge Hesket Newmarket, Hesket CA7 8JN 01697 478206   C. Stobart

Open all year
3 bedrs (1 twin ba/wc) 1 ba, 1 wc ⚓
£B&B £16, D £10.

SELF CATERING

AMBLESIDE 10B2

Fell Foot Farm Little Langdale, Ambleside LA22 9PE 01539 437294 Mrs. Harryman

🐎(9)

BRAMPTON 10B1

High Nook Farm Low Row, Brampton CA8 2LU 01697 746273   Mrs. Forster

🐎 ♞
£Wk £70

CARLISLE 10B1

Arch View Midtodhills Farm, Roadhead, Carlisle CA6 6PF 01697 748213 Mrs. James

320 acre dairy, beef and sheep farm. Luxury cottages with four poster beds, oak beams, and log fire. Facilities include colour TV, video, dishwasher, microwave, washer/dryer, fridge/freezer and payphone. Use of swimming pool and mountain bikes.

M6, A7 Longtown, B6318 roadhead beside Bailey School.

3 units; 11 bedrs ♿ 🐎 ♞ ♟♟♟♟
£Wk £120-£398

Green View Lodges & Well Cottage

Green View, Welston, nr Dalston, Carlisle CA5 7ES 01697 476230   Mr. Ivinson

Every home comfort provided for a relaxing country holiday. Tiny picturesque hamlet, unspoilt views over rolling pastures to the Caldbeck Dells 3 miles away. Just bring yourselves and your food!

Chapel cottage - 1 bedroom, sleeps 2. Well House - 2 bedrooms, sleeps 4. Lodge 1 - 2 bedrooms, sleeps 4. Lodge 2/3, 3 bedrooms, sleeps 6. Well Cottage - 3 bedrooms, sleeps 7. All have microwaves, TV, CH, linen/towels, washing machines, direct dial phones.; Take B5299 for 9 miles to Welston.

6 units; 11 bedrs ♿ 🐎 ♞ cc Vi
£Wk £135-£440

Holmhead Farm Hadrian's Wall, Greenhead-in-Northumberland, Carlisle CA6 7HY 01697 747402   Mrs. Staff

For full farm description see B&B Entry. Take B6318 to A69, go east 3 miles.

♿ 🐎 ⚓ ♟♟♟ cc Vi
£Wk £125-£317

COCKERMOUTH 10A1

High Stanger Farm Cockermouth CA13 9TS 01900 823875   Mrs. Hewitson

🐎 ♞ ⚓ ♟♟♟ Listed

Jenkin Farm Embleton, Cockermouth CA13 9TN 01768 776387   Mrs. Teasdale

For full farm description see B&B Entry.

1 unit; 2 bedrs 🐎 ♟♟♟
£Wk £230-£350

Stanger Farm Cockermouth CA13 9TS 01900 824222   C. A. Heslop

For full farm description see B&B Entry. From town centre take B5292, 2 miles out of town turn right at crossroads, 150 yards turn left, farm on right.

1 unit; 2 bedrs 🐎
£Wk £85-£275

KENDAL 10B2

High Swinklebank Farm
Longsleddale, Kendal LA8 9BD
01539 823682   Olive Simpson

1 unit ☒ ☒ ☒ ☒ *Commended*

Hyning Cottages Hyning, Grayrigg,
Kendal CA8 9BX 01539 824627
Mr. & Mrs. Marshall

4 units; 1-2 bedrs ☒ ☒

Brunt Knott Farm Brunt Knott, Over
Staveley LA8 9QX 01539 821030
Mrs. Dace

☒

KESWICK 10B2

Bassenthwaite Hall Farm
Bassenthwaite, Keswick 01768 776393
Mrs. Trafford

For full farm description see B&B Entry. From
Keswick take A591 at the roundabout on
outskirts of Keswick, for approx 6 miles. Then
R at Black & White house.

3 units; 7 bedrs ☒(8) ☒
£Wk £70-£500

KIRKBY STEPHEN 10C2

Augill House Farm Brough, Kirkby
Stephen CA17 4DX   ☒ RAC
017683 41305   Mrs. Atkinson

For full farm description see p39. There are 2
self-catering properties on the farm, with 1-2
bedrooms, sleeping 2-3.

☒

MILNTHORPE 10A2

Preston Patrick Hall Cottage
Crooklands, Milnthorpe LA7 7NY
01539 567200   Mrs. Armitage

A self contained wing of a Medieval Manor
House built in traditional Lake District stone
and slate, set within 250 acres of farmland.

Follow the A65 towards the M6 (junction 36),
turn left opposite village hall and first right in
½ mile.

1 unit; 2 bedrs ☒ ☒
£Wk £100-£275

PENRITH 10B1

Skirwith Hall Skirwith, Penrith CA10
1RH 01768 88241   Mrs. Wilson

☒ ☒ ☒ ☒ *Approved*
£Wk £95-£320

PLACES TO VISIT

APPLEBY

Appleby Castle Conservaton Centre
Appleby Castle, Appleby CA16 6XH
017683-51402
The Castle and grounds provide a
beautiful riverside setting for rare breeds
of farm animals, cattle, sheep, goats and
pigs. Also a large collection of birds
including owls, flamingoes, parakeets,
domestic and ornamental waterfowl etc.
The Great Hall of the House and Norman
Keep are open to the public. The centre
now incorporates 'The National School of
Falconry'. Tarzan Trail.
Location: 12 miles southeast of Penrith
on the A66. M6 junctions 38
(northbound) and 40 (southbound).
Open: April-Oct daily 1000-1700 (1600 in Oct).
Entrance: adult £3.50, child £1.50, under
5s free, OAP £2 ☒ ☒ ☒ ☒

DERBYSHIRE

ALKMONTON 8A2

Dairy House Farm Alkmonton DE6 3DG 01335 330359 A. Harris

81 acre, stock rearing farm with old oak beamed farmhouse, inglenook fireplace own dining room and lounges. Log fires and good home cooking. A515 to Ashbourne.

Open All Year except Xmas
7 bedrs (1 twin ba/wc; 3 double inc 2 sh/wc; 3 single inc 1 sh/wc) 3 ba, 2 wc ⌸ ✂ 🛏🛏🛏 *Highly Commended*
£B&B £16-£23, D £12-£15, WR £105-£154, WR/D £175-£224.

ASHBOURNE 8A2

Air Cottage Farm Ilam, Ashbourne DE6 2BD 01335 29475 Mrs. Wain

A small hill farm, farming sheep and beef cattle. Peaceful and quiet with wonderful views overlooking Dovedale. A515 from Ashbourne, turn left where signposted to Ilam, then turn right at memorial. First cattlegrid gateway on right.

Open Mar-Nov
3 bedrs (1 twin; 1 double; 1 single) 1 ba, 1 wc ☒ 🛏 *Listed*
£B&B £14-£16, WR £98-£112, child rates.

Beechenhill Farm Ilam, Dovedale, Ashbourne DE6 2BD 01335 27274 Mrs. Prince

Warm farmhouse facing south on a traditional dairy farm in the Peak National Park. House and cottages are beautifully decorated and very welcoming. Take A515 north towards Buxton. After 1 mile turn left for Ilam. In Ilam turn right at monument. Farm one mile on left.

Open Feb-Dec
2 bedrs (1 double sh/wc; 1 family sh/wc) ☒ ⌸ ✂ 🛏🛏 *Highly Commended*
£B&B £17-£21, child rates.

Bent Farm Tissington, Ashbourne DE6 1RD 01335 390214 Mrs. Herridge

A Peak District National Park working dairy farm offering homely accommodation in the 17th century farmhouse. Some rooms are ensuite. Visitors lounge with TV and log fires. Tea and coffee facilities in all rooms.

Open all year
3 bedrs (2 twin ba/wc; 1 double ba/wc) ☒(4)
£B&B £15.50, WR £105, child rates.

Collycroft Farm Clifton, Ashbourne DE6 29N 01335 342187 Mrs. Hollingsworth

Open all year
3 bedrs (1 double; 1 twin; 1 family) ☒

Little Park Farm Mappleton,
Ashbourne DE6 2BR 01335 29341
Mrs. Harrison

Open all year
3 bedrs (1 twin; 2 double) 1 ba, 1 wc ☎(5)
🐝Commended

Sidesmill Farm Snelston, Ashbourne
DE6 2GQ 01335 342710   Mrs. Brandrick

Sidesmill farm is a working dairy farm on the
banks of the River Dove. A rippling mill
stream flows past the 18th century stone-built
farmhouse. A515 Lichfield Road out of
Ashbourne. Clifton village, Norbury Lane.

Open Apr-Oct
2 bedrs (1 twin; 1 double) 1 ba ☎(2) *Listed*
£B&B £14-£15, WR £91.

Throwley Hall Farm Ilam, Dovedale,
Ashbourne DE6 2BB 01538 308202
M. A. Richardson

Open all year
5 bedrs (1 twin; 2 double inc 1 sh/wc; 1
family; 1 single) 1 ba, 2 wc ☎ 🏠 🛏 🐝🐝
Commended
£B&B £16-£19, WR £98-£112, child rates.

ASHOVER   8A2

Old School Farm Uppertown, Ashover
S45 0JF   RAC
01246 590813   J.A. Wootton

Open Mar-Oct
4 bedrs (1 double; 2 family sh/wc; 1 single)
1 ba, 1 wc ☎ ✄ 🐝
£B&B £16, D £6, WR £112, WR/D £154,
child rates.

BELPER   8B2

Dannah Farm *Highly Acclaimed*
Bowman's Lane,Shottle, Belper DE5 2DR

01773 550273 Fax 01773 550590   RAC

7 bedrs (inc 6 en suite) 1 ba cc Ac Vi

Lawn Farm Whitewells Lane, (off Holly
Lane), Ambergate DE56 2DN
01773 852352   Mrs. Oulton

Open all year.
2 bedrs (1 double ba/wc; 1 family) ☎ 🛏 🐝
£B&B £15-£25, WR £90-£150, child rates.

BRAILSFORD   7F2

Mercaston Hall Mercaston, Brailsford
DE6 3BL 01335 360263   Mr. Haddon

Historic, listed buildings in a quiet location.
A52 Derby to Ashbourne Rd in Brailsford.
Take turning to Hulland, 1st crossroads turn R,
signpost Mercaston, 1 ¼ ml R.

Open Jan-Dec
3 bedrs (1 twin ba/wc; 2 double inc 1
sh/wc) 1 ba, 2 wc ☎(10) 🛏 🐝🐝
£B&B £29-£33, WR £191-£219, child rates.

BUXTON   8A1

Cotesfield Farm Parsley Hay, Buxton
SK17 0BD 01298 83256   Mr. Mckerrow

Open Feb-Oct
3 bedrs (1 twin; 1 double; 1 family) 1 ba, 1
wc ☎(6) 🏠

Fernydale Farm Earl Sterndale, Buxton
SK17 0BS 01298 83236   J Nadin

Working dairy/sheep farm.

Open Jan-Nov
2 bedrs (2 double sh/wc) 🐝🐝
£B&B £18-£20.

Mosley House Farm Maynestone Road, Chinley, Buxton SK12 6AH 01663 750240 Mrs. Goddard

Enjoy a stay on our lovely Dairy Farm surrounded by superb countryside. Lovely spacious rooms with central heating, TV, washbasins, delicious breakfasts, garden and patio. 10 minutes walk to village. Chinley is off the A624 Glossop to Buxton Road.

Open Jan-Dec
2 bedrs (1 double ba/wc; 1 family ba/wc) 1 ba, 1 wc ✿ ♿ Listed
£B&B £14-£15, WR £90-£95, child rates.

Shallow Grange Chelmorton, Buxton SK17 0DY 01298 23578 Mrs. Holland

Open all year
3 bedrs (1 twin ba/wc; 1 double ba/wc; 1 family ba/wc) ✿(5) ♿ ♛♛♛

Wolfscote Grange Farm Hartington, Nr Buxton SK17 0AX 01298 84342 Mrs. Gibbs

Open Jan-Dec
4 bedrs (1 twin; 2 double inc 1 sh/wc; 1 family) ✿ ♿
£B&B £16, child rates.

CHINLEY 7F1

Cote Bank Farm Buxworth, Whaley Bridge, Buxton SK12 7NP 01663 750566 Mr. Broadhurst

Cote Bank, home of the Broadhursts for 200 years, is an 150 acre hill sheep farm in the Peak National Park. The guests' lounge has a log fire. Bedrooms with tea/coffee making facilities. Enjoy wonderful walks, spectacular views and warm hospitality. B6062 to Chinley, right at 'Squirrels', left up Stubbins Lane, left at first fork.

Open Mar-Nov
2 bedrs (1 double sh/wc; 1 family ba/wc) ✿(6) ♛♛ Highly Commended
£B&B £17-£18.50, WR £110-£115, child rates.

DERBY 8B2

Parkview Farm Weston Underwood, Ashbourne DE6 4PA 01335 360352 Mrs. Adams

Parkview is a 370 acre mixed farm with an attractive Victorian farmhouse set in large, lawned gardens in beautiful countryside. Country house hospitality, delightful rooms and four poster beds.

The farm can either be approached from the A38 or A52 from Derby. Follow the National Trust signs for Kedleston Hall.

Open all year
3 bedrs (2 double; 1 single) 2 ba, 3 wc
🛏(4) 👑👑
£B&B £18.50-£25, child rates.

The Beeches Farmhouse Waldley, Doveridge, Derby DE6 5LR 01889 590288 Mrs. Tunnicliffe

160 acre dairy farm with 18th century farmhouse with licensed restaurant. Won national award for farm based catering. Derby Rd from Uttoxeter to Doveridge village, turn L opposite Cavendish pub Maiston Ln, 2ms grass triangle, R, 1st on L.

Open Jan-Dec
10 bedrs (1 twin ba/wc; 2 double sh/wc; 7 family ba/wc) 3 wc 🛏 🏠 👑👑👑 *Highly Commended* cc Ac AmEx DC Vi
£B&B £22.50-£38.50, D £9.50-£18.50, WR £157.50-£269.50, WR/D £224-£399, child rates.

MATLOCK 8A2

Farley Farm Farley, Matlock DE4 5LR 01629 582533 Mrs. Brailsford

Open Jan-Dec
3 bedrs (1 twin; 1 double; 1 family) 2 ba, 2 wc 🛏 🏠 🐕 👑👑
£B&B £15-£16, D £6, WR £105, WR/D £147, child rates.

Henmore Grange Hopton, Wirksworth, Matlock DE4 4DF 01629 540420 Mrs. Brassington

Open Jan-Dec
14 bedrs (5 twin inc 3 ba/wc, 1 sh/wc; 7 double inc 2 ba/wc, 4 sh/wc; 2 family inc 1 ba/wc, 1 sh/wc) 1 ba, 3 wc 🛏 🐕 👑👑👑
£B&B £20-£31, child rates.

Packhorse Farm Tansley, Matlock DE4 5LF
01629 582781 Mrs. Haynes

Packhorse Farm is quietly situated in extensive grounds on the edge of the Peak District, a couple of miles east of Matlock on the A615. It is a working farm with 40 acres. Its location makes it ideal as a touring base. Good walking country.

Closed Xmas and New Year
4 bedrs (1 twin; 2 double; 1 family) 🛏(3) 🏠 🐕
£B&B £15.

Tithe Farm Aldwark, Grange Mill, Matlock DE4 4HX 01629 540263 D. Forsey

Open Apr-Oct
2 bedrs (1 twin ba/wc; 1 family ba/wc) 🛏 🏠 👑👑
£B&B £17-£22.50, WR £119-£150.50, child rates.

MICKLEOVER 8A2

Bonehill Farm Etwall Road, Derby, Mickleover DE3 5DN 01332 513553 Mrs. Dicken

Georgian farmhouse in rural setting. 120 acre

All towns listed in this guide
are shown on the maps
at the back.

sheep, beef, turkey & arable farm. On A516 3 miles from town centre.

Open Jan-Dec
3 bedrs (1 twin; 1 double, 1 family) ☎
🏠Listed
£B&B £15-£18, WR £105-£125, child rates.

RIPLEY 11D3

Bowes Green Farm Bishop Thornton, Ripley, Harrogate HG3 3JX 01423 770114 Mrs. Sowray

Open all year

SELF CATERING

ASHBOURNE 8A2

Beechenhill Farm Ilam, Dovedale, Ashbourne DE6 2BD 01335 27274 Mrs. Prince

For full farm description see B&B Entry. Take A515 north towards Buxton. After 1 mile turn left for Ilam. In Ilam turn right at monument. Farm one mile on left.

☎ 🏠 Highly Commended
£Wk £110-£375

Throwley Hall Farm Ilam, Dovedale, Ashbourne DE6 2BB 01538 308202 M. A. Richardson

Follow A52, then A523 turn right for Calton. Go straight over crossroads, right at T junction and follow road 2 miles.

☎ 🏠 Commended
£Wk £180-£450

BAKEWELL 8A2

Old House Farm Newhaven, Hartington, SK17 0DY 01629 636268 Mrs. Flower

A warm, spacious and beautifully appointed cottage. High standards are also maintained on our 400 acre dairy/sheep farm.

Half way between Ashbourne & Burton on A515 at Newhaven turn onto A5012, farm is around corner on left.

☎ 🏠 Commended
£Wk £150-£280

BELPER 8B2

Chevin House Farm The Chevin, Belper DE56 2UN 01773 823144 Mr. Jordan

☎ 🏠 Commended
£Wk £100-£220

BUXTON 8A1

Shallow Grange Chelmorton, Buxton SK17 0DY 01298 23578   Mrs. Holland

The Grange has 3 self-catering units, with 1-2 bedrooms, sleeping 2-4.

☎(5)

Wolfscote Grange Farm Hartington, Nr Buxton SK17 0AX 01298 84342 Mrs. Gibbs

For full farm description see B&B Entry. A515 take B5054 to Hartington, L in Hartington after phone box, up hill, chapel L, 20 yds, then R, follow signs 2mls.

☎ 🏠
£Wk £140-£250

DERBY 8B2

Parkview Farm Weston Underwood, Ashbourne DE6 4PA 01335 360352 Mrs. Adams

For full farm description see B&B Entry. The farm can either be approached from the A38 or A52 from Derby. Follow the National Trust signs for Kedleston Hall.

☎(4) 🏠
£Wk £120-£350

PLACES TO VISIT

ALKMONTON

Bentley Fields open farm
Alkmonton, Longford, Derby
01335-330240
This 240-acre livestock farm rears rare breeds alongside modern ones. There are cows, sheep, pigs and poultry plus a farm trail through a lost village.
Location: 2 miles from A515 Ashbourne/Sudbury road or 7 miles from

A52 Derby/Ashbourne road.
Open: 11.00am-6.00pm April 16th-22nd,
May Day, Sun/Mon May 28th-3rd June
and Sun only July/August plus August
Bank Holiday Mon.
Entrance: adult £1.50,
child/OAP/concessions £0.80 WC & ✗ 🏊

BURTON UPON TRENT

**Bass Museum, Visitor Centre & Shire
Horse Stables**
Horninglow Street, Burton upon Trent
DE14 1JZ 01283-51000

Guided brewery tours, audio-visual
history of brewing, shire horses and
brewery wagons.
Location: on the main A50 opposite the
police station.Open all year, daily 1000-
1700.
Entrance: adult £3.45 child £1.85
OAP/concession £2.35 WC & ✗ 🏊

DEVON

BAMPTON   4B2

Newhouse Farm Oakford, Tiverton,
Bampton EX16 9JE 013985 347
Mrs. Boldry

Newhouse is a 17th century farmhouse with
oak beams and inglenook fireplace. All
bedrooms individually furnished with ensuite
bathrooms and drink-making facilities. Farm
entrance on B3227 5 miles West of Bampton.

Open all year
3 bedrs (1 twin ba/wc; 2 double ba/wc)
😺😺
£B&B £16-£18, D £10, WR £105-£110,
WR/D £165-£170.

Huxtable Farm West Buckland,
Barnstaple EX32 0SR 01598 760254
Jackie Payne

Secluded sheep farm with a medieval
longhouse and barn furnished with antiques.
4 course, candlelit dinner with complimentary
homemade wine. Log fires in winter. Sauna
and fitness room. Farm walks, wild flowers,
badger sets. 5 mls on A361 towards Taunton,
L turn off (signpost W/E Buckland), through
W Buckland, 1 ml E Buckland, entrance on R.

Open Jan-Dec
6 bedrs (1 twin ba/wc; 3 double inc 1
ba/wc; 2 family ba/wc) 🐕 🏛 😺😺😺
Commended
£B&B £20-£25, D £12, child rates.

Rowden Barton Roundswell,
Barnstaple, Bampton EX31 3NP
01271 44365   Mrs. Dallyn
Open all year
2 bedrs (1 twin; 1 double) 2 ba, 2 wc
🐕(12) 🏛 *Listed*

Waytown Farm Shirwell, Barnstaple
EX31 4JN 01271 850396   Mrs. Kingdon

240 acre beef and sheep farm, set in the
lovely, rolling Devonshire countryside. 17th
century farmhouse offering every comfort with
delicious home cooking. Take A39 Lynton Rd
out of Barnstaple, farm on right hand side of
main Rd before Shirwell Village.

Open Jan-Dec
4 bedrs (1 twin; 1 double sh/wc; 1 family; 1
single) 1 ba, 1 wc 🐕 😺😺 *Commended*
£B&B £16-£18.50, D £7.50, WR £110-£125,
WR/D £145-£160, child rates.

BARNSTAPLE 2C2

Haxton Down Farm Bratton Fleming, Barnstaple EX32 7JL 01598 710275 Mrs. Burge

Working beef and sheep farm, parts of house 17th century. Set in peaceful surroundings with no passing traffic. Wildlife and farm animals. Excellent food and service guaranteed. Leave Barnstaple head to Bratton Fleming at top of village fork R, farm 1 mile on, on R.

Open Apr-Nov
3 bedrs (inc 1 double;1 single) 1 wc ☎ ♘*Listed*
£B&B £14-£16, D £7.50-£8, WR £95-£100, WR/D £140-£150, child rates.

Home Park Farm *Highly Acclaimed*
Lower Blakewell, Muddiford, Barnstaple
EX31 4ET   RAC
01271 42955   Mrs. Lethaby

Open Jan-Dec
3 bedrs (1 twin; 1 double; 1 family) ☎ ⌕
♚♚
£B&B £15-£17.50, D £7.50, WR/D £150-£160, child rates.

Meadow Farm East Buckland, Barnstaple EX32 0TB 01598 760375 Mrs. Hopkins

Spacious bungalow surrounded by beautiful gardens, meadows, and wonderful views to Exmoor. Ideal base for touring Exmoor National Park, North Devons rugged coastline and sandy beaches. Between South Molton and Barnstaple on A361, turn west to Buckland, approx. 2 ½ miles to farm.

Open Jan-Dec
2 bedrs ♚♚
£B&B £16-£20, D £10, WR £112, WR/D £165.

Stone Farm Brayford, Barnstaple EX32 7PJ 01271 830473   L. P. A. Joslin

Open Jan-Dec
4 bedrs (1 twin; 1 double ba/wc; 2 family ba/wc) 1 ba, 1 wc ☎ ⌕
£B&B £16-£17, D £6-£9, WR/D £155, child rates.

Denham Farm *Acclaimed* North
Buckland, Braunton EX33 1HY   RAC
01271 890297   J. Barnes

A 100 acre beef and sheep farm in unspoilt hamlet built around 1712. On Braunton to Ilfracombe A361 take 2nd turning left past Knowle village, signposted North Buckland, continue 1 mile.

Open Jan-Dec
10 bedrs (2 twin sh/wc; 6 double inc 2 ba/wc, 4 sh/wc; 2 family) 1 ba, 1 wc ☎
♚♚♚ *Commended* cc Ac Vi
£B&B £20-£25, D £12, WR £140-£147, WR/D £198-£217, child rates.

> ## For a full explanation of a farm entry, see page 5.

BIDEFORD 2C2

Higher Venn Farmhouse
Woolfardisworthy, Nr Bideford EX39 5RQ
01237 431017   Mr. Thomas

Family-run, small holding offering a range of
ensuite, twin, double and family rooms.
Generous farmhouse breakfast served as
standard. Tea/coffee facilities in all rooms.
Guest's TV lounge and dining room with log
fire. Free babysitting. A39 from Bideford to
Bucks Cross take R turn signposted
Woolfardisworthy. From village take rd to
Meddon, farm 1 ml on R

Open Jan-Dec
5 bedrs (1 twin ba/wc; 3 double inc 2
ba/wc, 1 sh/wc; 1 family ba/wc) 2 ba ♂ ♄
£B&B £13-£15, WR £78-£90, child rates.

Summerwell Farm Hartland, Bideford
EX39 6HB 01237 441304   R. Macer

Open March-Oct
3 bedrs (1 twin; 1 double; 1 single) 1 ba, 1
wc ♂
£B&B £13-£15, D £6, WR £98, WR/D £115-
£120, child rates.

BOVEY TRACEY 3D3

Frost Farm Hennock, Bovey Tracey
TQ13 9PP 01626 833266   Mr. Harvey

A pretty, pink-washed, thatched old
farmhouse on working organic farm in our
green valley. Good farmhouse food, fresh
meats, vegetables, fruits, local ice-cream. Large
spacious bedrooms en suite with tea/coffee
facilites, colour TV, CH.

Open all year
3 bedrs (3 twin sh/wc) ♂ ⊁ ♠*Commended*

BUCKFASTLEIGH 2C3

Mill Leat Farm Holne, Ashburton,
Newton Abbot TQ13 7RZ 01364 3283
Mrs. Cleave

Traditional, stone-built farmhouse cut into the
hillside on a traditionally run Dartmoor Hill
farm consisting mainly of sheep and beef
cattle. Take Holne/Scorriton Road and follow
until you see granite cross and oak tree on
triangle of grass - then turn right.

Open all year
2 bedrs (2 family) 1 ba ♂*Listed Approved*
£B&B £13, D £7.50, WR £89, WR/D £130.

CLOVELLY 2C2

Burscott Farm Clovelly, Nr Bideford,
Clovelly 01237 431252   Mrs. Jewell

Open Mar-Nov
3 bedrs (twin; 1 family, 1 double) 1 ba,
1wc
♂ ⌂

COLYTON 3D3

Higher Cownhayne Farm Cownhayne
Lane, Colyton EX13 6HD 01297 552267
Elise Pady

Open all year
♂
£B&B £13.50-£15.

Smallicombe Farm Northleigh, EX13 6BU 01404 831310 Mrs. Todd

A small working farm in an Area of Outstanding Natural Beauty, with Jersey cows, pigs, sheep and goats. Family suite on ground floor, the twin room is equipped for elderly or partially disabled. Good farmhouse cooking. Cot, highchair, laundry. Situated south of A35 Axminster-Honiton road.

Open all year-except Xmas
4 bedrs (1 twin ba/wc; 1 double ba/wc; 1 family ba/wc; 1 single ba/wc)
Commended
£B&B £17.50-£19, D £6-£10.50, WR £115-£129.

CREDITON 3D3

Brindiwell Farm Cheriton Fitzpaine, Nr Crediton EX17 4HR 01363 866357 Mrs. Lock

Open all year
3 bedrs (1 twin; 1 double; 1 single) 1 ba 1 wc *Listed*
£B&B £12-£15, D £8-£10, WR £84, WR/D £110.

Hele Barton Black Dog, Thelbridge, Crediton EX17 4QJ 01884 860278 Mrs. Gilblard

The 236 acre family-run beef and sheep farm lies ten miles west of Tiverton (B3137/B3042). The listed 17th century farmhouse has a thatched roof and many period details inside. Tea/Coffee making facilities in rooms. TV lounge and traditional cooking. M5 junction 27 to Tiverton, then B3137 (Tiverton-S Molton Rd) 10 miles to Witheridge then B3042, 2 miles turn L ½ mile on L.

Open all year
5 bedrs (2 twin inc 1 sh/wc; 2 double inc 1 sh/wc; 1 family sh/wc) 1 ba, 2 wc
Commended
£B&B £14-£18, D £7-£8, WR £90-£110, WR/D £135-£155, child rates.

Hensley Farm Worlington, Crediton EX34 0NE 01884 860346 Rosemarie Webber

16th century, thatched oak farmhouse situated near picturesque country villages. 80 dairy cattle, sheep and beef cattle. Guests are welcome to roam around farm. Wonderful walks with river on farm. North Devon link road A361, take B3137 to Wintleigh, No Mans Land, Witheridge, Drayford, Worlington, farm ½ mile.

Open Apr-Oct
2 bedrs (1 double ba/wc; 1 family) 1 ba, 2
wc ☎(4) 🏠 ✝ cc Ac Vi
£B&B £13.50, D £7.50, child rates.

Stockham Farm Thelbridge, Crediton
EX17 4SJ 01884 860308   Mrs. Webber

Open Feb-Nov
4 bedrs (1 twin; 2 double ba/wc; 1 single)
2 wc ☎ 🏠 ⚡ 🐴🐴
£B&B £16-£18, D £9.50, WR £105-£125,
WR/D £160-£175, child rates.

CROYDE   2C2

Combas Farm Braunton EX33 1PH
01271 890398   Mrs. Adams

This traditional 17th-century Devon longhouse
with inglenook fireplaces is set in a secluded
valley, off the B3231 out of Braunton, within
walking distance of the beaches and coastal
path. Combas is a mixed farm covering 140
acres.

Open Apr-Nov
☎ 🏠 Listed Commended

CULLOMPTON   3D2

Sunnyside Farm Butterleigh,
Cullompton EX15 1PP 01884 855322
Mrs. Hill

Open Jan-Dec
3 bedrs (2 double sh/wc; 1 family) 1 ba, 1
wc ☎ ✝
£B&B £15-£17, D £9, WR £90, WR/D £140,
child rates.

DAWLISH   3D3

Smallacombe Farm Aller Valley,
Dawlish EX7 0PS 01626 862536

A. J. Thomson

Open all year
3 bedrs (1 twin ba/wc; 1 double ba/wc; 1
family) 3 ba, 2 wc ☎ 🐴

EXETER   3D3

Marianne Pool Clyst St George, Exeter
EX3 0NZ 01392 874939   Mrs. Bragg

Open all year
2 bedrs (1 twin; 1 family) 1 ba, 1 wc ☎ 🏠
✝ Listed

Mill Farm Kenton, Exeter EX6 8JR
01392 832471   Mr. Lambert

Open all year
5 bedrs (1 twin; 2 double; 2 family) 1 ba, 2
wc ☎ 🏠 ✝ Listed Commended

Whitemoor Farm Doddiscombsleigh,
Exeter EX6 7PU 01647 52423   Mrs. Lacey

16th Century thatched farmhouse surrounded
by own farmland and garden. Peaceful and
quiet mixed farm. M5-A38 turn off L, top of
Haldon Hill for Dunchideock. R under road,
4th signposted turning L 1/2ml R at bottom of
hill

Open Jan-Dec
4 bedrs (1 twin; 1 double ba/sh/wc; 2
single) 1 ba, 2 wc ☎ 🏠 ✝ ⚡ 🐴
£B&B £16-£16.50, D £8, WR £105-£108.50,
WR/D £157.50, child rates.

EXMOOR 3D2

Hindon Farm Nr Minehead, Exmoor
TA24 8SH 01643 705244   P. M. Webber

Superbly positioned 18th century farm with 500 acres set in moorland, between Minehead (3 miles) and village of Selworthy 1 mile. Real working farm with sheep, cows, pigs, poultry, horses, etc. Turn off A39 (Minehead to Porlock road) signed to village of Bratton, through lane to Hindon Farm.

Open all year
3 bedrs; (1 twin 2 double inc 1sh/wc) 1 ba, 1 wc ☌ ⌦ ✝ *Listed Commended*
£B&B £18-£20, D £13-£15, child rates.

Little Brendon Hill Wheddon Cross, Exmoor TA24 7DG 01643 841556
Mrs. Maxwell

Small sheep farm with horses and many 'free range' birds. 9mls from Minehead turn L at Wheddon Cross (A396) to B3224 about 1ml up hill on L.

Open Jan-Dec
3 bedrs (2 twin ba/wc; 1 double ba/wc) ☌ ⌦ ✗ ☙☙
£B&B £16, D £10.

Little Quarme Farm Wheddon Cross, Exmoor TA24 7EA 01643 841249
Mr. Cody-Boutcher

Lovely old farmhouse standing amid 18 acre horse and sheep farm. Outstanding southerly views. Very well furnished, TV lounge, sun lounge. Friendly family atmosphere. Very peaceful and many animals. ¼ mile past Wheddon Cross on Exford road B3224.

Open Apr-Nov
3 bedrs (1 twin, 1 double, 1 family) 2 ba, 1 wc ☌ ⌦ *Listed*

£B&B £15-£17, D £8-£10, WR £100-£110, child rates.

EXMOUTH 3D3

Gulliford Farm Lympstone, Exmouth
EX8 5AQ 01392 873067   Mrs. Hallett

Open Jan-Dec
7 bedrs (2 twin; 2 double; 1 family; 2 single) 1 ba, 1 wc ☌
£B&B £18-£20, WR £126-£140, child rates.

HOLSWORTHY 2C3

Elm Park Farm Bridgerule, Holsworthy
EX22 7JT 01288 81231   Mrs. Lucas

Open Mar-Oct
4 bedrs (1 twin, 3 family inc 2 sh/wc) 1 ba 1wc ☌ ✝ ☙☙

Leworthy Farm Holsworthy EX22 6SJ ⛪
01409 253488   Mr. Cornish

Open all year
12 bedrs (2 twin inc 1 ba/wc, 1 sh/wc; 3 double ba/wc; 6 family inc 4 ba/wc, 2 sh/wc; 1 single ba/wc) 2 ba, 3 wc ☌ ✝ ☙☙
£B&B £14.50-£19, D £10, WR/D £144-£186.

Ley Farm Milton Damerel, Holsworthy
EX22 7NY 01409 261259   Mrs. Holdcroft

Thatched 16th century farmhouse on a 100 acre dairy farm.

Open April- October
2 bedrs (2 family) 1 ba, 1 wc ☌
£B&B £13-£15, WR £85-£95, child rates.

Lodgeworthy Bridgerule, Holsworthy
EX22 7EH 01288 81351   Mrs. Hale

Attractive, 15th century, Devon longhouse in a
secluded position on a 250 acre dairy farm
bordered by the river Tamar. Pretty ensuite
bedrooms. 3 miles south off the A3072
Holsworthy-Bude road. Farm entrance by
bridge in village.

Open all year
5 bedrs (1 twin sh/wc; 2 double sh/wc; 1
family sh/wc; 1 single) 1 ba, 1 wc ⛺ ☼☼☼
Commended
£B&B £15, D £7, WR/D £140, child rates.

The Barton Pancrasweek, Holsworthy
EX22 7JT 01288 81315   Mrs. Cole

Open May-Sept
3 bedrs (inc 1 twin ba/wc) ⛺ ☼☼☼
£B&B £13-£14, D £7-£8, WR £91-£98, WR/D
£140-£147, child rates.

West Nethercott Whitstone, Holsworthy
EX22 6LD 01288 84394   Mr. Hopper

Open all year

ILSINGTON   3D3

Narracombe Farm Ilsington, Newton
Abbot TQ13 9RD 01364 661243 Mrs. Wills

Mixed farm, with charming old farmhouse, set
in pleasant surroundings. Spacious and
comfortable rooms, communal bathroom with
shower. Delicious breakfasts and evening
meals. Take Haytor road from Bovey. Follow
signs for Haytor. After cattle grid take 1st left,
then take 2nd right into farm.

Open Jan-Dec
2 bedrs (1 twin; 1 family) ⛺
£B&B £15-£16, D £8-£10, WR £98, WR/D
£154-£168, child rates.

IVYBRIDGE   2C4

Venn Farm Ugborough, Ivybridge
01364 73240   Mrs. Stephens

Open Feb-Nov
4 bedrs (2 twin inc 1 ba/wc; 2 family inc 1
sh/wc) ⛺(2) 🐕 ☼☼☼ *Commended*
£B&B £17, D £9, child rates.

Weeke Farm Modbury, Ivybridge PL21
0TT 01548 830219   Mr. Rogers

Open Mar-Nov
2 bedrs (1 double, 1 family) 1 ba, 1wc ⛺
🐕 *Listed*

KINGSBRIDGE   2C4

Burton Farm Galmpton, Kingsbridge
TQ7 3EY 01548 561210   Mr. Rossiter

Working dairy/sheep farm with recently
renovated 15th century farmhouse with
tasteful decor. Ensuite facilities, guest lounge
with TV, stereo and video. Home cooking
using farm produce. Hope Cove 1 mile,

Salcombe 3 miles. Kingsbridge take Salcombe Rd 3mls to Hope Cove sign (R) then to giveway T-junction. Go 600yds, take L-hand slip Rd, L.

Open Jan-Dec
7 bedrs (2 twin inc 1 ba/wc; 2 double inc 1 sh/wc; 2 family ba/wc; 1 single) 2 ba, 2 wc
🐕 ⌗ ♨♨
£B&B £17-£20, D £9, WR £119-£140, WR/D £182-£203, child rates.

Coombe Farm Kingsbridge TQ7 4AB
01548 852038   Mrs. Robinson

Open all year

South Allington House Galmpton, Chivelstone, Kingsbridge TQ7 2NB
01548 511272   B.J. Baker

Georgian house in four acres of lovely grounds on an arable farm. Bowls, croquet, and fishing available. Kingsbridge follow sign to Frogmore, bottom Frogmore turn R for East Prawle to Chivelstone Cross, L, farm ½ ml on R.

Open Jan-Dec
11 bedrs (3 twin inc 1 ba/wc; 4 double inc 1 ba/wc, 2 sh/wc; 2 family inc 1 ba/wc; 2 single) 1 ba, 2 wc 🐕 ⌗ ✂ ♨♨♨ *Commended*
£B&B £18-£24, child rates.

LODDISWELL   2C4

Crannacombe Farm Hazlewood, Loddiswell, Kingsbridge TQ7 4DX
01548 550256   Mr. Bradley

Open all year

MORETONHAMPSTEAD   3D3

Little Wooston Farm
Moretonhampstead TQ13 8QA
01647 40551   Mrs. Cuming

Open Apr-Oct
3 bedrs (1 double; 1 family; 1 single) 🐕 ⌗ 🐦 *Listed*
£B&B £12.50-£13, D £16-£17, WR/D £15-£16, child rates.

NEWTON ABBOT   3D3

Great Sloncombe Farm
Moretonhampstead, Newton Abbot TQ13 8QF 01647 440595   Mrs. Merchant

13th century farmhouse in a magical Dartmoor valley. Dairy farm with meadows, woodland, wildflowers and animals. En-suite bedrooms, farmhouse breakfasts with newbaked bread, delicious suppers - everything provided for an enjoyable country break. Moretonhampstead take A382 towards Chagford for 1½ mls. At sharp double bend take L turning, farm is 1/2ml on R.

Open Jan-Dec
3 bedrs (1 twin sh/wc; 2 double sh/wc)
🐕(8) ⌗ 🐦 ♨♨♨ *Commended*
£B&B £18-£20, D £10-£10.50.

Kellinch Farm Bickington, Newton Abbot TQ12 6PB 01626 821252 Mrs. Pike

Open Easter-Sept
2 bedrs (1 twin ba/wc; 1 double ba/wc) 1 ba, 2 wc 🐕 ⌗ *Commended*

Milton Farm East Ogwell, Newton Abbot TQ12 6AT 01626 54988 Mrs. Stone

Open Apr-Oct
3 bedrs (1 twin; 1 double; 1 single) 1 ba, 1 wc 🐕

£B&B £14-£15, D £6-£7, WR £90, WR/D £133, child rates.

New Cott Farm Poundsgate, Newton Abbot TQ13 7PD 01364 631421 Mrs. Phipps

Working cattle/sheep farm with a friendly welcome. Beautiful views and lovely home cooking. Follow Two Bridges/Pricetown rd. for 4 mls, through Poundsgate village. Follow road for 1 mile, turn left & follow signs

Open all year
4 bedrs (1 twin; 3 double inc 1 ba/wc, 2 sh/wc) ☎(3) 🏠 ♨♨ Commended
£B&B £16.50-£17, D £9.50, WR/D £160-£170.

OKEHAMPTON   2C3

Higher Cadham Farm Jacobstowe, Okehampton EX20 3RB 01837 85647 J. A. King

Open Mar-Jan, except Xmas
10 bedrs (2 twin inc 1 sh/wc; 4 double inc 3 sh/wc; 2 family inc 1 sh/wc; 2 single) 1 ba, 2 wc ☎(3) ♿ 🏠 ♨ Commended
£B&B £14.50-£18, D £7, WR £90-£120, WR/D £125-£170, child rates.

The Knole Farm Bridestowe, Okehampton EX20 3RB 01837 86241 Mrs. Bickle

Early 19th Century farmhouse offering glorious views of Dartmoor. Comfortable rooms that contain tea making facilities. Marvellous food provided. 89 % of guests return annually.

Open Easter-Nov
4 bedrs (2 double; 1 family; 1 single) 2 ba, 2 wc ☎ ✝ ♨ Commended

£B&B £15-£16, D £7-£8, WR £105-£112, WR/D £154-£161, child rates.

OTTERY ST MARY   3D3

Pitt Farm Fairmile, Ottery St Mary EX11 1NL 01404 812439   Mrs. Hansford

Attractive, 16th century, thatched farmhouse on a family working livestock/arable farm. Friendly atmosphere in a beautiful setting. Take the Fairmile rd. from Ottery St. Mary, farm is located ½ mile down the road on the left.

Open all year
5 bedrs (1 twin; 2 double; 2 family) 3 ba, 3 wc ☎ cc AmEx
£B&B £16-£20, D £17-£10, WR £112-£140, WR/D £161-£210, child rates.

PAIGNTON   3D4

Elberry Farm Broadsands, Paignton TQ4 6HJ 01803 842939   Mrs. Tooze

Working farm with beef, poultry and arable farming. Large walled garden. Plenty of traditional farmhouse food. Tea and coffee facilities in all rooms.

Open February to November
4 bedrs (1 twin; 3 family) 1 ba, 1 wc ☎ ✂
£B&B £12-£13, D £5-£6, WR £91, WR/D £127, child rates.

PARKHAM   2C2

The Old Barn Bocombe Farm, Parkham, Nr Bideford EX39 5PH 01237 451255   Mr. Scambler

Open all year

PLYMOUTH   2C4

Slade Barn Netton, Noss Mayo, Plymouth PL8 1HA 01752 872235 Mr. Cherrington

Farm with open plan spacious accommodation with sliding doors into the garden. Nearby, sandy beaches and a picturesque village and estuary.

Open all year
3 bedrs (1 twin; 2 double) ☎
£B&B £16.50-£18.50.

SIDMOUTH 3D3

Higher Coombe Farm Tipton St John, Sidmouth EX10 0AX 01404 813385 Kerstin Farmer

Late Victorian house on beef and sheep farm, see the lambs in the spring. Garden with a variety of plants, some unusual . Peaceful, quiet position, abundance of wildlife and birds. Take road towards Ottery St Mary, 1.5 miles from the Bowd Inn turn right, we are the 2nd farm up lane.

Open all year
3 bedrs (1 twin; 1 double; 1 family) 1 ba, 1 wc ♿ ☕
£B&B £18, D £10, WR £105, WR/D £165, child rates.

Pinn Barton Farm Peak Hill, Pinn Lane, Sidmouth EX10 0AX 01395 514004 Mrs. Sage

Open all year
3 bedrs (1 twin ba/sh/wc; 1 double ba/sh/wc; 1 family ba/sh/wc) ♿(8) 🏠 🐎 ☕☕ *Commended*

SOUTH MOLTON 2C2

Crangs Heasleigh Heasley Mill, North Molton, South Molton EX36 3LE 01598 740268 Mary Yendell

Open all year
4 bedrs (1 twin; 1 double; 1 family; 1 single) 1 ba, 2 wc ♿ 🐎 ☕☕
£B&B £13.50-£14.50, WR £90, child rates.

Kerscott Bishop's Nympton, South Molton EX36 4QG 01769 550262 T. A. Sampson

Peaceful, friendly, 16th century, beef and sheep farm. Mentioned in the Domesday Book. Wonderful setting overlooking Exmoor. Beautiful yester year interior. Hearty varied breakfast and dinner. Non-smokers only.

Open Jan-Dec
3 bedrs (1 twin sh/wc; 2 double inc 1 sh/wc) 1 ba, 2 wc ♿(8) ☕☕ *Commended*
£B&B £14.50-£16.50, D £6.50-£7, child rates.

Partridge Arms Farm West Anstey, South Molton EX36 5NU 01398 4217 Mrs. Milton

Open all year
7 bedrs (2 twin inc 1 sh/wc; 3 double inc 2 sh/wc; 2 family inc 1 sh/wc) 1 ba ♿ 🏠 🐎 ☕☕ *Approved*
£B&B £17.50-£22, D £8, WR/D £175-£203, child rates

STOCKLAND 3D3

The Stable Heathstock Farm, Stockland, Honiton EX14 9EU 01404 88267 Mrs. Patch

Open all year

TAVISTOCK 2C3

Wringworthy Farm Mary Tavy,
Tavistock PL19 9LT 01822 810434
Mr. Anning

Mainly Elizabethan house, mentioned in
Domesday Book. Beef and sheep farm in
quiet valley. Good beds, central heating, tea
and coffee making facilities in rooms.
Comfortable lounge. Take A386 signed
Okehampton, 2 miles on look for farm sign
on left.

Open Mar-Nov
3 bedrs (1 twin; 2 double) 2 ba 🏇 ⌖ *Listed*
£B&B £15-£16, child rates.

TIVERTON 3D2

Harton Farm Oakford, Tiverton EX16
9IIII 01398 5209 L. J. Head

Stone built, south facing 17th Century
farmhouse in quiet position. 53 acres mainly
sheep. Also cattle, pigs, etc. Large organic
vegetable garden. A396 N out of Tiverton to
Minehead, then B3227 to South Molton.

Open Jan-Dec
3 bedrs (2 twin; 1 family) 1 ba, 2 wc 🏇(4)
⌖ 🛏 ♨ ⅄
£B&B £13-£15, D £6, WR £91, WR/D £133,
child rates.

Lodge Hill Farm Ashley, Tiverton EX16
5PA **RAC**
01884 252907 B. Reader

Open all year
9 bedrs (2 twin sh/wc; 2 double sh/wc; 2
family inc 1 sh/wc; 3 single inc sh/wc) 2 ba
🏇(4) ⌖ 🛏 ♨♨ *Approved* cc Ac Vi
£B&B £16-£32, WR/D £155.

Marchweeke Farm Witheridge,
Tiverton EX16 8NY 01884 860418
Mrs. Webber

This Devon longhouse has lovely views and
lies 11 miles west of Tiverton B3137/B3042.
Good home cooked food using own produce.
Tea/coffee facilities in rooms. The farm is 107
acres of cereals, beef and sheep.

Open Feb-Nov
2 bedrs (1 twin ba/wc; 1 double ba/wc) 🏇
🛏 ♨♨
£B&B £14-£16, D £22-£24, WR £95-£105,
WR/D £140-£160, child rates.

Weir Mill Farm Willand, Cullompton,
Tiverton EX15 2RE 01884 820803
Mrs. Parish

Weir Mill is a working beef, sheep and arable
farm of 105 acres. The farmhouse overlooks
the fields beside the River Culm. TV and
tea/coffee facilities in all rooms. From M5, J27
take B3181 towards Willand (3 miles), 50
yards past Uffculme turning, turn L.

Open May-Dec
3 bedrs (2 double; 1 family sh/wc) 1 ba
🏇(4) ⌖ 🛏 ♨♨ *Commended*
cc Ac Vi

TORRINGTON 2C2

Bakers Farm Torrington EX38 7ES
01805 23260 Mr. Ridd

Open all year

TOTNES 3D3

Buckyette Farm Littlehempston, Nr
Totnes, Tiverton RAC
01803 762638 Mrs. Miller

Grassland farm in attractive countryside. From
Totnes take A381 towards Newton Abbot,
follow signpost to Littlehempston, turn right at
phone box, farm 3rd to left

Open Mar-Oct
6 bedrs (1 twin ba/sh; 1 double ba/wc; 4
family inc 3 ba/wc, 1 sh/wc) ☎ ♨♨
£B&B £17-£21, D £9, WR £114, WR/D
£172-£179, child rates.

Charford Farm Avonwick, Totnes TQ9
7LT 01364 73263 Mrs. Barons

300 year old farmhouse on 340 acre dairy and
stock farm with calves, horses etc. Very
comfortable, clean and friendly. From Totnes
A3121 towards Plymouth, after 5 miles turn
left at bottom of hill. Second house on right.

Open Jan-Dec
3 bedrs (1 twin; 1 double ba/wc; 1 family
ba/wc) 1 ba, 1 wc ☎ ⊞ ♞ ✂ ♨♨
£B&B £15-£18, D £8, WR £105-£110, WR/D
£145-£150, child rates.

Hatchlands Farm Bluepost, Avonwick,
Totnes TQ9 7LR 01364 72224 S. Palmer

Open All year
2 bedrs (2 family sh/wc) ☎ ♞ ✂
£child rates.

UPOTTERY 3D3

Lower Luxton Farm Upottery, Honiton
EX14 9PB 01823 60269 Mrs. Tucker

Olde Worlde farmhouse offering every
comfort in an area of outstanding natural
beauty. Guests made very welcome . Take
A30 to Upottery, then take Churchingford
Road for 3 miles, take right turning, pass
Fernleigh House,1st farm on left

Open all year
3 bedrs (1 twin; 1 double; 1 family) 1 ba, 2
wc ☎ ♞
£B&B £12-£14, D £6-£7, WR £80-£90, WR/D
£105-£115, child rates.

WIDECOMBE-IN-THE-MOOR 2C3

Lower Southway Farm Widecombe-in-
the-Moor, Ashburton TQ13 7TE
01364 2277 Mrs. Nosworthy

Open Jan-Dec
3 bedrs (1 twin; 2 double) 1 ba, 1 wc
☎*Listed*
£B&B £14-£15, WR £91, child rates.

WIVELISCOMBE 3D2

Greenway Farm Wiveliscombe,
Taunton TA4 2UA 01984 623359
Mrs. Wollaston

Open Mar-Oct
5 bedrs (2 double; 2 family; 1 single) 1 ba,
3 wc ☎ ⊞ ♞ ♨
£B&B £15, D £7, WR £105, WR/D £154,
child rates.

SELF CATERING

BARNSTAPLE   2C2

Denham Farm North Buckland,
Braunton EX33 1HY   **RAC**
01271 890297   J. Barnes

For full farm description see B&B Entry. There
are 2 self-catering units, one with 4 bedrooms,
sleeping up to 8 people. The other has 1
bedroom and sleeps up to four people. On
Braunton to Ilfracombe A361 take 2nd turning
left past Knowle village, signposted North
Buckland, continue 1 mile.

2 units; 4 & 1 bedrs ☆ ♌♌♌ *Commended*
cc Ac Vi
£Wk £250-£575

BIDEFORD   2C2

Higher Venn Farmhouse
Woolfardisworthy, Nr Bideford EX39 5RQ
01237 431017   Mr. Thomas

For full farm description see B&B Entry.
Fridge, washing machine, microwave, colour
TV, garden Bar-B-Q, patio. A39 from Bideford
to Bucks Cross take R turn signposted
Woolfardisworthy. From village take rd to
Meddon, farm 1 ml on R

1 unit; 1 bedr ☆ ♌

Winscott St Giles, Great Torrington
EX38 7JP 01805 23120   Mrs. Millman

400 acre mixed working farm. Cottage ½ mile
from farmhouse in peaceful countryside.

S Molton Rd from Torrington, R at High
Bullen, at end of St. Giles village L to Wards
Stony Ford, cottage on L.

☆
£Wk £120-£200

CHULMLEIGH

Manor Farm Riddlecombe, Chulmleigh
EX18 7NX 01769 520335   Mrs. Gay

Picturesque farmhouse with glorious views.
Dairy and sheep farm where guests can see
the animals, watch milking, and feed baby
lambs, etc. Guests can also make use of a
Games room that has been designed to
entertain all age groups.

Follow A337 to Dolton Beacon Garage. Turn
onto the B3217, after 50 yards turn right, into
Riddlecombe - farm on left.

☆ ♌ ♌♌♌
£Wk £150-£385

COLYTON   3D3

Higher Cownhayne Farm Cownhayne
Lane, Colyton nr. Seaton EX13 6HD
01297 552267   Elsie Pady

3 units; sleeps 4-8 ☆
£Wk £100-£350

Smallicombe Farm Northleigh,
EX13 6BU 01404 831310   Mrs. Todd

There are 4 converted barns sleeping 2-10.
These have retained their original character
but have all modern facilities. One ground
floor unit has been specifically designed to
accommodate wheel chairs. Cots, highchairs
available.

Situated south of A35 Axminster-Honiton road.

♿ ☆ ♌ ♌♌♌ *Commended*
£Wk £95-£525

CREDITON   3D3

Brindiwell Farm Cheriton Fitzpaine, Nr
Crediton, EX17 4HR 01363 866357
Mrs. Lock

Brindiwell is a sheep farm of 120 acres
situated north of St Eketer. The delightful
longhouse is a listed building with oak
beamed ceiling and panelling.

☆*Listed*
£Wk £120-£150

Hele Barton Black Dog, Thelbridge,
Crediton EX17 4QJ 01884 860278
Mrs. Gillard

For full farm description see B&B Entry. M5
junction 27 to Tiverton, then B3137 (Tiverton-
S Molton Rd) 10 miles to Witheridge then
B3042, 2 miles turn L ½ mile on L.

☆ *Commended*

EXETER   3D3

Lochinvar Shepherds Park Farm,
Woodbury, Exeter EX5 1LA 01395 232185
Mrs. Glanvill

The farm has a 3 bedroom bungalow sleeps 6
plus cot. Shepherds Park Farm is south of
Exeter (A376/B3179), and its location offers a
wide choice of activities.

ᗺ ᛏ

EXMOOR   3D2

Hindon Farm Nr Minehead, Exmoor
TA24 8SH 01643 705244   P. M. Webber

For full farm description see B&B Entry. Turn
off A39 (Minehead to Porlock road) signed to
village of Bratton, through lane to Hindon Farm.

ᗺ ᛏ ⅍ ꟿꟿꟿ
£Wk £150-£400

Little Quarme Country Cottages
Wheddon Cross, Exmoor TA24 7EA
01643 841249   Mr. Cody-Boutcher

For full farm description see B&B Entry. ¼ mile
past Wheddon Cross on Exford road B3224.

ᗺ *Listed*
£Wk £80-£425

Wintershead Farm Simonsbath,
Exmoor TA24 7LF 01643 83222
Mrs. Styles

ᗺ ᛏ ꟿꟿꟿ
£Wk £110-£420

EXMOUTH   3D3

Gulliford Farm Lympstone, Exmouth
EX8 5AQ 01392 873067   Mrs. Hallett

ᗺ
£Wk £200-£300

HOLSWORTHY   2C3

Ley Farm Milton Damerel, Holsworthy
EX22 7NY 01409 261259   Mrs. Holdcroft

See also B&B Entry.

ᗺ
£Wk £100-£190

Thorne Manor Holsworthy EX22 7JD
01492 53342   Mr. Clarke

ᗺ ᛏ ꟿꟿꟿ
£Wk £130-£350

IVYBRIDGE   2C4

Oldaport Farm Cottages Modbury,
Ivybridge PL21 0TG 01548 830842
Mr. Evans

ꟿꟿꟿ/ꟿꟿꟿꟿ *Highly Commended*

KINGSBRIDGE   2C4

Burton Farm Galmpton, Kingsbridge
TQ7 3EY 01548 561210   Mr. Rossiter

For full farm description see B&B Entry.
Kingsbridge take Salcombe Rd 3mls to Hope
Cove sign (R) then to giveway T-junction. Go
600yds, take L-hand slip Rd, L.

ᗺ ꟿꟿꟿ
£Wk £70-£400

South Allington House Galmpton,
Chivelstone, Kingsbridge TQ7 2NB
01548 511272   B.J. Baker

For full farm description see B&B Entry.
Kingsbridge follow sign to Frogmore, bottom
Frogmore turn R for East Prawle to
Chivelstone Cross, L, site ½ ml on R.

ᗺ *Commended*
£Wk £110-£360

LYNTON   2C2

West Ilkerton Farm Barbrook, Lynton
EX35 6QA 01598 52310   Mrs. Eveleigh

West Ilkerton Farm, in Exmoor National Park,
is off the A39 Lynton-Barnstaple road near
Barbrook and borders open moorland. This
luxurious semi-detached cottage sleeps 6 and
is on a secluded Exmoor hill farm with sheep,
cattle and heavy horses.

From Lynton go to Barbrook A39. Take
turning signposted Ilkerton & Shallowford
1/2ml, 1st R, 1/2ml to site.

ᗺ ᛏ ꟿꟿꟿ *Commended*
£Wk £120-£380

MORETONHAMPSTEAD 3D3

Budleigh Farm Moretonhampstead
TQ13 8SB 01647 40835 Mrs. Harve

& ❧ ♝ ⅋⅋/⅋⅋⅋ *Commended*

NEWTON ABBOT 3D3

Kellinch Farm Bickington, Newton
Abbot TQ12 6PB 01626 821252 Mrs. Pike

Accommodation is available in a self-contained
well-equipped annex to the farmhouse, 1
bedroom, sleeps 3. Evening meals can be
provided in the farmhouse if required.

Shippen and Dairy Cottages c/o
Lookweep Farm, Liverton, Newton Abbot
TQ12 6HT 01626 833277 Mr. Corrick

Open all year

PLYMOUTH 2C4

Slade Barn Netton, Noss Mayo,
Plymouth PL8 1HA 01752 872235
Mr. Cherrington

For full farm description see B&B Entry. ❧ ⅋

£Wk £215-£1380

SOUTH MOLTON 2C2

Nethercott Manor Farm Rose Ash,
South Molton EX36 4RE 01769 550483
Mr. Woollacott

Thatched listed house on mixed 200 acre farm.

❧ ♝ ⅋⅋⅋
£Wk £90-£350

TOTNES 3D3

Hatchlands Farm Bluepost, Avonwick,
Totnes TQ9 7LR 01364 72224 S. Palmer

❧ ♝

WIDECOMBE-IN-THE-MOOR 2C3

Wooder Manor Widecombe-in-the-
Moor, Ashburton TQ13 7TR 01364 2391
Angela Bell

Wooder is a 180-acre, family-run, beef and
sheep farm surrounded by woodlands, moors
and granite tors. It lies 6 miles north west of
Ashburton under a mile from Widecombe
village. The 4 cottages have 2-5 bedrooms,
sleeping 4-12. Clean and well-equipped.

& ❧ ♝ *Commended*

Middle Stoke Farm Holne,
Widecombe-in-the-Moor TQ13 7SS
01364 631444 Mrs. Neal

£Wk £200-£500

PLACES TO VISIT

EXMOOR

Exmoor Rare Breeds Farm
Week-St-Mary, Holsworthy EX22 6UX
01566-781366
A trail over modern and traditional
farmland with rare and commercial breeds
of cattle, pigs, sheep, goats and ponies in
natural surroundings. With 38 different
breeds, this is one of the largest collections
in North Cornwall. Conservation area has 2
ponds with waterfowl, ducks and geese.
Picnic area, pets corner, antique farming
artifacts on display. On sale: souvenirs.
New for 1995 season coarse fishing dawn
until dusk £2.50 per rod separate charge.
Location: east of the Camelford-Bude
road at Wainhouse Corner.
Open Easter-Oct.
Entrance: Adult £2, child £1,
OAP/Concessions £1 WC & by appointment

SEATON

Beer Quarry Caves
Quarry Lane, Beer Seaton
01297-80282
One hour guided tour of vast man-made
caverns started by the Romans. The stone
was mined until the 1900's and has been
used in many famous buildings. Folklore
and smugglers tales abound.
Location: signposted from B3174 between
Exeter and Lyme Regis.
Open: daily, Apr-Sept 1000-1800, Oct
1100-1630.
Entrance: adult £2.65 child/OAP £1.90.
WC ✗ ⅃

UFFCULME

Coldharbour Mill Working Wool Museum

Coldharbour Mill, Nr Cullompton, Uffculme EX15 3EE
01884-840960
A guided tour shows all the stages in the production of knitting yarn and woven cloth. A water wheel and steam engine also exhibited.
Location: off B3181, 2 miles from M5 Jn.27.
Open: Easter-Oct, daily 1100-1700; Nov-Mar Mon-Fri ring for times.
Entrance: adult £3.85, child £1.95. WC &
✕ ☕

BARNSTAPLE

Exmoor Animal and Bird Gardens

South Stowford, Bratton Flemming, Nr Barnstaple EX31 4SG
01598-763352
Landscaped animal and bird gardens with many water fowl, penguins and animals roaming at liberty. Tarzanland to entertain children. Picnic areas.
Location: on A399 (M5 J27/A361) between Blackmoor Gate and Bratton Flemming.
Open: Apr-Oct daily 1000-1800, Nov-Mar daily 1000-1600.
Entrance: adult £3.50, child £2.00, OAP/concession £2.75. WC ☕

OKEHAMPTON

Finch Foundry

Sticklepath, Okehampton EX20 2NW
01837-840046
Fascinating early 19th century forge, powered by three water wheels, which produced sickles, sythes and shovels for both agriculture and mining. The power of the massive tilt hammers and heat from the furnace, rumbling of the water wheels and screeching of the grinding stone make the whole building vibrate during regular demonstrations, transporting the visitor back to Dartmoor's industrial past. The forge is situated in the centre of this picturesque village with attractive countryside and river walks adjoining. Picnic area and refreshments available.
Location: centre of Sticklepath village, 4 miles east of Okehampton.
Open: Apr-Oct daily except Tuesdays 1100-1500. Last admission 30 mins. before closing.
Entrance: adults £2.20 child £1, National Trust members free WC & ✝ ✕ ☕

Museum of Dartmoor Life

West Street, Okehampton EX20 1HQ
01837-52295
Exhibition tells the story of the people who have lived and worked on Dartmoor from prehistoric times to the present day. Displays also examine issues such as the environment and the effects of social change. On sale: crafts, books, gifts. Flower shop, Opal studio, visitor centre and tea rooms.
Location: signposted from A30 into Okehampton.
Open: Easter-31Oct, Mon-Sat (Suns Jun-Sep), 1000-1700, in winter weekdays only.
Entrance: adult £1.50, child 75p, OAP/concession £1.20. WC ✝ ✕ ☕.

TIVERTON

Grand Western Horseboat Co

The Wharf, Canal Hill, Tiverton EX16 4HX 01884-253345
Horse-drawn transport of a bygone era. 2-3 hour trips by barge pulled by a heavy horse along the west country's most beautiful canal. Advisable to book. On sale: canal painted giftware.
Location: signposted from Tiverton.
Open: April-early Oct, daily.
Trip charges: adult £5.95 child £3.95.
WC ✝ ✕ ☕

CLOVELLY

The Milky Way & North Devon Bird of Prey Centre

Downland Farm, Clovelly, Bideford EX39 5RY 01237-431255
Nominated for ETB Best Tourist Attraction 1992. Pet and feed baby animals, hand milk a cow, watch a

falconry display, even throw your own pot. Adventure playground. Pilder Countryside Collection. Face painting. Laser clay pigeon shooting. Lyn-Barn ride on railway. Sheep dog display: from the North Devon sheep dog training and breeding centre. Archery: Tuition with

National Longbow Champion. On sale: dairy products, local crafts, books. Location: A29 Bideford-Bude road, 2 miles south of Clovelly. Open: April-Oct, daily 1030-1800 WC 🐴 ♿ ✗ 🎒

DORSET

BLANDFORD FORUM   3F2

Manor House Farm Ibberton, Blandford Forum DT11 0EN
01258 817349   C. Old

A small 15th century manor house, with oak beams and nail studded doors. It was Henry VIII's gift to his fifth wife, Katherine Howard. Now it is a farmhouse surrounded by a large colourful garden in a quiet village. 250 acre dairy & sheep farm. 10 miles west of Blandford Forum via A350/A357, 5 miles south of Shillingstone.

Open all year
3 bedrs (1 twin; 2 double sh/wc) 1 ba, 1 wc 🛉 🐴
£B&B £12-£15, WR £70-£90.

BRIDPORT   3E3

Dunster Farm Broadoak, Bridport DT6 5NR 01308 424626   Mrs. Hutchings

Open Apr-Oct
2 bedrs (2 double) 1 ba, 2 wc 🛉
£B&B £13-£15, D £6, WR £91-£98, WR/D £127-£134, child rates.

All towns listed in this guide are shown on the maps at the back.

Frogmore Farm Chideock, Bridport
01308 456159   Mrs. Norman

17th century stone farmhouse on an arable, stock and small animal farm. Wildlife pond area. 2 miles west of Bridport ½ mile before Chideock off A35.

Open Jan-Dec
3 bedrs (1 twin; 2 double sh/wc) 1 ba, 1 wc ☺ 🏤 🐴
£B&B £14-£16, D £7, WR £92, WR/D £141, child rates.

Rudge Farm Chilcombe, Bridport DT6 4NF 01308 482630   Mr. Diment

Open all year

CORFE CASTLE   3F3

Bradle Farmhouse Bradle, Wareham, Corfe Castle BH20 5NL 01929 480712 Gillian Hole

Beautiful manor farmhouse which was built in 1862, is situated on over 500 acres. A mixed farm with splendid views of Corfe Castle and surrounding Purbeck Hills. Turn R at Corfe Castle to Church Krowle. Turn L at crossroads. 1 mile to farm.

Open all year

3 bedrs (1 twin ba/wc; 1 double ba/wc; 1 family) 1 ba, 1 wc ☺ 🏤 🐴 *Commended*
£B&B £16-£19, WR £105-£123, WR/D £165-£188, child rates.

DORCHESTER   3E3

Lamperts Farmhouse Sydling St Nicholas, Dorchester DT2 8QR
01300 341790   Mrs. Bown

Open all year
3 bedrs (1 twin ba/wc; 1 double ba/wc; 1 family ba/wc) ☺ 🐴
£B&B £18-£20, D £10-£12, WR £126, WR/D £196, child rates.

Maiden Castle Farm Dorchester DT2 9PR 01305 262356   Mrs. Hoskin

A large, Victorian farmhouse on a mixed farm in the heart of Thomas Hardy country. Take A354 towards Weymouth. Farm on right.

Open all year
8 bedrs (2 twin inc 1 ba/wc, 1 sh/wc, 3 double inc 1 ba/wc, 1 sh/wc; 1 family sh/wc; 2 single inc 1 ba/wc) 1 ba, 1 wc ☺ 🏤 🐴 🐴 🐴 *Commended* cc Ac Vi
£B&B £18-£22, WR £126-£154, child rates.

GILLINGHAM 3F2

Huntingford Oak Gillingham SP8 5QH
01747 860574 G. B. James

The modern house of Huntingford Oak stands on a working farm amid the unspoilt Dorset countryside. Enjoy a peaceful atmosphere with marvellous views and walks. Ground floor bedroom, highchair and playroom available. A303 from London.

Open all year
3 bedrs (1 twin ba/wc; 1 double ba/wc; 1 family ba/wc) 2 wc ➥ ♿ ⊞ ♛♛
£B&B £20-£25, WR £120-£145, child rates.

Kington Manor Farm Church Hill, Kington Magna, Gillingham SP8 5EG
01747 838371 G. Gosney

This newly-built, stone farmhouse, attractively sited with views over Blackmore Vale, is located in a quiet and pretty village. The 30 acre farm has beef and pigs. Good home cooking, tea/coffee facilities and TV in room. From East Stour, turn right onto A30, after West Stour turn right (Sandley & Bourton), take 2nd road on left to farm.

Open Jan-Nov
2 bedrs (1 twin ba/wc; 1 double sh/wc) ➥

★ *Listed*
£B&B £15, WR £100, child rates.

SHAFTESBURY 3F2

Culverhouse Farm Motcombe, Shaftesbury SP7 9HU 01747 52273
Mrs. Menlove

Open Apr-Oct
3 bedrs (3 twin inc 1 ba/wc) 1 ba, 1 wc ➥

SHERBORNE 3E2

Almshouse Farm Hermitage, Sherborne DT9 6HA 01963 210296 Mrs. Mayo

This family-run dairy farm of 150 acres overlooks the Blackmoor Vale. The farmhouse was a monastery during the 16th century and was restored in 1849. It lies 6 miles south of Sherborne. The comfortable rooms have tea/coffee making facilities. A352 towards Dorchester for 5 miles. At Holnest crossroads right hand turning to Hermitage, farm 1 mile up this road .

Open all year
3 bedrs (1 twin; 1 double ba/wc; 1 family) 2 ba, 2 wc ➥ ♛♛
£B&B £15.50-£18.

STURMINSTER MARSHALL 4A4

Henbury Farm Dorchester Road, Sturminster Marshall, Wimborne BH21 3RN 01258 857306 Mr. Tory

300 year old farmhouse facing large front lawn and pond. Situated on 200 acre dairy farm. Guest lounge with colour TV, 2 en suites available. We are situated on Wimborne side of the A350/A31 junction (we are on the A31).

Open Jan-Dec
6 bedrs (2 twin inc 1 ba/wc, 1 sh/wc; 2 double; 2 single) 1 ba ☻ ♚♚
£B&B £18-£22.

STURMINSTER NEWTON   3F2

Holebrook Farm Lydlinch, Sturminster Newton DT10 2JB 01258 817348
Sally Wingate-Saul

Accommodation in a Georgian farmhouse with many original features or in delightful converted stables with own shower, sitting room and kitchen. Breakfast is taken in lovely old farmhouse kitchen. Peaceful all grass working farm; cattle & rare-breed pigs. Take A357 westwards to Lydlinch, 300 yards after garage turn left (signposted Church), farm is 1 mile from main rd on R.

Open all year
6 bedrs (5 twin inc 4 sh/wc; 1 single) 1 ba, 1 wc ☻ ♿ *Highly Commended*
£B&B £21-£23, D £11-£12, WR £147-£161, WR/D £224-£245, child rates.

Lower Fifehead Farm Fifehead St Quinton, Sturminster Newton
01258 817335   Mrs. Miller

Open May- Sep
3 bedrs (1 twin; 1 double; 1 single) 2 ba, 2 wc ☻ ♿ 🏠 🐈 *Approved*
£B&B £13-£15, WR £175, child rates.

Moorcourt Farm Moorside, Marnhull, Sturminster Newton DT10 1HH
01258 820271   Mrs. Sheila Martin

Come and relax in an informal family atmosphere at this Georgian farmhouse with delightfully converted stables, situated a mile south of the A357, 3 miles west of Sturminster Newton. Suitable for the disabled. Good home cooking. Grass & cattle farm.

Open Apr-Oct
3 bedrs (1 twin; 2 double) 2 ba, 2 wc ☻ ♿ 🏠 ♚ cc Ac
£B&B £13-£14, WR £91, child rates.

SWANAGE   3F3

Downshay Farm Haycrafts Lane, Swanage BH19 3EB 01929 480316
Mrs. Pike

On a 130-acre family-run dairy farm stands this delightfully situated Victorian Purbeck stone farmhouse overlooking Corfe Castle and the Purbeck Hills. Downshay Farm is 3 miles from Swanage, signposted from Harmans Cross on the A351 Wareham-Swanage road.

Open Apr-Oct
2 bedrs (1 double, 1 family) 2 ba, 2wc ☻ *Listed*

WAREHAM   4A4

Chaldecotts Swalland Farm, Kimmeridge, Wareham BH20 5PE
01929 480936   Mrs. Vearncombe

Open Mar-Oct
2 bedrs (1 double; 1 family) ☻(5) 🏠 *Listed*
£B&B £16-£18, WR £110-£120.

Knitson Old Farmhouse Corfe Castle, Wareham BH20 5JB 01929 422836
Mrs. Helfer

Open March-Oct.
3 bedrs (1 double; 1 family; 1 single) 2 ba, 2 wc ☻ *Listed*
£B&B £16.50-£18, D £7-£12, WR £105-£120, child rates.

Luckford Wood Farmhouse East Stoke, Wareham BH20 6AW 01929 463098
Mrs. Barnes

Open Jan-Dec
4 bedrs (1 twin; 1 double; 2 family sh/wc) 1 ba, 1 wc ☻ 🏠 🐈*Listed* cc Vi
£B&B £15-£22, WR £105-£140, child rates.

Newlands Farm West Lulworth, Wareham BH20 5PU 01929 41376   Leslie Sumpson

Open except Xmas
2 bedrs (1 double sh/wc; 1 family sh/wc) 1 ba, 1 wc ☻(5) 🏠 🐈 *Listed Approved* cc Vi
£child rates.

YETMINSTER 3E2

Manor Farmhouse High Street, Yetminster, Sherborne DT9 6LF
01935 872247 Ann Partridge

Modernised to a high standard, a 17th century farmhouse with many original features, in the centre of an historic village, described as the best stone-built village in the south of England. Fresh produce cooked to traditional recipes.

Open All year except Xmas
4 bedrs (2 twin inc 1 ba/wc, 1 sh/wc; 2 single sh/wc) 🚿 ♨️♨️♨️ cc Vi
£B&B £25, D £10-£15, WR £150-£180, WR/D £240-£270.

SELF CATERING

BRIDPORT 3E3

Frogmore Farm Chideock, Bridport
01308 456159 Mrs. Norman

For full farm description see B&B Entry. 2 miles west of Bridport ½ mile before Chideock off A35.

🐴 🐦
£Wk £160-£315

DORCHESTER 3E3

Clyffe Farm Tincleton, Dorchester DT2 8QR 01305 848252 Mrs. Coleman

Mixed dairy/arable/beef farm with woodland and meadow walks. Beautiful bird watching in the Frome Valley. Horses/ducks and calves. 4 miles due East of Dorchester towards Wareham via village of Puddletown.

🐴 🎣 *Commended*
£Wk £140-£325

Lamperts Farmhouse Sydling St Nicholas, Nr Dorchester, Dorchester DT2 8QR 01300 341790 Mrs. Bown

🐴 🐦
£Wk £100-£200

GILLINGHAM 3F2

Cole Street Farm Cole Street Lane, Gillingham SP8 5JQ 01747 822691
Mrs. Hawkett

SHAFTESBURY 3F2

Hartgrove Farm Shaftesbury SP7 0JY
01747 811830 Susan Smart

🐴 🐦 ✂️ 🎣🎣🎣🎣
£Wk £100-£395

STURMINSTER NEWTON 3F2

Holebrook Farm Lydlinch, Sturminster Newton DT10 2JB 01258 817348
Sally Wingate-Saul

For full farm description see B&B Entry. Take A357 westwards to Lydlinch, 300 yards after garage turn left (signposted Church), farm is 1 mile from main rd on R.

♿ 🐴 *Highly Commended*
£Wk £140-£240

Lower Fifehead Farm Fifehead St Quinton, Sturminster Newton
01258 817335 Mrs. Miller

For full farm description see B&B Entry. 🐴 🐦
🎣🎣🎣 *Approved*
£Wk £90-£200

Moorcourt Farm Moorside, Marnhull, Sturminster Newton DT10 1HH
01258 820271 Mrs. Sheila Martin

For full farm description see B&B Entry. 🐴 cc Ac
£Wk £125-£200

PLACES TO VISIT

WEYMOUTH

Radipole Lake RSPB Nature Reserve
The Swannery car park, Weymouth DT4 7TZ 01305-778313
A lake with major reed banks supporting rare bearded tits and Cetti's warblers. Location: by Swannery public car park near Weymouth.
Open: at all times.
Entrance: adult £1.50, child 50p, OAP/concession £1 WC ♿ 🐾

CO. DURHAM

BARNARD CASTLE 10C2

East Mellwaters Farm Bowes, Barnard Castle DL12 9RH 01833 628269 Mrs. Milner

Open Jan -Dec
5 bedrs (3 double inc 2 ba/wc; 1 family ba/wc; 1 single sh/wc) 🛏 🏠 🐕 ♨♨♨ cc Ac Vi
£B&B £15-£20, D £10-£15, WR £100-£130, WR/D £165-£220, child rates.

Snaisgill Farm Middleton-in-Teesdale, Barnard Castle DL12 6RP 01833 640343 Mrs. Parmley

Open May-Oct
2 bedrs (2 double) 1 ba, 2 wc 🛏(10) *Listed*
£B&B £13.50-£14.50, child rates.

West Roods Farm West Roods Farm, Boldron, Barnard Castle DL12 9SW RAC 01833 690116 Mrs. Lowson

Open Mar-Oct
3 bedrs (1 double sh/wc; 1 family; 1 single) 1 ba, 2 wc 🛏 ♨♨♨ cc Ac Amex
£B&B £16, D £10, WR £100, child rates.

BISHOP AUCKLAND 10C1

Low Cornriggs Farm Cowshill-in-Weardale, Bishop Auckland DL13 1AQ 01388 537600 Mrs. Ellis

Situated on the Weardale Way 1 ½ miles from Killhope Wheel. A working stock farm with riding. Stay in our beautifully restored farmhouse. Fresh homecooked food, licensed. Tea trays. Warm and friendly. A689 10 miles

to Alston - 10 miles Stanhope.

Open Jan-Dec
6 bedrs (2 twin inc 1 sh/wc; 1 double ba/wc; 1 family sh/wc; 2 single) 1 ba, 1 wc
🛏 🏠 🐕 ♨♨ *Highly Commended*
£B&B £17.50-£18, D £9, WR £120-£125, WR/D £180-£188, child rates.

STANLEY 13F4

Bushblades Farm Harpeley, Stanley DH9 9UA 01207 232722 Mrs. Gibson

60 acre sheep farm with Georgian farmhouse set in large garden. Take A639, ½ mile after Stanley follow sign for Harperley. Farm on right ½ mile after crossroads.

Open all year
3 bedrs (1 twin ba/wc; 2 double) 1 ba, 1 wc 🛏(12) 🏠 *Listed*
£D&D £16-£25.

WESTGATE 13F4

Lands Farm Westgate DL13 1SN 01388 517210 Barbara Reed

Peace and a high standard of comfort are to be found in this old stone-built farmhouse with large gardens encircled by a stream. Enjoy the tranquility of the North Pennines - an area of outstanding natural beauty. Travel to Westgate on the A689, then follow signposts

Open April-October
2 bedrs (1 twin; 1 double sh/wc) 🐴 ⅄ 🌼🌼
£B&B £17-£18, WR £110-£120, child rates.

WOLSINGHAM   10C1

Greenwell Farm Tow Law, Bishop Auckland DL13 4PH 01388 527248 Linda Vickers

Quality bed and breakfast or self catering in comfortable antique furnished rooms. Beautiful views, country walks and nature

trail. At Tow Law War Memorial take B6297 for 1 ½ miles, turn L after ¼ mile, fork R up lane.

Open Jan-Dec
5 bedrs (2 twin inc 1 ba/wc, 1 sh/wc; 2 double inc 1 ba/wc, 1 sh/wc; 1 family ba/wc) 🐴 ♿ 🛁 🐕 ⅄ 🌼🌼 cc Vi
£B&B £15-£18.50, D £8.50-£10, WR £105-£130, WR/D £165-£200, child rates.

SELF CATERING

DURHAM   11D1

Baxter Wood Farm Crossgate Moor, Durham DH1 4TG 01091 3865820 Mrs. Jones

2 units, sleeps 2-4 🐴(10) 🏠 🐕 *Highly Commended*

WOLSINGHAM   10C1

Greenwell Farm Tow Law, Bishop Auckland DL13 4PH 01388 527248 Linda Vickers

For full farm description see B&B Entry. At Tow Law War Memorial take B6297 for 1½ miles, turn L after ¼ mile, fork R up lane.

♿ 🐴 🐕 ⅄ 🏠 cc Vi
£Wk £165-£350

EAST SUSSEX

BATTLE 8E4

Little Hemingfold Farmhouse
Acclaimed Telham, Battle TN33 0TT **RAC**
01424 774338 Mr. Slatter

Open all year
13 bedrs 10 en suite ☎ ♂ cc Ac AmEx Vi
£B&B £30-£65, D £19.50, WR/D £273-£294.

Moonshill Farm *Highly Acclaimed* The
Green, Moons Hill, Ninefield, Battle
TN33 9JL **RAC**
01424 892645 June Ive

Farmhouse in 10 acres in village.

Open all year
3 bedrs; 1 ba ✠

Gifford Farm Cottage Battle Road,
Dallington TN21 9LH 01424 8221
Mrs. Izzard

Open all year
3 bedrs (inc 1 twin; 1 double) 1 ba, 1 wc
☎ ♂
£B&B £13.50, D £6-£8, WR £13.50, child rates.

BRIGHTON 5D4

Poynings Manor Farm Poynings,
Brighton BN45 7AG 01273 857371
Mrs. Revell

Old manor farmhouse nestling under the
South Downs with 260- acres. Sheep and
arable farm. From M/A 23 on to Henfield 281.

Open March-Dec.
3 bedrs (2 twin; 1 double) ☎ 🏠
£B&B £18.50-£22, D £10, child rates.

BURWASH

Woodlands Farm Etchingham, Burwash
TN18 7LA 01435 882794 Mrs. Sirrell

Woodlands Farm stands well back from the
A265, 4 miles east of Heathfield, surrounded
by fields and woods. The peaceful and
beautifully modernised farmhouse offers
comfortable and friendly accommodation, one
room even has a four poster bed.

Open Easter-Nov
4 bedrs (2 twin inc 1 ba/wc; 2 double inc 1
sh/wc) 2 ba, 2 wc ☎ 🏠
£B&B £15.

HAILSHAM 5D4

The Stud Farm Bodle Street Green,
Hailsham BN27 4RJ 01323 833201
Mr Gentry

Open Jan-Dec
3 bedrs (2 twin inc 1 sh/wc; 1 double) 1 ba
☎ 👑👑👑
£B&B £17-£25, D £8.50, WR £119-£140,
WR/D £178.50-£199.50, child rates.

Old Barn Farm Halesham BN27 1RS
01323 833346   Mrs. Parkes

Open all year
3 bedrs (1 twin sh/wc; 1 family sh/wc; 1
single sh/wc) ☒ �& ☗
£B&B £17-£20, D £8, WR £100, WR/D £156,
child rates.

HARTFIELD   5D3

Stairs Farmhouse High Street, Hartfield
TN7 4 AB 01892 770793   Mrs. Pring

Open all year
3 bedrs (1 twin; 1 double; 1 family) 2 ba, 3
wc ☒ ⊞ ✂ *Listed*
£B&B £19-£25, D £5-£12.

HASTINGS & ST LEONARDS   5E4

Westwood Stonestile Lane, Hastings
TN35 4PG 01424 751038   Mrs. A York

Working farm with sheep, goats, chickens and
ducks. Elevated position with outstanding
views over the Brede Valley. Quiet rural
location off a country lane. 2 ground floor
bedrooms. Hastings seafront take A259 to Rye,
1st set of traffic lights turn L. Past crematorium
2nd turning on R.

Open Jan-Dec
3 bedrs (1 twin; 1 double sh/wc; 1 family
sh/wc) ☒(5) ✂
£B&B £15-£21, child rates.

LEWES   5D4

Stud Farm House Telscombe Village,
Lewes BN7 3HZ 01273 302486 Mr. Armour

15th century farm house on a working sheep
farm (1000 sheep) with race horses and beef
herd. Situated on the South Downs, near the
sea. Family-run. Lewes, train station on L,
follow through. Ilford, Rodmel, Southease, R
into Telscombe village. Opposite church on R.

Open Jan-Dec
4 bedrs (2 twin; 1 double; 1 family) ⊞
£child rates.

RYE   5E3

Cliff Farm Iden Lock, Rye TN31 7QE ☒
01797 280331   Mr. Sullivin

190 year old, Sussex, peg-tile hung farmhouse.
Farm's elevated position offers an
uninterrupted view over Romney Marsh.
Ideally positioned as a centre for touring,
walking, fishing, bird watching, or just for a
quiet rest.

Open all year
3 bedrs, 1 ba

SEDLESCOMBE   5E3

Platnix Farm Oast Harts Green, Nr
Battle TN33 0RT 01870 214 Mrs. Howard

This delightful oasthouse with beamed interior
is on a working 100-acre sheep farm,4 miles
north of Hasting (A21/A229). One bedroom is
circular. Farm is surrounded by beautiful
countryside.

Open all year
3 bedrs (1 twin; 2 double inc 1 ba/wc, 1
sh/wc) 3 ba, 3 wc ❧
£child rates.

UCKFIELD   5D3

Sliders Farm Furners Green, Uckfield
TN22 3RT 01825 790258   D. Salmon

Listed 16th Century farmhouse with oak
beams and inglenooks. Peacefully situated on
edge of Ashdown Forest. Surrounded by own
fields and woodlands. Swimming pool, tennis
court & fishing. From Haywards Heath take
A272 E. A275 N for 2 1/2mls. Sliders Lane is
on L 1ml S of Danehill.

Open Jan-Dec
4 bedrs (1 twin ba/wc; 2 double ba/wc; 1
family ba/wc) ❧ 🖶 ♈
£B&B £19, D £12.50, child rates.

SELF CATERING

HASTINGS & ST LEONARDS   5E4

Westwood Stonestile Lane, Hastings
TN35 4PG 01424 751038   Mrs. A York

For full farm description see B&B Entry.
Hastings seafront take A259 to Rye, 1st set of
traffic lights turn L. Past crematorium 2nd
turning on R.

❧(5)⊁

UCKFIELD   5D3

Sliders Farm Furners Green, Uckfield
TN22 3RT 01825 790258   D. Salmon

For full farm description see B&B Entry. From
Haywwards Heath take A272 E. A275 N for 2
1/2mls. Sliders Lane is on L 1ml S of Danehill.

❧ ♈
£Wk £200-£400

PLACES TO VISIT

EASTBOURNE

Seven Sisters Sheep Centre
East Dean, Nr Eastbourne BN20 0DG
01323-423302
Everything sheepish on this family-run
farm. Over 40 breeds of British sheep,
seasonal demonstrations, lambing,
shearing, sheep milking, cheese making.
Other young farm animals - pigs, goats,
calves, rabbits and chicks - to feed and
cuddle both outside and under cover. 17th
century flint barn. On sale: sheep's milk,
cheese, yoghurt and ice cream. Coloured
fleeces, knitwear and sheep gifts.
Location: a mile from Beachy Head, off
A259.
Open: Mar-Sept, daily 1400-1700
(restricted opening in May)
Entrance: adult £2, child £1.25,
OAP/concessions £1.60. WC ♿ ✗

ESSEX

BRAINTREE 5E1

School Green Farm Blackmore End, Braintree CM7 4DS 01371 850679
B. A. Deacon

Open Jan-Dec
2 bedrs (2 family) 1 ba, 2 wc *Listed*
£B&B £15, WR £90, child rates.

Spicers Farm Rotten End, Wethersfield, Braintree CM7 4AL 01371 851021
Delia Douse

Spicers is a mixed farm with arable crops in a quiet rural area designated of special landscape value. The farmhouse provides comfortable accommodation, with TV, tea/coffee facilities & lovely views. 2 rooms, 1 with shower, 1 with private bathroom. Take B1053 from Braintree to Shalford. At Shalford turn 1st right signed to Rotten End, farm is 2nd house on right.

Open Jan-Dec
3 bedrs (2 twin inc 1 ba/wc, 1 Double sh/wc) *Commended*
£B&B £15-£18, child rates.

CHIPPING ONGAR

Bumbles Moreton Road, Chipping Ongar CM5 0EZ 01277 362695 Mr. Whitley

Open Jan-Dec
3 bedrs (3 twin) 2 ba, 2 wc (12) *Listed*
£B&B £15-£16.50, WR £95-£105.

New House Farm Mutton Row, Stanford Rivers, Nr Ongar CM5 9QH
01277 362132 Mrs. Martin

Open all year

COLCHESTER 5E1

Kings Vineyard Fossetts Lane, Fordham, Colchester CO6 3NY
01206 240377 Mrs. Tweed

Warm welcome awaits you in rural countryside overlooking Colne Valley. Traditional/vegetarian breakfast served in elegant conservatory. TV, tea/coffee making facilities. From A12 take A604 NW for 1ml, R to Fordham, R into Fossetts Ln, opp. 3 Horseshoe pub. Sign 'Kings B & B', 3/4ml.

Open Jan-Dec
3 bedrs (1 twin; 1 double; 1 family) 1 ba, 2 wc
£B&B £16.50-£22, child rates.

KELVEDON 5D2

Highfields Farm Kelvedon, Colchester CO5 9BJ 01376 570334 Deanna Bunting

Open all year
3 bedrs (3 twin inc 2 ba/wc, 1 sh/wc)
£B&B £16-£20.

SAFFRON WALDEN 5D1

Duddenhoe End Farm Duddenhoe End, Nr Saffron Walden CB11 4UU
01763 838258 Mrs. Foster

Open all year
3 bedrs (1 twin ba/wc; 2 double inc 1 ba/wc, 1 sh/wc) (10)
Highly Commended
£B&B £18-£22.

Parsonage Farm Arkesden, Saffron Walden CB11 4HB 01799 550306
Mrs. Forster

Open all year
3 bedrs (1 twin; 2 double ba/wc) 1 ba, 1 wc
£B&B £15-£18, child rates.

Rockells Farm Duddenhoe End, Saffron Walden CB11 4UY 01763 838053
Mr & Mrs. Westerhuis

Open all year
3 bedrs (1 twin ba/wc; 1 family sh/wc; 1
single ba/wc) 3 ba, 3 wc 🛏 🐕 ♨♨
£B&B £17-£19, D £7, child rates.

WIX   5E1

New Farm House *Acclaimed* Spinnells
Lane, Manningtree, Wix CO11 2UJ   RAC
01255 870365   Mrs. Mitchell

Modern farmhouse on a 50-acres working
farm, set in large gardens with a play area and
delightful countryside views.

Open all year
6 bedrs; (1 sh/wc) 2 ba 🛏 & 🐕*Listed*
cc Ac Vi £B&B £19.50-£37, D £10.50,
WR/D £179.50.

SELF CATERING

SAFFRON WALDEN   5D1

Rockells Farm Duddenhoe End, Saffron
Walden CB11 4UY 01763 838053
                 Mr & Mrs. Westerhuis
& 🛏 🐕
£Wk £120-£180

PLACES TO VISIT

SOUTH WOODHAM FERRERS

Marsh Farm Country Park
Marsh Farm Road, South Woodham
Ferrers, Chelmsford CM3 5LD
01245-321552
A working farm with beef cattle,
sheep, free range chickens and pigs.
Hand milking demonstration, pets
corner, adventure play area, country
walks and nature reserve. On sale: free
range eggs.
Location: signposted from A130
Rettendon Turnpike roundabout.
Open: mid Feb-Nov, Mon-Fri 1000-1630,
weekends & Bank Holiday 1000-1730
Entrance: adult £2.10, child £1.45,
OAP/concessions £1.45 WC & (restricted
access) 🐕 ✗ 🦽

GLOUCESTERSHIRE

BOURTON-ON-THE-WATER   4A1

Upper Farm Clapton-on-the-Hill,
Bourton-on-the-Water GL54 2LG
01451 820453   Helen Adams

This 17th century farmhouse on a 140 acre
mixed farm enjoys a beautiful hill position
with uninterrupted views across Windrush
Valley. The house has been lovingly restored
with individually designed rooms. Upper Farm
is situated off the A429.

Open Mar-Nov
🛏(8) ⌦ 6 bedrs (2 twin inc 1ba/wc; 2

double inc 1sh/wc 1 family, 1 single)
♨♨

CHELTENHAM   7E4

Hartbury Farm Chedworth,
Cheltenham GL54 4AL 01285 720350
Mrs. Booth

Open Apr-Oct
3 bedrs (1 twin ba/wc; 1 double; 1 family)
2 ba, 2 wc 🛏 🐕*Listed*
£B&B £14-£15.50, D £7.50, child rates.

CHIPPING CAMPDEN 7F4

Weston Park Farm Dovers Hill,
Chipping Campden 01386 840835
Mrs. Whitehouse

Open Jan-Dec
2 bedrs (1 double; 1 family) 🛁 ⚘⚘
£B&B £36-£38, child rates.

CIRENCESTER 7F4

College Farm Ampney St Mary,
Cirencester GL7 5SW 01285 851382
Mrs. Bennett

A dairy farm with pedigree freesian cows
where guests are welcome to look round. The
farmhouse sits in a large garden separate from
the farm buildings. Take the Cirencester to
Fairford Rd A417, L past Ampney St. Peter by
Red Lion pub, L into Ampney, farm in village.

Open Jan-Dec
3 bedrs (1 twin; 1 double sh/wc; 1 family
sh/wc) 1 ba, 1 wc 🛁 ⚘⚘
£B&B £14-£16.50, D £10, WR £98-£115,
WR/D £165-£185, child rates.

COLEFORD 7E4

Lower Tump Farm Eastbach, English
Bicknor, Coleford GL16 7EU
01594 860253   Mrs. Sylvia Davis

Open all year
3 bedrs (2 twin sh/wc; 1 double ba/wc)
🛁 ⚘⚘
£B&B £13-£14, WR £85-£91, child rates.

DYMOCK 7E4

Lower House Farm Kempley, Dymock
01531 890301   Mrs. Bennett

Warm welcome on dairy farm. Superb food,
idyllic countryside, many animals and play
area. Easy access for touring the Wye Valley,
Cotswolds and Forest of Dean. Take road
from Newent to M50 via Gorsley. Over
motorway bridge, next R past Ross on Wye
Golf Club, 2 1/2mls to Kempley.

Open Mar-Dec
2 bedrs (1 twin sh/wc; 1 double sh/wc) 🛁
⚘ 🐕
£B&B £16-£20, D £9-£10, WR £119-£140,
WR/D £182-£210, child rates.

FALFIELD 3E1

Green Farm Guest House Falfield
GL12 8DL 01454 260319 Mrs. B.C.Burrell

Open all year
8 bedrs; 1 ba, 1 wc 🛁 🐕
£B&B £16-£30, D £10-£17, child rates.

GLOUCESTER 7E4

Gilberts Gilberts Lane, Brookthorpe,
Gloucester GL4 0UH
01452 812364   Jenny Beer

Gilbert's is a listed, 400 years old, Jacobean
manor house, sympathetically restored and
modernised. The surrounding small organic
farm has livestock, including bees, fruit and
vegetables. Gilbert's is off the A4173 south of
Gloucester.

Open all year
4 bedrs (1 twin sh/wc; 2 double sh/wc; 1
single sh/wc) 1 wc 🛁 ⚘⚘
£B&B £21, child rates.

Hill Farm Wainlode Lane, Norton, Gloucester GL2 9LN 01452 730351
D. E. Blanchard

Closed Xmas and New Year
4 bedrs (1 twin; 3 double inc 2 sh/wc) 1 ba, 3 wc ⛺ ♿ ♕♕♕
£child rates.

MINSTERWORTH 7E4

Severn Bank Minsterworth GL2 8JH
01452 750357 R. A. Carter

Open all year
6 bedrs (2 twin; 2 double; 1 family; 1 single) 1 ba, 1 wc ⛺ ♕♕
£B&B £17.50-£19.50, child rates.

MORETON-IN-MARSH 7F4

Banks Farm Upper Oddington, Moreton-in-Marsh GL56 0XG
01451 830475 Mrs. Adams

Mixed farm. Cotswold stone farmhouse in elevated position in centre of Oddington, overlooking fields to 11th Century Church. A436 from Stow, R B4450 to Bledington, 1st L Oddington, 1st R in village (no thru rd), approx. 3/4ml between each turn.

Open Mar-Oct
2 bedrs (1 twin; 1 double) 1 ba, 1 wc
⛺(10) ♿ Listed
£B&B £16.50-£18, WR £109-£112.

STONEHOUSE 7E4

Nastend Farm Nastend, Stonehouse GL10 3RS 01453 822300 Mr. Guilding

Open Feb- Nov
2 bedrs (2 family inc 1 ba/wc) 1 ba, 1 wc
⛺ ♿ ♕♕

£B&B £15-£16.50, D £10, WR £105-£115.50, WR/D £175-£185.50, child rates.

STOW-ON-THE-WOLD 4A1

Corsham Field Farmhouse Bledington Road, Stow-on-the-Wold GL54 1JH
01451 831750 Mr & Mrs. Smith

Open all year
3 bedrs (1 twin; 1 double; 1 family ba/wc) 1 ba, 2 wc ⛺ 🐕 ♕♕
£B&B £13.50-£18, WR £94.50-£126, child rates.

Fairview Farmhouse Bledington Road, Stow-on-the-Wold GL54 1AN
01451 830279 Mrs. Davis

Fairview Farmhouse is set in 1 acre of garden with outstanding panoramic views. Bedrooms are en suite, beautifully furnished with canopy beds, colour TV, tea/coffee making facilities and other thoughtful items. From Stow on the Wold take A436 to Chipping Norton, approx 1 ml turn R (B4450) - 350 yds, farm is on L.

Open Jan-Dec
3 bedrs (1 twin sh/wc; 2 double inc 1 ba/wc, 1 sh/wc) ♕♕♕
£B&B £38-£40, D £26.

South Hill Farm House Fosseway,
Stow-on-the-Wold GL54 1JY
01451 831219   Mr. Kenneally

Victorian Cotswold stone farmhouse furnished
to a high standard. House is centrally heated
and televisions are avaliable in all rooms.
Ample parking. An excellent base for touring.
¼ mile south of Stow-on-the-Wold via the A429.

Open all year
5 bedrs (1 twin sh/wc; 3 double inc 2
sh/wc; 1 family sh/wc) 1 ba, 1 wc 🏇 🏠
🌄🌄
£B&B £15-£18, WR £100-£112.50.

TEWKESBURY   7E4

Barn Hill Farmhouse Bredons Norton,
Tewkesbury GL20 7HB 01684 72704
                    Mrs. Archer

Open Jan-Dec
2 bedrs (1 twin ba/sh/wc; 1 double
ba/sh/wc) 🐓 ✂

TWYNING   7E4

Abbots Court Church End, Twyning,
Tewkesbury GL20 6DA 01684 292515
                    Mr. Williams

Open Jan-Dec
8 bedrs (4 twin inc 1 ba/wc, 2 sh/wc; 2
double inc 1 ba/wc, 1 sh/wc; 2 family
sh/wc; 4 single) 1 ba, 3 wc 🏇 🏠 🐓 🌄🌄 cc Vi
£B&B £14-£16, WR £93-£108, child rates.

WINCHCOMBE   7F4

Postlip Hall Farm Winchcombe,
Cheltenham GL54 5AQ 01242 603351
                    Mrs. Albutt

Attractive spacious and comfortable farmhouse
in superb location. Tastefully furnished
bedrooms with TV and beverages. Sheep and
beef enterprises on this family farm.
Outstanding scenery. Towards Cheltenham on
B4632 1ml from Winchcombe L, follow signs
up drive & keep bearing L.

Open Jan-Dec
3 bedrs (1 twin sh/wc; 1 double sh/wc; 1
family sh/wc) 1 ba, 1 wc 🏇 🏠 ✂
🌄🌄 *Commended*
£B&B £16-£20, WR £116, child rates.

Sudeley Hill Farm Winchcombe GL54
5JB 01242 602344   Mrs. Scudamore

15th Century listed farmhouse. Working
sheep/arable farm 800 acres.

Open Jan-Dec
3 bedrs (1 twin ba/sh/wc; 1 double ba/sh/
wc; 1 family ba/sh/wc) 1 wc 🏇 🌄🌄
£B&B £40, WR £252, child rates.

SELF CATERING

CHELTENHAM   7E4

Bangrove Farm Teddington, Tewkesbury
GL20 8JB 01242 620223   Pat Hitchman

🏇
£Wk £170-£300

CHIPPING CAMPDEN 7F4

Weston Park Farm Dovers Hill,
Chipping Campden 01386 840835
Mrs. Whitehouse

⌇
£Wk £150-£350

CIRENCESTER 7F4

Westley Farm Chalford, Cirencester GL6
8HP 01285 760262 Mr. Usborne

Secluded family hill farm with cattle, sheep
and horses. Spectacular views over Golden
Valley. Good walking country.

Just off A419 halfway Cirencester/Stroud.

⌇ ⚘
£Wk £120-£280

DYMOCK 7E4

Lower House Farm Kempley, Dymock
01531 890301 Mrs. Bennett

For full farm description see B&B Entry. Take
road from Newent to M50 via Gorsley. Over
motorway bridge, next R past Ross on Wye
Golf Club, 2 1/2mls to Kempley.

⌇ ⚘
£Wk £200-£220

PLACES TO VISIT

GUITING POWER

Cotswold Farm Park
Guiting Power, Cheltenham GL54 5UG
01451-850307
The most comprehensive collection of
rare breeds of farm livestock in the
country in a beautiful farm setting high in
the Cotswolds. Pets corner, adventure
playground, farm trail, lambing, shearing
and other seasonal attractions. On sale:
gifts.
Location: off the B4077 Stow-on-the-Wold
to Tewkesbury road.
Open: April-Sept, daily 1030-1700
Entrance: adult £3.50, Child £1.50, OAP
£2. WC ♿ ✗ ▮

CINDERFORD

Dean Heritage Centre
Camp Hill, Soudley, Cinderford GL14
7UG 01594-822170
A museum of forest life telling the story
of the forest and its people with nature
trails, adventure playground, picnic and
barbecue area.
Location: off the B4227 between
Blakeney and Cinderford.
Open: Feb-Mar daily 1000-1700, Apr-Oct
daily 1000-1800, Nov-Jan Sat/Sun 1000-
1600.
Entrance: adult £2.60 child £1.60
OAP/concession £2.10 (1994) WC ♿ ✗ ▮

GLOUCESTER

Gloucester Folk Museum
99-103 Westgate Street, Gloucester GL1
2PG 01452-526467
Toys and games, a Victorian classroom
with period lessons in costume, model
steam engines, farming, fishing,
shoemaker's workshop and lots more. All
housed in Tudor, timber-framed
buildings. "A dairy, wheelwright and
carpenters workshops and an ironmaker's
shop in new extensions."
Open: all year, Mon-Sat 1000-1700, July-
Sept, Suns 1000-1600. Entrance free. WC
♿ (limited access) ▮

Nagshead RSPB Nature Reserve
Parkend, Gloucester 01594-832632
Rich in woodland wildlife: birds,
butterflies and dragonflies.
Location: entrance off B4431 Coleford
road immediately after leaving Parkend
village. Seasonal information centre.

HAMPSHIRE

LYNDHURST 4B4

Fritham Farm Fritham, Lyndhurst SO43
7HH 01703 812333   P. A. Hankinson

Lovely farmhouse on working farm in heart of
the glorious New Forest. All grass farm with
lambs, foals and calves in spring. Leave
Junction 1 on M27, take Fordingbridge Rd,
follow signs to Fritham. Farm 300m on RHS
after Fritham & Eyeworth sign.

Open Jan-Dec
3 bedrs (2 twin sh/wc; 1 double ba/wc,
sh/wc) ☎(10) ♞ ♨♨
£B&B £16.50-£18, child rates.

PETERSFIELD

The Bailiff's Cottage Home Farm,
Hollycombe, Liphook GU30 7LR
01428 722171   Angela Jeaner

Open all year
2 bedrs (1 twin; 1 single) 1 ba, 1 wc

RINGWOOD 4A4

Bisterne Farmhouse Lower Bisterne
Farm, Bisterne, Ringwood BH24 3BW
01425 475170   L.M. Binfield

Bisterne is a Grade II listed 17th-century
farmhouse set on a 300-acre dairy and arable
farm in the Avon valley close to the New Forest.
Good home cooking from local produce. The
farm is on the B3347, 3 miles south of Ringwood.
Riding, sea and river fishing, golf and sailing.

Open Mar-Oct.
3 bedrs (1 twin; 1 double ba/wc; 1 family
sh/wc) ☎(7) ⊞

SELF CATERING

RINGWOOD 4A4

Bisterne Farmhouse Lower Bisterne
Farm, Bisterne, Ringwood BH24 3BW
01425 475170   L.M. Binfield

The farm is on the B3347, 3 miles south of
Ringwood. Riding, sea and river fishing, golf
and sailing.

☎(7)

Dunain Farm Hangersley, Ringwood
BH4 3JN 01425 472611   Mrs. Griffin

♿ ☎(7) ♞

ROGATE 4C3

Mizzards Farm Rogate GU31 5HS
01730 821656   Mrs. Francis

☎(7) ♞

HEREFORD & WORCESTER

BEWDLEY 7E3

Bullockhurst Farm Rock, Bewdley
DY14 9SE 01299 832305 Mr. Nott

Georgian farmhouse with large garden on a mixed farm. Decorated and furnished to a high standard. W of Bewdley travel on A456 turn L at Royal Pub. 1 ml to Bliss Gate Inn, over crossroads follow Rock Village sign 1 ml.

Open Mar-Nov
2 bedrs (1 twin ba/wc; 1 family) ⏰ 🐾🐾
£B&B £17-£18, WR £110-£120, child rates.

BROADWAY 7F4

Manor Farm Wormington, Broadway
01386 73302 Pauline Russell

This 15th-century Tudor house boasts leaded casements in the sitting room, a stone inglenook in the hall, slabs of Welsh slate on the floors, and a cheese room from its time as a dairy farm. Manor Farm has 600 acres of arable and beef. Off the B4632, between Broadway and Cheltenham.

Open All year
3 bedrs (1 twin; 2 double inc 1 sh/wc) 1 ba, 2 wc ⏰ 🐴 🐾🐾
£child rates.

BROMSGROVE 8A4

Lower Bentley Farm Lower Bentley Lane, Lower Bentley, Bromsgrove B60 4JB 01527 821286 Mrs. Gibbs

Victorian farmhouse on dairy/beef farm in quiet countryside close to the M5, M42 & M40, Stratford, Birmingham NEC, Worcester and Warwick. Ideal base for business and touring. M5 Jn 5, follow signs for Stoke Works, R into Weston Hall Rd, over crossroads, 1st R into Woodgate Rd, 3rd L, farm on L.

Open Jan-Dec
3 bedrs (1 twin ba/wc; 1 double ba/wc; 1 family) ⏰ 🏠 🐾🐾
£B&B £17.50-£25, child rates.

DROITWICH 7E3

Phepson Farm Himbleton, Droitwich
01905 391205 Mr. Havard

Closed Xmas and New Year
5 bedrs (2 twin inc 1 ba/wc; 2 double inc 1 ba/wc; 1 family) 1 ba, 1 wc ⏰ 🐴

HEREFORD 7D4

Cwm Craig Farm Little Dewchurch, Hereford 01432 840250 Mrs. Lee

Our spacious, Georgian farmhouse with large garden is surrounded by superb, unspoilt countryside. The working farm, 6 miles from Hereford, covers 190 acres with arable and beef. Games room, billiards/snooker table, cot and highchair available. 6 miles from Hereford A49/B4399.

Open all year
3 bedrs (1 twin, 1 double, 1 family) 2 ba, 2 wc ⏰ 🏠 🐾🐾
£B&B £14-£17, WR £91-£112, child rates.

Grafton Villa Farm Grafton, Hereford
01432 268689 Jenny Layton

This beautifully decorated farmhouse is set on a 200-acre farm which rears a variety of animals from chickens and sheep to horses. Superb home cooking. The farm lies in the heart of the Wye valley, on the A49 Hereford-Ross-on-Wye road.

Closed Xmas
3 bedrs (1 twin sh/wc; 1 double sh/wc; 1 family ba/sh/wc)

Sink Green Farm Rotherwas, Hereford
HR2 6LE 01432 870223 Mr. Jones

This beautiful, 16th century, farmhouse is set on a 180 acre livestock farm on the banks of the River Wye. The farm is 3 miles south of the city of Hereford on the B4399. Hereford Cathedral, museums and attractions are all within easy reach.

Open all year
3 bedrs (1 twin sh/wc; 2 double ba/wc)
£B&B £18-£24, WR £119-£168, child rates.

KINGTON 7D3

Bucks Head House School Farm, Upper Hergest, Kington HR5 3EW
01544 231063 Mrs. Protheroe

Open Jan-Dec
6 bedrs (3 twin; 1 double; 2 family) 4 ba, 4 wc
£B&B £15-£16, D £8-£9, WR £102-£105, WR/D £158-£160, child rates.

LEDBURY 7E4

Church Farm Coddington, Ledbury
HR8 1JJ 01531 640271 Mrs. West

Working mixed farm with a 16th century, black & white, Grade II listed farmhouse situated in a quiet rural hamlet. Happy relaxed atmosphere. All home cooking.

Open Feb-Nov
3 bedrs (1 twin; 2 double) 1 ba, 2 wc
Listed
£child rates.

Moor Court Farm Ledbury HR8 2TR
01531 670408   E. Godsall

Enjoy a relaxing holiday on a traditional working Herefordshire hop and livestock farm. Good farmhouse cooking. Situated 6 miles from Ledbury, Moor Court is well-placed for touring the Malverns, the Wye Valley and Welsh borders.

Open all year
3 bedrs (2 twin ba/wc ; 1 double ba/wc)
🛏 🐴 🐕 ⅍ ♨♨ *Commended*

New House Farm Much Marcle,
Ledbury HR8 2PH 01531 660604
Mrs. Jordan

Open all year
2 bedrs (1 twin; 1 double) 1 ba, 1 wc 🛏(5)
♨
£B&B £15, D £10, WR £70, child rates.

Underhill Farm Putley, Ledbury HR8
2QR 01531 670695   Mrs. Blandford

Open Apr-Oct
2 bedrs (1 double ba/sh/wc; 1 family sh/wc) 2 ba, 2 wc 🛏 🖶 *Listed*
£B&B £13-£16, child rates.

LEOMINSTER   7D3

Holgate Farm Kingsland, Leominster
HR6 9QS 01568 708275   J. A. Davies

Holgate is a listed, 17th century farmhouse set in beautiful countryside on a family-run, stock and arable farm about 4 miles northwest of Leominster. Delicious food and comfortable accommodation is offered. Berrington Hall 6 miles.

Closed Xmas
2 bedrs (1 double, 1 family) 1 ba, 1 wc
🛏 🐕

The Hills Farm Leysters, Leominster
HR6 0HP 0156 887205   Mrs. Conolly

Open Feb-Oct
4 bedrs (1 twin sh/wc; 3 double ba/wc) 🐕
♨♨♨ *Highly Commended*   cc Vi
£B&B£20-£22, D £15, WR £140, WR/D £245.

MALVERN   7F4

Grove House Farm Guarlford, Malvern
WR14 3QZ 01684 574256 Helen Simpson

This tastefully furnished and spacious farmhouse is at the centre of a 370-acre livestock and arable farm, at the foot of the

Malvern Hills. Just under 2 miles east of Malvern off the B4211 Guarlford road.

Open Feb-Nov
3 bedrs (1 twin; 1 double; 1 family) 2 ba, 2 wc ☂ ⛩⛩ *Commended*

ROSS-ON-WYE 7E4

Aberhall Farm St Owens Cross, Ross-on-Wye HR2 8LL 01989 730256
Mrs. Davies

Open Mar-Oct
3 bedrs (1 twin; 2 double inc 1 sh/wc) 1 ba, 1 wc ☂(10) ⌗ ⚹ ⛩⛩
£B&B £15.50-£17.

UPTON-UPON-SEVERN 7E4

Tiltridge Farm & Vineyard Upper Hook Road, Upton-on-Severn WR8 0SA
01684 592906 Mrs. Barker

Period family farmhouse lying between the Malvern Hills and the attractive riverside town of Upton-on-Severn. Set in its own vineyard, the house has been fully renovated and is warm and comfortable throughout. Warm welcome, good food & wine. Turn down 'New St' and follow road past a fruit farm & over an old railway bridge.

Open Jan-Dec
2 bedrs (1 double ba/wc; 1 family sh/wc) 1 ba, 2 wc ☂ ⌗ ⛩ ⛩⛩
£B&B £18-£20, D £9.50-£11, WR £112-£126, WR/D £178.50-£192.50, child rates.

WHITBOURNE 7E3

Upper Elmores End Linley Green Road, Whitbourne WR6 5RE
01886 821245 Mrs. Simpson

Open Apr-Oct
3 bedrs (1 twin; 2 double) 1 ba, 2 wc ☂ ⚹ ⛩
£B&B £15-£16, D £9, WR £100, WR/D £160.

WHITCHURCH 12A2

Bradeley Green Farm Tarporley Road, Whitchurch SY13 4HD 01948 663442
Mr. Mulliner

Open all year
☂ ⌗ ⚹

WORCESTER 7E3

Church House Farm Shelsley Beauchamp, Nr Worcester, WR6 6RA
01886 812393 Mrs. Moore

Our large 18th-century farmhouse is situated on the River Teme, 10 miles from Worcester. Family run farm with sheep and poultry.

Open April-Oct
2 bedrs (2 twin ba/wc) ☂ ⛩ ⛩⛩
£B&B £15-£18, D £9.50, WR £10.50, WR/D £171.50, child rates.

SELF CATERING

BROMSGROVE 8A4

Hill Farm Rocky Lane, Bournheath, Bromsgrove BG1 9HU
01527 72403 Lilian Rutter
☂(4)

Lower Bentley Farm Lower Bentley Lane, Lower Bentley, Bromsgrove B60 4JB 01527 821286 Mrs. Gibbs

For full farm description see B&B Entry. M5 Jn 5, follow signs for Stoke Works, R into Weston Hall Rd, over crossroads, 1st R into Woodgate

Rd, 3rd L, farm on L.

ᕰ ᛏ

DROITWICH 7E3

Phepson Farm Himbleton, Droitwich
01905 391205 Mr. Havard

The Granary is a one-bedroomed self-catering flat sleeps 2-4, with lovely views across the farmland.

ᕰ ᛏ

HEREFORD 7D4

Bankside Dilwyn, Hereford HR4 8HD
01544 318329 Mrs. Wellings

A spacious house, overlooking unspoilt farmland and the Black Mountains. Sleeps 6 plus nursery. 2 WC's, shower and bathroom.

From Leominster take the A4112 towards Brecon then A4110 Hereford Road. Dilwyn signposted on left.

ᕰ ⅄ ꝯꝯꝯ
£Wk £195-£240

Grafton Villa Farm Grafton, Hereford
01432 268689 Jenny Layton

The farm lies in the heart of the Wye valley, on the A49 Hereford-Ross-on-Wye road.

ᕰ ᛏ

LEDBURY 7E4

Church Farm Coddington, Ledbury
HR8 1JJ 01531 640271 Mrs. West

For full farm description see B&B Entry.
ᕰ ᛏ Listed

Moor Court Farm Ledbury HR8 2TR
01531 670408 E. Godsall

For full farm description see B&B Entry.ᕰ ᛏ

LEOMINSTER 7D3

Holgate Farm Kingsland, Leominster
HR6 9QS 01568 708275 J. A. Davies

ᕰ ᛏ cc Ac Vi

The Hills Farm Leysters, Leominster
HR6 0HP 0156 887205 Mrs. Conolly

See also B&B Entry. A49 N, turn onto A4112 through Kimbolton to Leysters 200yds past Leysters Garage turn R down lane.

ᛏ cc Vi

WORCESTER 7E3

Church House Farm Shelsley
Beauchamp, Nr Worcester, WR6 6RA
01886 812393 Mrs. Moore

For full farm description see B&B Entry.
ᕰ ᛏ ⅄

PLACES TO VISIT

BROMSGROVE

Avoncroft Museum of Buildings
Stoke Heath, Bromsgrove B60 4JR
01527-813886
An open air museum spanning 600 years of history, including 25 buildings which have been rescued and re-erected on 15 acres of Worcestershire countryside. Location: off the A38 bypass, 2 miles south of Bromsgrove. Entrance: adult £3.50, child £1.75, OAP concession £2.80. WC ⅄ ᛏ ✗ ᕬ

HEREFORD

Cider Museum & King Offa Distillery
Pomona Place, Off Whitecross Road, Hereford HR4 0LW 01432-354207 Housed in a former cider works, the Museum tells the facinating story of cider making through the ages. There is a full programme of events and temporary exhibitions throughout the year. In the distillery cider is distilled, the first time (legally) in Britain for over 200 years. Location: off A438, near town centre. Open: Apr-Oct., daily 10.00 to 5.30 Nov-Mar., Mon to Sat. 1.00 to 5.00. Last admissions 45 mins earlier Entrance: adults £2, children, OAP's, full-time students £1.50, group concessions.WC ⅄ (ground floor access only) ✗ (guide dogs only) ᕬ

EVESHAM

Domestic Fowl Trust
Honeybourne Pastures, Honeybourne,
Evesham WR11 5QJ
01386-833083 Fax 0386-833364
The only Conservation Centre
specialising in the display and breeding
of all domestic ducks, hens, bantams and
turkeys. All breeds are in labelled

paddocks. Also children's farm and
adventure playground. On sale: poultry
equipment, books, feedstuffs, housing
and young stock.
Location: signposted off A46 Broadway-
Stratford-on-Avon road.
Open: all year, Sat-Thur 1030-1700.
Entrance: adult £3, child £2,
OAP/concessions £2.50 WC ঠ 🐾

HERTFORDSHIRE

PLACES TO VISIT

ST ALBANS

Bowman's Open Farm
Coursers Road, London Colney, St Albans
AL2 1BB 01727-822106
A chance for the public to see a real
commercial farm at work. Lots of animals
to see and stroke and farm machinery.
Large farm shop.
Location: Follow signs from M25 Jn.22.
Open: daily 0900-1730.
Entrance: adult £3, child OAP
concessions £2 WC ঠ ✗ 🐾

HATFIELD

Mill Green Museum
Mill Green, Hatfield AL9 5PD
01707-271362
Local history museum and fully restored,
water-powered, corn mill. Visitors can
see corn grinding in the traditional way.
Small local history museum with
changing programme of temporary
exhibitions in the former miller's house
adjoining the mill. Craft demonstrations
on summer weekends. On sale: flour,
souvenirs, books.
Location: signposted from A1000 and
A414.
Open: Jan-Dec, Tues-Fri 1000-1700, Sat-
Sun & Bank hols 1400-1700. Entrance
charges on application WC ঠ (partial
access) 🐾

HODDESDON

**Rye House Marsh RSPB
Nature Reserve**
Rye Road, Hoddesdon 01992-460031
Riverside marsh containing a variety of
habitats; flood meadows, pools, fen,
scrub and wet woodland.
Location: near Rye House station, east of
Hoddesdon.Open daily 0900-1700.
Entrance: adult £2, child 50p,
OAP/concessions £1. WC ঠ 🐾
(weekends only)

LETCHWORTH GARDEN CITY

Standalone Farm
Wilbury Road, Letchworth Garden City
SG6 4JN
01462-686775
An open working farm of 170 acres with
cattle, sheep, pigs and poultry plus the
traditional farmyard animals - goats,
ducks, donkeys, ponies and Shire horses.
Milking demonstrations 1400/1430 daily.
Picnic areas, wildfowl area.
Location: signposted from A1M J9.
Open: Mar-Sept inclusive Sun-Mon 1100-
1700
Entrance:1995: adult £2.50, child £1.25,
OAP/concessions £1.25, Under 3 FOC,
day ticket (6) £9.00, group discount on
application. WC ঠ ✗ 🐾

HUMBERSIDE

BEVERLEY   11E3

Crowtree Farm Arram, Beverley HU17
7NR 01964 550167   Mrs. Hart

Smallholdings with lots of friendly animals.
Tranquil gardens with croquet and games
inside and out. Driffield Rd out of Beverley. In
Leconfield R 1 ¼ ml over railway crossing
bridge,R in centre of village, up driveway.

Open Jan-Dec
2 bedrs (inc 1 twin ba/wc) 1 ba, 1 wc ఆ 扁
卜 *Listed*
£B&B £15-£16, D £7.50-£8, WR £85-£90,
WR/D £135-£140, child rates.

BRIDLINGTON   11F3

The Grange Bempton Lane,
Flamborough, Bridlington YO15 1AS
01262 850207   Mrs. Thompson

Open Jan-Dec
3 bedrs (1 twin; 1 double; 1 family) 2 ba, 2
wc ఆ 卜
£B&B £13-£14.50, WR £91, child rates.

MARKET WEIGHTON   11E3

Arras Farmhouse Arras, Market
Weighton Y04 3RN 01430 872404
Mrs. Stephenson

Open all year
3 bedrs (1 twin; 2 double inc 1 ba/wc, 1
double sh/wc) 1 ba, 1 wc ఆ 扁 卜
£B&B £30-£34, D £5, child rates.

PLACES TO VISIT

BRIDLINGTON

Bempton Cliffs RSPB Nature Reserve
Cliff Lane, Nr Bridlington 01262-851179
England's largest breeding seabird colony
with over 200,000,000 birds, including
gannets and puffins.
Location: take cliff road from Bempton
village on B1229 from Flamborough to
Filey.
Open: reserve at all times. Visitor centre:
Mar-Oct, daily 1000-1700. Car park £1.50
WC ఆ

HORNSEA

Hornsea Museum
Burn's Farm, 11 Newbegin, Hornsea
HU18 1AB 01964-533443
An exhibition of Victorian domestic and
village life housed in an 18th century
farmhouse and outbuildings. Craft
displays in summer and a large garden.
The museum has won many awards.
Open: Apr-Sept, daily Mon-Sat 1000-1700,
Sun 1500-1700
Entrance: adult £1.50,
child/OAP/concessions £1 WC (partial
access) ✗ (summer afternoons) ఆ

ISLE OF WIGHT

NEWPORT   16A3

Cheverton Farm Shorwell, Newport
PO30 3JE 0983 741017   Mrs. Hodgson

Open all year
3 bedrs (2 twin; 1 double) 2 ba, 2 wc ఆ 卜
cc Ac Vi

KENT

AYLESFORD 5E3

Court Farm Village High Street,
Aylesford, Maidstone ME20 7AZ
01622 717293 D. Tucker

Beamed farmhouse dating back to 14th
Century in village location. All bedrooms,
colour TV, tea & coffee making facilities.
Quiet and comfortable. Take A229 towards
Chatham.1st off 2nd roundabout
signposted 'Aylesford' approx. 1 ¼ miles on
left.

Open Jan-Dec
3 bedrs (1 twin; 1 double; 1 single) 1 ba, 2
wc 🏠 ✄
£B&B £14-£21, WR £98-£147.

CANTERBURY 5E3

Crockshard Farmhouse Wingham,
Canterbury CT3 1NY 01227 720464
Nicola Ellen

Very attractive farmhouse in beautiful
gardens in the heart of the Kentish
countryside. Sheep, cattle, poultry and
many other domestic animals. Home
produce. From A2 between Dover and
Canterbury take B2046 Wingham Rd. After 4
miles, 2nd turn to Goodnestone on R, farm
1st L.

Open Jan-Dec
4 bedrs (1 twin; 3 family inc 1 sh/wc) 2 ba,
2 wc 🐂 🐓
£B&B £17.50-£20, WR £105-£120, child
rates.

Great Field Farm Misling Lane, Stelling
Minnis, Canterbury CT4 6DE

01227 709223 Mrs. Castle

Lovely, spacious farmhouse overlooking
beautiful countryside. Wealth of old pine, fine
furnishings, paddocks with friendly ponies
and arable land. Ensuite facilites available.
Canterbury take B2068 8 miles, past Stelling
Minnis turn 1 mile, Misling Lane on R before
the George Inn.

Open Jan-Dec
3 bedrs (1 twin; 2 double ba/wc) 1 ba, 2
wc 🐂 Listed
£B&B £16-£20, child rates.

CHARING 5E3

Barnfield Charing, Ashford TN27 0BN
01233 712421 Mrs Pym

A lovely, romantic, 15th century Kent
farmhouse peacefully set in its own garden,
surrounded by 500 acres of sheep and arable
farm land. Go to the roundabout on the A20
at Charing and leave by A20 exit to Lenham.
Go 400 yards and turn left. 2½ miles on l.

Open all year
4 bedrs (1 twin; 1 double; 1 family; 1
single) 1 ba, 2 wc 🐂 Listed cc Vi

£B&B £18.50-£20.50, D £12.50, WR £111-£123, WR/D £186-£198, child rates.

DOVER 5F3

Coldred Court Farm Church Road, Coldred, Dover CT15 5AQ 01304 830816 Mrs. Kelly

Open Jan-Dec
3 bedrs (1 twin ba/wc; 2 double ba/wc)
Highly Commended
£B&B £19-£30, D £10-£12, WR £133-£210, WR/D £200-£270.

FAVERSHAM 5E3

Leaveland Court Leaveland, Faversham ME13 0NP 01233 740596 Mrs. Scutt

Enchanting 15th Century timbered farmhouse on 300 acre downland farm. Delightful gardens with heated outdoor swimming pool. All rooms en suite with colour TV. From Faversham S on A251 towards Ashford, past Sheldwich then 2nd R at Leaveland corner by bus stop.

Open Jan-Dec
3 bedrs (inc 1 twin sh/wc) 1 ba
cc Ac Vi
£B&B £18-£20, D £8-£12, WR £120, WR/D £160-£180, child rates.

FOLKESTONE 5F3

Beachborough Park Newington, Folkestone CT18 8BW 01303 275432 Mrs. Wallis

Converted farm buildings designed to give character, comfort, and peace. Set in a 30 acre area that houses a swimming pool, and coarse and trout fishing facilities. Rare farm animals also bred on site. Leave Folkestone on M20. Leave via exit no.12 to join the A20. Take B20 to Lyminze, farm is first house on the left.

Open all year.
8 bedrs (4 twin inc 1 ba/wc, 2 sh/wc; 4 double inc 1 ba/wc, 3 sh/wc)
£B&B £17.50-£25, D £4.50-£12.50, WR £15-£20, WR/D £25-£30, child rates.

SITTINGBOURNE 5E3

Palace Farmhouse Doddington, Sittingbourne ME9 0AU 01795 886820 Mrs. Leak

Open Jan-Dec
cc Vi
£B&B £20-£25, WR £125-£160.

SUTTON VALENCE 5E3

Sparks Oast Farm Forsham Lane, Sutton Valence, Maidstone ME17 3EW 01622 842213 Mrs. Clout

Converted oasthouse on small working sheep farm with waterfowl, barn owls, pygmy goats etc. Overlooking the Weald countryside amidst orchards and hop gardens. Junction 8 M20 past Leeds Castle Entrance 3mls, L at Plough A274, go 4mls, R at bottom of hill, 1/2ml down lane on L.

Open all year
£B&B £32-£35, child rates.

TESTON 5E3

Court Lodge Court Lodge Farm, The Street, Teston, Maidstone ME18 5AQ 01622 812570 Rosemarie Bannock

Court Lodge is a listed 16th Century

farmhouse brickfaced in 1784 and possessing oak beams, leaded windows and two inglenook fireplaces set in a delightful old world garden. Overlooks Medway Valley. Central heated, log fires, superb breakfast. From Maidstone take A26 signposted Tonbridge to Teston (4mls), R and immediately R again (within 2 metres) into drive.

Open Jan-Dec
3 bedrs (2 twin inc 1 sh/wc; 1 double ba/wc) ☎(10) 👑👑👑 cc Vi
£B&B £34-£45, WR £238-£275.

TONBRIDGE   5D3

Great Cheveney Farm Goudhurst Road, Marden, Tonbridge TN12 9LX
01622 831207   Doris Day

16th Century timber framed farmhouse on 300 acre fruit/arable farm. Offers comfortable accommodation in peaceful surroundings, situated midway between Goudhurst/Marden villages on B2079. Guest's lounge, TV, parking. A21 (Hastings) approx. 6mls, L onto A262 (Goudhurst). In centre of village L onto B2079 (Marden), go 3 1/2mls, farm on L

Open Jan-Dec
2 bedrs (1 double ba/wc; 1 single ba) 1 wc
☎(10) ✔ *Listed Highly Commended*
£B&B £21-£34, WR £130-£210.

Tanner House Tanner Farm, Goudhurst Road, Marden, Tonbridge TN12 9ND
01622 831214   Lesley Mannington

Open Jan-Dec
3 bedrs (2 twin sh/wc; 1 double sh/wc)
☎(5) 🏥 ✔ 👑👑👑 cc Ac AmEx Vi
£B&B £18-£20, D £12, WR £115-£125,
WR/D £200-£210, child rates.

WYE   5E3

Ripple Farm Godmersham, Nr Canterbury, Wye CT3 1NY 01227 730748
Mrs. Baur

16th Century farmhouse where we do B & B and 2 self contained cottages in coverted stables. Both sleep up to 5. We are a small mixed organic farm specialising in organic vegetables. A28 follow Ashford signs, L at Godmarsham crossroad under Railway Bridge, cont. 3/4ml, L, Gundale sign, site 200yds R.

Open all year
2 bedrs (2 family) 1 ba, 1 wc ☎ 🏥
£B&B £16.50-£17.50, child rates.

SELF CATERING

FOLKESTONE   5F3

Beachborough Park Newington, Folkestone CT18 8BW 01303 275432
Mrs. Wallis

For full farm description see B&B Entry. Leave Folkestone on M20. Leave via exit no.12 to join the A20. Take B20 to Lyminze, farm is first house on the left.

☎ 🐕 ????
£Wk £165-£500

SEVENOAKS   5D3

Ash Place Farmhouse Ash, Sevenoaks TN15 7HD 01474 872238   Mrs. Scott

☎ ????
£Wk £150-£220

SUTTON VALENCE 5E3

Sparks Oast Farm Forsham Lane,
Sutton Valence, Maidstone ME17 3EW
01622 842213 Mrs. Clout

For full farm description see B&B Entry. Bed
sitting room, kitchen, twin bed, bathroom.;
Junction 8 M20 past Leeds Castle Entrance
3mls, L at Plough A274, go 4mls, R at bottom
of hill, 1/2ml down lane on L.

1 unit; 1 bedrs ☎
£Wk £130-£250

TESTON 5E3

Court Lodge Court Lodge Farm, The
Street, Teston, Maidstone ME18 5AQ
01622 812570 Rosemarie Bannock

For full farm description see B&B Entry. From
Maidstone take A26 signposted Tonbridge to
Teston (4mls), R and immediately R again
(within 2 metres) into drive.

☎(10) cc Vi
£Wk £120-£325

WYE 5E3

Ripple Farm Godmersham, Nr
Canterbury, Wye CT3 1NY 01227 730748
Mrs. Baur

For full farm description see B&B Entry. 2
cottages in converted stables. A28 follow
Ashford signs, L at Godmersham crossroad
under Railway Bridge, cont. 3/4ml, L, Gundale
sign, site 200yds R.

& ☎
£Wk £170-£240

PLACES TO VISIT

STAPLEHURST

Brattle Farm Museum
Brattle Farm, Staplehurst TN12 OHE
01580-591222
A personal collection of agricultural
bygones including tractors, vintage cars,
motor cycles, bicycles, blacksmith's and
wheelwright's equipment and a pair of
working oxen. Many items of local
manufacture. On sale: souvenirs and
pottery.

Location: off the A229 in Staplehurst.
Open: Easter-Oct, Sun & bank hols 0930-
1830
Entrance: adult £1.50, child £1,
OAP/concessions £1 WC ♀ & ✗ ▨

LYDD

Dungeness RSPB Nature Reserve
Dungeness Road, Lydd, Romney Marsh
01797 321309
A unique shingle foreland with natural
and manmade pits. Important for
breeding seabirds, migrants and
wintering wild fowl. TR063196
Location: off Lydd-Dungeness road.
Open: 0900-2100 or sunset if earlier,
closed Tues.
Entrance: adult £2 child 50p
OAP/concessions £1. WC & ▨

HILDENBOROUGH

Hollanden Farm Park
Great Hollanden Farm, Mill Lane,
Hildenborough, Nr Sevenoaks TN15 0SG
01732-833858
Over 50 rare breeds, pets corner,
adventure playground, tractor-trailer
rides, recreation of an Iron Age
settlement. School visits catered for.
Picnic area. On sale: fresh fruit and
vegetables, meat and dairy produce, gifts.
Location: 7 miles south of M25, off A21
on B245.
Open: 26 Mar-30 Sept, daily 1030-1700.
Entrance: adult £3.95, child £2.60,
OAP/concession £3 WC & ✗ ▨

MAIDSTONE

Museum of Kent Life
Lock Lane, Sandling, Maidstone ME14
3AU 01622-763936
Hundreds of exhibits illustrate the
uniqueness of Kent's agricultural past as
the Garden of England.
Location: M20 Jn.6 then take the A229
Maidstone road.
Open: Easter-Oct, daily 1000-1730
Entrance: adult £3.50,
child/OAP/concession £2.00. WC & ♀ ✗ ▨

WOODCHURCH

South of England Rare Breeds Centre
Highlands Farm, Woodchurch, Ashford
TN26 3RJ
01233-861493
Kent's greenest atttraction. Ninety acres
of rolling Kent countryside, 65 rare
breeds of British farm animals - pigs,
poultry, cattle, sheep, goats, ducks and
geese. Children's Barn. Most animals can
be seen under cover. Gift shop. Farm
rides.
Location: on B2067 west of Ham Street
(M20 J10/A2070).
Open: all year, daily, summer 1030-1730,
winter 1030-1630.
Entrance: adult £3.25, child £1.25, OAP
£2.75 WC ♿ ✗ 🐾

PADDOCK WOOD

Whitbread Hop Farm
Beltring, Paddock Wood TN12 6PY
01622-872068 Fax 01622-872630
This leading Kent tourist attraction
features the largest collection of Victorian
oast houses in the world and is the home
of the famous Whitbread Shire horses.
Special weekend events. Hop story
exhibition, animal village, pottery
workshop, nature trail, play area. On
sale: gifts, souvenirs.
Location: M20 J4, A228 and B2016 to
Paddock Wood.
Open: all year, daily winter 1000-1600,
summer 1000-1800
Entrance: charges on application. WC 🐴
♿ ✗ 🐾

LANCASHIRE

BACUP 10C4

Pasture Bottom Farm Bacup OL13
9UZ 01706 873790   Mrs. Isherwood

100 acre beef cattle farm on the Lancashire
and Yorkshire border. Ideal for moorland
walking, within easy reach of many
attractions. A681 from Bacup, on Todmorden
Rd turn R down Greave Rd and farm signed
Pasture Bottom.

Open Jan-Dec
2 bedrs (2 twin) 🍳 🛏 🐴 ♨
£B&B £13, D £6.50, WR £91, WR/D
£136.50, child rates.

BURNLEY 10C3

Eaves Barn Farm Hapton, Burnley
BB12 7LP 01282 771591   Mrs. Butler

Eaves Barn Farm is a mixed working farm.
The accommodation is a spacious cottage
attached to the main house, furnished to a
high standard offering luxury facilities.
Burnley-Accrington Rd A679. Hapton Inn turn
R straight on.

Open Jan-Dec
3 bedrs (2 double inc 1 ba/wc, 1 sh/wc; 1
single) 1 ba, 2 wc ☎(10)*Listed*
£B&B £19.50-£22, D £9, child rates.

BURSCOUGH 10B4

Brandreth Barn Brandreth Farm, Tarlscough Lane, Burscough, Ormskirk L40 0RJ 01704 893510 Mrs. Wilson

Open all year
✠

CARNFORTH 10B3

Collingholme Farm Cowan Bridge, Nr Kirkby Lonsdale, Carnforth LA6 2JL 01524 271775 Mr. Burrow

Beautifully furnished, 250 year old stone farmhouse on a beef and sheep farm in a peaceful location by a stream, 1 mile from A65. Varied breakfasts. Warm and friendly atmosphere.

Open Mar-Oct
2 bedrs (1 twin; 1 double) ➎ *Listed*
£B&B £13-£15, WR £90-£100, child rates.

CLITHEROE 10C3

Wytha Farm Rimington, Clitheroe BB7 4EQ 01200 445295 Mrs. Oliver

Open Jan-Dec
➎ 🏠 🐕
£B&B £13.50-£17, D £7, WR £87.50-£119, WR/D £136.50-£168, child rates.

COLNE MAP

Higher Wanless Farm Red Lane, Colne BB8 7JP 01282 865301 Carol Mitson

The farm lies just north of Colne off the A682. Higher Wanless is luxuriously furnished, and nestles peacefully alongside one of the prettiest stretches of the Leeds-Liverpool Canal. Babysitting on request. The owners breed Shire Horses and sheep. Exit jct.13 M65 through Barrowford on A628. Turn R past 'Old Bridge Inn' turn R again. Signed 'Colne 2 mls', farm 1st L.

Open Jan-Nov
2 bedrs (1 twin inc 1 sh/wc; 1 family sh/wc) 1 ba, 1 wc ➎(3) 🏠 🐑🐑
£B&B £18-£23, D £10, child rates.

Parson Lee Farm Wycoller, Colne BB8 8SU 01282 864747 Mrs. Hodgson

Open Feb-Nov
3 bedrs (1 twin sh/wc; 1 double; 1 family ba/wc) 1 ba ➎(3) 🏠

GARSTANG 10B3

Stirzakers Farm Barnacre, Preston, Garstang PR3 1GE 01995 603335 Ruth Wrathall

Open all year
3 bedrs (1 double; 1 family; 1 single) 2 ba, 2 wc ➎ *Listed Highly Commended*
£B&B £14-£16, WR £70-£80, child rates.

LANCASTER 10B3

Fowgill Park Farm High Bentham, Lancaster LA2 7AH 01524 261630 Mr. Metcalfe

Open April- October
3 bedrs (2 twin inc 1 ba/wc; 1 double sh/wc) ➎ 🐕 🐑🐑
£B&B £13-£15.50, D £7.50, WR £84-£98, WR/D £136-£150, child rates.

OLDHAM 10C4

Globe Farm Huddersfield Road, Standedge, Oldham OL3 5LU
01457 873040 Jean Mayall

Smallholding 1100 foot in the Saddleworth Hills. Offering bed and breakfast or Youth Hostel facilities. TV and tea/coffee all rooms. Central heating. Walkers welcome. On A62 between Oldham and Huddersfield, ¾ mile from A670 junction.

Open all year
6 bedrs (2 twin; 2 double; 2 single) 2 ba, 2 wc ➎ ➍ cc Ac Vi
£B&B £17, D £6.50, WR £100, WR/D £140, child rates.

POULTON-LE-FYLDE 10B3

Todderstaffe Hall Farm off Fairfield Road, Poulton-le-Flyde, Nr Blackpool FY6 8LF 01253 882537 Mrs. Smith

Open all year

PRESTON 10B4

Jenkinsons Farmhouse Alston Lane, Longridge, Preston PR3 3BD
01772 782624 Mrs. Ibison

Open all year
6 bedrs (2 twin; 3 double; 1 single) 3 ba, 3 wc ➎ ➍ *Highly Commended*
£B&B £17, D £12.50, WR £140, WR/D £227.50, child rates.

ROCHDALE 10C4

Leaches Farm Ashworth, Rochdale OL11 5UN 01706 228520 Mrs. Neaye

This beautiful 17th-century 140 acre Pennine hill farm, with beef and sheep, has views over four counties. Take the A680 to Norden. Turn left into Ashworth road, farm is 1 mile down the road.

Closed Xmas and New Year
3 bedrs (1 twin; 1 double; 1 single) 1 ba, 1 wc ➎ ➌ ➍
£B&B £18, child rates.

SOUTHPORT 10B4

Martin Lane Farmhouse Martin Lane, Burscough L40 8HJ 01704 893527
Mr. Stubbs

Small farm with sheep and hens. Leave M6 at junction 27. Follow A5209 to junction with A59, turn L, then R onto B5242, 2nd R, then 1st r, then 1st R.

Open Jan-Dec
1 bedrs (1 family) ➎
£B&B £12.50-£18, WR £70-£105.

SELF CATERING

CARNFORTH 10B3

Brackenthwaite Farm Yealand Redmayne, Carnforth LA5 9TE
01539 563276 Mrs. Clarke

➎ ➌ ⌂⌂⌂
£Wk £85-£310

OLDHAM 10C4

Globe Farm Huddersfield Road, Standedge, Oldham OL3 5LU
01457 873040 Jean Mayall

For full farm description see B&B Entry. On A62 between Oldham and Huddersfield, ¾ mile from A670 junction.

➎ cc Ac Vi
£Wk £42

SOUTHPORT 10B4

Martin Lane Farmhouse Martin Lane, Burscough L40 8HJ 01704 893527
Mr. Stubbs

For full farm description see B&B Entry. Farm buildings converted into 2 first class cottages, both beatifully furnished and well equipped. Leave M6 at junction 27. Follow A5209 to junction with A59, turn L, then R onto B5242, 2nd R, then 1st r, then 1st R.

⌐ ♙♙♙♙
£Wk £215-£350

PLACES TO VISIT

CARNFORTH

Leighton Moss RSPB Reserve
Silverdale, Carnforth
01524-701601
Large reed bed with meres, willow and alder scrub. Home to rare bitterns. Location: off Yealand-Silverdale road just before station.

Open: daily 0900-2100
Entrance: adult £3 child 50p OAP £2. WC
&. ✗ 🖴

ORMSKIRK

Martin Mere Wildfowl & Wetlands Centre
Burscough, Ormskirk L40 0TA
01704-895181
A fun day out for the family to enjoy with nature walks, beautiful scenery and many species of waterfowl to be seen. New Wetland Adventure for children. On sale: books, gifts.
Location: 6 miles from Ormskirk, signposted from M6, M61, M58.
Open: all year, daily, Summer 0930-1730, Winter 0930-1600 WC &. ✗ 🖴

LEICESTERSHIRE

MARKET HARBOROUGH 8B3

The Wrongs Welford Road, Sibbertoft, Market Harborough LE16 9UJ
01858 880886 Mrs. Hart

Open Jan-Dec
2 bedrs (1 double; single) 1 ba, 1 wc ⌐ 🐎
✗ Listed
£B&B £15, WR £98, child rates.

MELTON MOWBRAY 8B3

Home Farm Church Lane, Old Dalby, Melton Mowbray LE14 3LB 01664 822622
Val Anderson

This peaceful Victorian farmhouse is set in an idyllic garden facing the church. Good food at

the Routier Best Pub in Great Britain (1991) at the nearby Crown Inn. Old Dalby lies west of the A606 Nottingham-Melton Mowbray road.

Open all year
5 bedrs (2 twin inc 1 sh/wc; 1 double sh/wc; 2 single sh/wc) 2 ba, 2 wc ⌐ 🐎 ✗
cc Ac Vi

OAKHAM 8C3

Yew Tree Farm Teigh, Oakham LE15
7RT 01572 84497 Mrs. Morley

Open Jan-Nov
2 bedrs (1 twin; 1 double) ⌐ 🚿 ✗
£B&B £13-£15, child rates.

REDMILE 8C2

Peacock Farm *Acclaimed*
Redmile NG13 0GQ ⊕RAC
01949 842475

Open all year
10 bedrs (inc 6 en suite) 2 ba 👑👑👑
£B&B £19.50-£42, D £12.50.

SELF CATERING

MELTON MOWBRAY 8B3

Elms Farm Long Clawson, Melton Mowbray LE14 4NG 01664 822395
R. S. Whittard

☙

PLACES TO VISIT

OAKHAM

Rutland County Museum
Catmos Street, Oakham, Rutland LE15 6HW 01572-723654

The Museum of Rutland Life includes farm equipment, machinery and wagons, rural tradesmen's tools, domestic collections and local archaeology. Accommodated in a splendid, late 18th century, indoor riding school. Special gallery on the "Volunteer Soldier in Leicestershire and Rutland".
Location: on A6003 near Oakham town centre.
Open: daily, Mon-Sat 1000-1700, Sun, April-Oct 1400-1700, Sun, Nov-Mar 1400-1700. Entrance free. WC ⮱

LINCOLNSHIRE

GAINSBOROUGH 8C1

Church Farm Fillingham, Gainsborough DN21 5BS 01427 668279 Christine Ramsay
Open all year

GRANTHAM 8C2

Sproxton Lodge Skillington, Grantham NG33 5HJ 01476 860307 E. M. Whatton

Sproxton Lodge, an arable farm with animals, lies south of Grantham, 3 miles west of the A1. In the comfortable farmhouse, built between 1790-1810, you can enjoy good home cooking, vegetarians also catered for. Cot available.

Closed Xmas and New Year
3 bedrs (1 double; 1 family; 1 single) 1 ba, 2 wc ☙ 🏠 *Listed*
£B&B £15, child rates.

Sycamore Farm *Acclaimed*
Bassingthorpe, Grantham NG33 4ED RAC
01476 585274 S. M. Robinson

Peaceful, Victorian Farmhouse in beautiful rural surroundings. Comfortable, attractively furnished bedrooms, colour TV, alarms and guest sitting room. Leave B6403 at railway bridge, 3 miles east of A1. Follow signs to Lower Bassingthorpe. Farm at end of village on left.

Open all year
3 bedrs (1 twin ba/wc; 2 double inc 1 sh/wc) 1 ba ☙(6) 🏠 ⤢ ♨♨
£B&B £17-£20, D £8-£10, child rates.

HORNCASTLE

Greenfield Farm Minting, Horncastle LN9 5RX 01507 578457 J. Bankes

Open all year
3 bedrs (1 twin sh/wc; 2 double inc 1

ba/wc, 1 sh/wc) 1 wc ⬠ ⚑ ⚒ ♨♨
£B&B £18-£19, WR £126, child rates.

Stamford House Farm Miningsby,
Horncastle PE22 7NW 01507 588682
Anne Morris

Open all year
2 bedrs (1 twin; 1 double ba/wc) 1 sh, 1
wc ⬠ ⊞ ⚑ ⚒ ♨♨

LINCOLN   8C1

Hainton Walk Farm Ludford, Lincoln
LN3 6AP 01507 313242   M. Thornalley

Open all year

Halfway Farm A46 Swinderby, Lincoln
LN6 9HN   RAC
01522 868749   Mr. Underwood

Open all year
17 bedrs (15 twin ba/wc) 1 ba ⬠(3)
cc Ac AmEx Vi

Honeyholes South Farm Hackthorn,
Lincoln LN2 3PW 01673 861868
M. Greenfield

The farmhouse is beside orchard, meadows
and a pond on a 230 acre, family-run, arable
farm 7 miles north of Lincoln. Good home
cooking and baking based on fresh local
produce. Horse stabling available. N from
Lincoln on A15 for 6 mls signed turning for
Hackforth further 1 ½ mls to village. Farm
signed on R, ½ ml on.

Open Jan-Dec
3 bedrs (1 twin; 2 double) 1 ba, 1 wc ⬠(2)
⊞ ⚒ Listed
£B&B £14, D £9, WR £90, WR/D £150,
child rates.

MARKET RASEN   8C1

East Farmhouse Buslingthorpe, Market
Rasen LN3 5AQ 01673 842283 Mrs. Grant

Open Jan-Dec
2 bedrs (1 twin sh/wc; 1 double sh/wc) ⬠
♨♨
£B&B £18-£20, D £12-£13, WR £120, WR/D
£205, child rates.

SLEAFORD   8C2

Manor Farm Leasingham, Sleaford
NG34 8JN 01529 302671   Mrs. Franks

Open All year
2 bedrs (2 twin) 1 ba, 2 wc ⬠ ⚑ Listed
£child rates.

STAMFORD   8C3

Midstone Farm House Southorpe,
Stamford PE9 3BX 01780 740136
Mr & Mrs. Harrison-Smit

Open all year
3 bedrs (1 twin; 1 double; 1 family sh/wc)
2 ba, 2 wc ⬠ ⚑ Listed
£B&B £17.50-£25, WR £115-£122.50, child
rates.

STURTON-BY-STOW   8C1

Gallows Dale Farm Stow Park Road,
Sturton-by-Stow LN1 2AH 01427 788387
B. Williams

Open all year
4 bedrs (1 twin; 1 double; 1 family; 1
single) 1 ba, 1 wc ⬠ ⚒
£B&B £14-£15, WR £90, child rates.

SELF CATERING

MARKET RASEN   8C1

East Farmhouse Buslingthorpe, Market
Rasen LN3 5AQ 01673 842283 Mrs. Grant

⬠
£Wk £150-£200

PLACES TO VISIT

SPALDING

Butterfly and Falconry Park
Long Sutton, Spalding PE12 9LE
01406-363833
A tropical butterfly garden with 500 butterflies flying around. In the attractive park the falconer gives daily displays with his eagles, owls and falcons. Large picnic area and adventure playground.
Location: signposted off A17 at Long Sutton.
Open: Apr-Aug, daily 1000-1800; Sep-Oct daily 1000-1700.
Entrance: adult £3.60 child £2.40 OAP/concession £3.20 Family ticket £10.00. WC ⅋ ✗ ⵿.

NORFOLK

BANHAM	9E3

East Farm Euston Road, Barnham, Thetford IP24 2PB 01842 890231 Mr. Heading

Open Jan-Dec
2 bedrs (1 twin ba/wc; 1 double ba/wc) ⴲ ⵿

£B&B £19-£22, child rates.

CROMER	9F2

Shrublands Farm Northrepps, Cromer NR27 0AA 01263 579297 Mrs. Youngman

Victorian farmhouse set in large garden on a 300 acre arable farm. A149 towards N Walsham, L to Northrepps Village 2mls from Cromer. Farm in village 50 yds past Tuesday Arms pub on L.

Open Jan-Dec
3 bedrs (2 twin inc 1 ba/wc, 1 sh/wc; 1 double ba/wc) ⴲ ⵿⵿
£B&B £18-£20, D £9-£11, WR £126-£140, WR/D £189-£217.

DISS	9E3

Abbey Farm Great Green, Thrandeston, Diss IP2 4BN 01379 783422   Mrs. Carlisle

Open all year
2 bedrs (1 double sh/wc; 1 single) 1 ba, 1 wc ⴲ ⵞ ⵿⵿
£B&B £20, child rates.

The Strenneth The Old Farmhouse, Old Airfield Road, Fersfield, Diss IP22 2BP 01379 888182   Mr. Webb

Family-run, fully renovated, former farmhouse with oak beams. Log fires in winter. Colour TVs. Tea and coffee making in all rooms. Executive and four posters for that special break. Hairdressing salon. Turn off A1066 to Fersfield village, through village to Airfield Road.

Open all year
7 bedrs (2 twin ba/wc; 4 double inc 2 ba/wc, 2 sh/wc; 1 single sh/wc) ⴲ ⵞ ⵿⵿
cc Ac Vi
£B&B £22-£29, D £13, WR £142-£187, WR/D £233-£278, child rates.

EAST DEREHAM	9E3

Bartles Lodge Church Farm, Church Street, Elsing, East Dereham NR20 3EA 01362 637177   Mrs. Bartlett

Open Jan-Dec
7 bedrs (3 twin inc 2 ba/wc, 1 sh/wc; 3 double sh/wc; 1 family ba/wc) 4 wc ⴲ ⵞ ⵿⵿ cc Ac Vi
£B&B £22, D £7.50, WR £140, WR/D £185.

Church Farm Cottages Brisley, East Dereham NR20 5LL 01362 668332 Mrs. Howes

The cottages stand beside the village green and back onto farmland belonging to the owner. They are both of brick and flint construction and were part of the original 400 year old farmhouse and cottage. Each is private with its own garden. Village is situated on B1145 and B1146 Crossroads.

Open all year
5 bedrs (2 twin; 2 double; 1 single) 2 ba, 3 wc ♿ ⌖
£B&B £20-£25, WR £110-£125, child rates.

Ivy House Farm Welgate, Mattishall, East Dereham 01362 850208   B. Jewson

Ivy House Farm is a Grade II listed building; part Jacobean, part Georgian with Elizabethan influences. This working farm, located south off the A47 west of Norwich, consists of a flock of breeding ewes and 3000 free range chickens.

Open all year
3 bedrs (2 twin; 1 double) 1 ba, 2 wc ♿ ⌖
£child rates.

Moor Farm Holidays Moor Farm,

Foxley, East Dereham NR20 4QM 01362 88523   Paul Davis

Open all year

FAKENHAM   9E2

Manor Farm House Stibbard Road, Fulmodeston, Fakenham NR21 0LX 01328 78353   Mrs. Savage

Open Jan-Dec
3 bedrs (1 twin; 2 double) 1 ba, 2 wc ♿(7)
⌖ ♨ *Commended* cc DC Vi
£B&B £18, D £10.50.

Old Coach House Thursford, Fakenham NR21 0BD 01328 878273   Mrs. Green

16th Century converted coach house. 70 acres of grassland farm with sheep, cows, ducks, hens. Self-catering also available in self-contained units, 1 is a converted hayloft, the other a converted stable block. From Fakenham take A148 to Cromer for 3mls. After Thursford boundary sign 1/2ml on left.

Open Jan-Dec
4 bedrs (3 twin inc 2 ba/wc; 1 double) 1 ba, 1 wc ♿ ⌖ *Listed*
£B&B £16-£19, D £7, WR £110-£130, child rates.

HARLESTON   9F3

Paynes Hill Farm Denton, Harleston IP20 0AW 01986 86628   Mrs. Pointer

Paynes Hill Farm is not a working farm. Old type house with beams and open fires if needed. Turn left into Tun-Beck Road, after roundabout. Third right, first left and first farm on left.

Open April-Sept
2 bedrs (1 twin; 1 family) 1 ba, 2 wc ♿

£B&B £12, D £5, WR £84, WR/D £119, child rates.

Weston House Farm Mendham, Harleston IP20 0PB 01986 82206 Mrs. Holden

This 17th century, Grade II listed, farmhouse is set in an acre of gardens overlooking pastureland. Weston House Farm is a stock and arable farm covering 300 acres. Cot, highchair and children's games available. Tea/coffee facilities. Turn off A143 Harleston by-pass to Mendham. Farm is signposted from centre of village.

Open Mar-Nov
3 bedrs (2 twin inc 1 sh/wc; 1 family sh/wc) 1 ba ♨ ♈ ♛♛ cc AmEx
£B&B £14.50-£17, D £9.50, WR £87.50-£101.50, WR/D £154-£168, child rates.

HOLT   9E2

Hempstead Hall Holt NR25 6TN
01263 712224   Linda-Lee Mack

This 19th century, Norfolk Flint Farmhouse is quietly set on a 300 acre working farm with ducks, geese and donkeys and a very large garden. Turn right off A148 Holt by pass sign posted Hempstead. In 1½ miles turn right s/p

Hempstead. In 400 yds turn right.

Open all year
2 bedrs (1 double ba/wc; 1 family ba/wc)
♨(3) ✁ ♛♛
£B&B £16-£20, WR £112-£140, child rates.

NORWICH   9F3

Highfields Farm Chandler Road, Upper Stoke Holy Cross, Norwich NR14 8RQ
01508 493247   Mrs. Golding

Open all year
1 bedrs (1 double sh/wc) ✁

Salamanca Farm Guest House Stoke Holy Cross, Norwich NR14 8QJ
01508 492322   Mrs. Harrold

Victorian 175 acre mixed farm with Victorian farm house, situated in the Valley of Tas. The Farm is located near the mill where Colman first began to produce mustard.

Open Jan 15th-Dec 15th
4 bedrs (1 twin sh/wc; 3 double inc 2 ba/wc, 1 sh/wc) ♨(6) ♛♛
£B&B £17-£19, child rates.

Hillside Farm Welbeck Road, Brooke, Nr Norwich NR15 1AU 01508 550260 Mrs. Holl

Open all year

THETFORD   9E3

Malting Farm Blo Norton Road, South Lopham, Diss IP22 2HT 01379 88201 Mrs. Huggins

Open all year
3 bedrs (1 twin; 2 double inc 1 sh/wc) 1 ba. 1 wc ♨ ♨ ✁ ♛♛
£B&B £17, WR £112, child rates.

WYMONDHAM 9E3

Rose Farm Suton, Wymondham NR18
9JN 01953 603512 Mrs. Durrant

Non-working 3 acre smallholding with ducks, geese, hens and bantams, also 3 donkeys which small children may like to ride. 4th L turning from traffic lights going S. Take Spooner Row Rd, then 1st L to School Lane.

Open Jan-Dec
4 bedrs (1 double; 1 family; 2 single) 2 ba, 1 wc ☼ 🖩 ✝Listed cc DC
£B&B £18-£21, WR £120-£140, child rates.

Willow Farm Wattlefield, Wymondham NR18 9PA 01953 604679 Mrs. Highton

This comfortable farmhouse is set in 4 acres of gardens and grounds with sheep and chickens. High standards of hospitality are offered in this peaceful spot. The farm lies just 3 miles southeast of Wymondham A11/B1135.

Open all year
3 bedrs (1 twin; 1 double; 1 single) 2 ba, 2 wc ☼ 🖩 ✝

YARMOUTH, GREAT 9F3

Homestead Farm Newbridge, Great

Yarmouth 01983 531270 Mr. Priddle
Open all year
☼ ✝

SELF CATERING

EAST DEREHAM 9E3

Church Farm Cottages Brisley, East Dereham NR20 5LL 01362 668332
Mrs. Howes

Village is situated on B1145 and B1146 Crossroads.

☼ ♟♟♟♟
£Wk £165-£380

FAKENHAM 9E2

Highfield Farm Great Ryburgh, Fakenham NR21 7AL 01328 78249
Mrs. Savory

✝ ♟♟♟

Old Coach House Thursford, Fakenham NR21 0BD 01328 878273 Mrs. Green

For full farm description see B&B Entry. From Fakenham take A148 to Cromer for 5mls. After Thursford boundary sign 1/2ml on left.

☼ ✝
£Wk £100-£280

PLACES TO VISIT

SNETTERTON

International League for the Protection of Horses
Overa Farm, Snetterton NR16 2RL
01953-498682
Look around the stables and fields, meet the various horses the ILPH has stabled and find out about the work of the ILPH. Location: off the A11 Thetford-Norwich road. Open all year, Weds & Sun (or by appointment) 1430-1600. Entrance free
WC ⅙ ✝ ⅃

DISS

Bressingham Steam Museum and Gardens
Diss IP22 2AB 01379-88382

A live steam museum with hundreds of steam related exhibits including the world famous Scot locomotive. Also a fire museum and Victorian steam roundabout. Daily train rides. Beautiful 6-acre famous Dell garden.
Location: off the A1066, 2.5 miles West of Diss.Open Apr-Oct. Phone in advance for full details of opening times. WC & ♥ ✿

WELLS-NEXT-THE-SEA

Bygones at Holkham and Holkham Hall
Holkham Park, Wells-next-the-Sea
01328-710227
A special exhibition of the history of farming with reference to Coke of Norfolk and Turnip Townshend with over 4000 historic vehicles, implements and domestic items.
Location: signposted on the A149 coast road midway between Cromer and Kings Lynn.
Open: May-Sep, Sun-Thurs 1330-1700. Bygones
Entrance: adult £3.00, child £1.50. WC & ♞ ✗ ✿.

EAST DEREHAM

Norfolk Rural Life Museum
Beech House, Gressenhall, East Dereham
01362-860563
A working farm with rare breeds of livestock, an Edwardian cottage garden, Craftmen's Row and many other exhibits.
Location: signposted from the A47, 2 miles from East Dereham.
Open: Apr- Oct, Mon-Sat 1000-1700, Sun 1200-1730, Bank Hols 1000-1700.
Entrance: adult £3.50 child £1.50 OAP/concession £2.50. WC ✗ ✿

WEST RUNTON

Norfolk Shire Horse Centre
West Runton Stables, West Runton, Cromer NR27 9QH 01263-837339
Shire horses on diplay and seen working. Farm animals to play with.
Location: singposted off the A148 and

A149 between Cromer and Sheringham. Open: April 2 to Oct 29 Sun to Fri 1000-1700 Admission: adult £3.50 child £2.50 OAP/concessions £2.00. Group concession now includes children's farm and kiddie corner.WC & ♞ ✗ ✿

STRUMPSHAW

Strumpshaw Fen RSPB Nature Reserve
Low Road, Strumpshaw, Norwich
01603-715191
Norfolk Broads habitat with marsh, fen and shallow water, supporting many species of bird, in particular marsh harriers, bearded tit, grebes, wildfowl, kingfisher, osprey and many others. In winter; bean geese, whitefronts and 10,000 wigeon. Swallowtail butterflies in June. Orchids and many other rare plants June-Aug.
Location: off A47 road to Great Yarmouth. Entrance across level-crossing from car park reached from Brundell.
Open daily 0900-2100
Entrance: adult £2.50 child 50p OAP/concessions £1.50 WC &

TITCHWELL

Titchwell Marsh RSPB Nature Reserve
Titchwell, King's Lynn PE31 8BB
01485-210432
Extensive salt, brackish and freshwater marsh backing onto the beach and dunes make Titchwell the home of a wide variety of species.
Location: off A149 midway between Thornham and Titchwell villages.Open at all times. Car park £2 WC ♞ ✿

NORTH YORKSHIRE

AMPLEFORTH 11D2

Carr House Farm Ampleforth YO6 4ED
01347 868526 Mrs. Taylor

Our 16th century farmhouse stands on a family-run mixed farm in peaceful Herriot countryside. We are situated in undulating pastureland in the Hambleton Hills. 18 miles north of York (south of the A170).

Open all year
3 bedrs (3 double sh/wc) ☎(7) ⅄ ♨♨♨

BEDALE 11D2

Ainderby Myers Farm Hackforth, Bedale DL8 1PF 01609 748668
Mrs. Anderson

Ancient manor house. Once farmed by the monks of Jervaulx Abbey. From A1 exit at Hackforth turn off. ¾ mile on left.

Open all year
3 bedrs (1 double; 1 family; 1 single) 2 ba, 3 wc ☎ *Commended*

GOATHLAND 11E2

Dale End Farm Green End, Goathland, Whitby 01947 895371 Mrs. Cockrem

Open all year
☎ ♞ ⅄

GREAT AYTON 11D2

Manor House Farm Ingleby Greenhow, Great Ayton TS9 6RB
01642 722384 Mrs. Bloom

Closed Xmas
3 bedrs (2 twin ba/wc; 1 double ba/wc)
☎(12) ♨ ♞ ♨♨
£B&B + dinner £34-£37, WR/D £238.

HARROGATE 11D3

North Pasture Farm Brimham Rocks, Summerbridge, Harrogate 01423 711470
Mrs. Payne

Open Mar-Oct
3 bedrs (1 twin ba/wc; 2 double ba/wc) ⅄
♨♨♨
£B&B £17.50-£18.50, D £9.

HELMSLEY 11D2

Barn Close Farm Rievaulx, Helmsley YO6 5HL 01439 798321 Mrs. Milburn

Farmhouse is luxurious. Hill farm is set in a valley of outstanding beauty. From Helmsley B1257, L turn to Rievaulx at Old Byland, R turn at bridge, next R at sign.

Open Jan-Dec
2 bedrs; 1 ba, 3 wc ♿ 🏠 🐴 ♛♛♛
£B&B £16-£18, D £10, child rates.

Cringle Carr Farm Hawnby, Helmsley
YO6 5LT 01439 6264   S. Garbutt

Open March - November
2 bedrs (1 twin; 1 double) 1 ba ♿ ♛
£B&B £15-£17, D £10, WR £105-£119,   –
WR/D £175-£189, child rates.

Hill End Farm Chop Gate, Bilsdale,
Helmsley TS9 7JR 01439 798278
Mrs. Johnson

Working farm where guests are welcome to
wander around and meet the animals; pigs,
sheep, lambs, calves, etc. The farmhouse has
ensuite facilities, a comfortable lounge and
separate dining room. Take the B1257 Rd from
Helmsley to Stokesley. 9 miles from Helmsley.

Open Apr-Nov
2 bedrs (1 double; 1 family ba/wc) 1 ba, 1
wc ♿ ♛♛♛
£B&B £15.50-£18, D £10.50, child rates.

Laskill Farm Hawnby, Helmsley YO6
5NB 01439 798268   Sue Smith

Attractive farmhouse with own lake and large
walled garden for visitors' use. High standard of
food and comfort. Ideal centre for surrounding
places of interest and scenic beauty, or simply
enjoy peace and tranquility in idyllic surroundings.

Open all year
5 bedrs (2 twin inc 1 ba/wc; 2 double inc 1
ba/wc; 1 single) ✄

Lockton House Farm Bilsdale,
Helmsley YO6 5NE 014396 303
Mrs. Easton

This 16th century, oak-beamed farmhouse is

set on a working cattle and sheep farm with
ponies and horses, 7 miles from Helmsley at
the heart of the Yorkshire Moors. Good home
cooking. Horse riding 2 miles.

Open Mar-Oct
3 bedrs (1 twin; 1 double; 1 family) 1 ba, 2
wc ♿ 🏠 🐴 ✄

Manor Farm Old Byland, Helmsley,
York YO6 5LG 01439 798247 Mr. Garbutt

Comfortable farmhouse on, family run dairy
and sheep farm. B1257 from Helmsley, turn
left after 1 ½ miles follow signs for Old Byland,
farm in village.

Open April- October
3 bedrs (1 twin; 1 double; 1 family) ♿ 🐴
♛
£B&B £15, D £10, WR £105, WR/D £175,
child rates.

Wether Cote Farm Bilsdale, Helmsley,
York YO6 5NF 01439 798260   Mr. Wood

Open March -October
3 bedrs (1 twin; 1 double; 1 family) 2 ba, 2
wc 🏠 *Listed*
£B&B £14-£15, D £10, WR £98, WR/D £168,
child rates.

INGLETON 10B3

Gatehouse Farm Far Westhouse,
Carnforth, Ingleton LA6 3NR
01524 241458 Nancy Lund

Open Jan-Dec
3 bedrs (1 twin sh/wc; 2 double inc 1
ba/wc) ☒ 🚻 🛉 ♨♨
£B&B £15-£17, D £8, WR £100-£110, WR/D
£150-£165, child rates.

Langher Country House Tatterhorne
Lane, Ingleton, via Carnforth LA6 3DT
01524 241587 Mrs. Bell

Open all year
7 bedrs (2 twin ba/wc; 2 double ba/wc; 2
family; 1 single) 1 ba, 3 wc ☒ 🚻 🛉 ♨♨
£B&B £14.50-£18.50, WR £95-£119, WR/D
£127-£150, child rates.

Stacksteads Farm Tatterthorn Road,
Carnforth, Ingleton LA6 3HS
01524 241386 Mr. Charlton

Open Jan-Dec
3 bedrs (1 twin; 2 double sh/wc) 1 ba, 1
wc ☒ 🚻
£B&B £14, D £8, child rates.

KIRKBYMOORSIDE 11E2

Sinnington Common Farm
Kirkbymoorside YO6 6NX 01751 431719
F. M. Wiles

Open Jan-Dec
3 bedrs (1 twin ba/wc; 1 double ba/wc; 1
family ba/wc) ☒ 🚻 🛉 ♨♨♨
£B&B £15.50-£17.50, D £7.50-£8.50, WR
£108.50-£116, WR/D £161-£168, child rates.

MALHAM 10C3

Miresfield Farm Malham, Skipton
BD23 4DA 01729 830414 Mr. Sharp

Open all year
☒ 🛉 ♨♨♨
£B&B £20-£22, D £10-£12, WR £133-£154,
WR/D £203-£238, child rates.

MASHAM 11D2

Haregill Lodge Ellingstring, Masham,
Ripon HG4 4PW 01677 460272
Mrs. Greensit

Attractive 18th Century stone farmhouse set
on a family run mixed farm. Secluded gardens
with play area for children overlook
Hambleton Hills. Good home cooking with
supper tray. Log fires & satellite television. Tea
making facilities provided. Take A6108
towards Leyburn for 2 miles. Turn left to High
Ellington & Ellenstring. The only farm in
between villages

Open all year-except Xmas
2 bedrs (2 family inc 1 sh/wc) 1 ba, 1 wc
☒ 🚻 🛉 ⅍ ♨♨
£B&B £15-£18, D £9.50, WR £100-£120,
WR/D £160-£185, child rates.

Lamb Hill Farm Masham, Ripon HG4
4DJ 01765 689274 Mrs. Robinson

A spacious and comfortable old farmhouse set
on a mixed farm with views of the Dales.
There are pretty bedrooms with tea/coffee
facilities. The farm is on the edge of the
National Park, ideal for exploring. Situated off
the A6108 between Masham and West
Tanfield.

Open Feb-Nov.
3 bedrs (1 twin sh/wc; 1 double sh/wc; 1

family ba/wc) ☎(8) ⊁ ☙☙
£B&B £16-£17, WR £112-£119, child rates.

NORTHALLERTON   11D2

Lovesome Hill Farm Lovesome Hill,
Northallerton DL6 2PB 01609 772311
Mrs. Pearson

Open Feb-Nov.
6 bedrs ☎ ☙☙ *Commended*

Wellfield House Farm North
Otterington, Northallerton DL7 9JF
01609 772766   Mrs. Hill

Comfortable part 17th century sheep/arable
working farm. Large garden contains ponds
and a croquet lawn. Take the A167 southbound from Northallerton, follow for 2 ½
miles.

Open Jan-Nov
3 bedrs (1 twin; 1 double sh/wc; 1 family)
1 ba, 2 wc ☎ 🖶 ⊁ ☙☙
£B&B £15-£18, D £11, WR £105, WR/D
£182, child rates.

PICKERING   11E2

Rawcliffe House Farm *Acclaimed*
Newton-upon-Rawcliffe, Stape, Pickering
YO18 8JA   🔲 RAC
01751 473292   Mrs. Ducat

Open all year
3 bedrs ☎
£B&B £18.50-£39, WR/D £171.50-£122.50.

Seavy Slack Farm Stape, Pickering
YO18 8HZ 01751 473131   Mrs. Barrett

Open Easter-Oct
2 bedrs (1 double; 1 family) 1 ba, 1 wc ☎
🐓

£B&B £13-£16, D £10-£12, WR £90-£100,
WR/D £160-£175, child rates.

RAVENSCAR   11E2

Church Farm Ravenscar YO13 0NA
01723 870479   Mrs. Wheeler

18th Century traditional York Stone farmhouse
on small working farm in North Yorks Moors
National Park. Within the farmhouse amongst
the oak beams & the exposed stone walls are
a number of large homely open fires.
Ravenscar is signposted on the A171
Scarborough to Whitby road. Enter Ravenscar,
Church Farm is the 1st farm therein.

Open all year
4 bedrs (1 twin; 2 double; 1 family) 1 ba, 1
wc ☎ 🐓 ⊁
£B&B £14-£15, D £7.50, WR £98-£105,
WR/D £135-£141, child rates.

RICHMOND   10C2

Wilson House Barningham, Richmond
DL11 7EB 01833 21218   Mrs. Lowes

Period farmhouse with newly renovated guest
accommodation on a 475 acre working farm.
Spacious, comfortable en suite bedrooms with
televisions and beverage making facilities. A
kitchenette is provided for guest use.

Open March-Oct.
4 bedrs (1 twin sh/wc; 1 double sh/wc; 1
family sh/wc; 1 single) 1 wc ☎ 🖶 ☙
£B&B £12-£15, D £8-£10, WR £95, WR/D
£151, child rates.

RIPON   11D3

St George's Court Old Home Farm,
High Grantley, Ripon HG4 3EU
01765 620618   S. Gordon

At St George's Court you can sleep in renovated farm buildings, then breakfast in our beautiful 17th-century farmhouse. All rooms ground floor. We are 200 yards from any road, and in this secluded spot we have a third acre pond where wildlife thrives.

Open all year
5 bedrs (1 twin ba/wc; 3 double ba/wc; 1 single ba/wc) ♿ ⟲(8) ⊞ ⋔ ✕

SCARBOROUGH   11E2

Plane Tree Cottage Farm Staintondale, Scarborough YO13 0EY 01723 870796
Mrs. Edmondson
Open all year
2 bedrs (1 twin; 1 double) 1 ba, 1 wc
⟲(3) ⋔ *Listed*
£B&B £15, D £9, WR £160, WR/D £150.

Tofta Farm Staintondale, Scarborough YO13 0EB 01723 870298   D. Dobson

There are glorious views of both sea and countryside from this modernised 300-year-old farmhouse with extensive landscaped gardens. Tofta Farm stands on the edge of the North Yorkshire Moors, and is ideally suited for walkers. Just off the A171 north of Scarborough.

Open all year
4 bedrs (3 double inc 1 sh/wc; 1 family sh/wc) 1 ba, 2 wc ⟲ ⋔
£B&B £14-£20, D £8, WR £98-£140, WR/D £154-£196, child rates.

SELBY   11D3

Lund Farm Gateforth, Selby YO8 9LE 01757 228775   Mr. Middleton

18th Century farmhouse on working farm with pine beams and log fires. Safe enclosed garden, eggs to collect, lambs to feed in winter. Families and business people welcome. Very convenient for the historic city of York. Take A19, turn right into Brayton. The farm is then on the left 1½ miles up the road.

Open all year.
2 bedrs (1 twin; 1 family) 1 ba ⟲ ⊞
£B&B £18-£22, D £8-£12, WR £120-£130, WR/D £204-£214, child rates.

SKIPTON   10C3

Wenningber Farm Hellifield, Nr Skipton BD23 4JR 01729 850856
Mrs. Phillip

Wenningber Farm is a cottage type farmhouse with oak beams, log fire, full central heating, renovated to a very high standard. We have 110 acres of mixed farming. Take the Airton-Malham Road out of Hellifield, which is on the A65.

Open all year
2 bedrs (inc 1 twin) 1 ba, 1 wc ⟲ ⋔ ⛟
£B&B £16-£18, WR £112-£125, child rates.

Bondcroft Farm Embsay, Skipton BD23 6SF 01756 793371   Mrs. Clarkson

Open Easter-Oct
3 bedrs (1 twin; 2 double) 1 ba, 2 wc
⟲(10) ⊞ ✕ *Listed Approved*
£B&B £14.50-£18, D £7-£8.

STAMFORD BRIDGE   11E3

High Catton Grange Stamford Bridge, York 01759 371374   Sheila Foster

Open Feb-Nov
3 bedrs (1 twin; 1 doubleba/wc; 1 single)
⟲ ⋔ ✕
£B&B £25.

THIRSK   11D2

Eldmire Hill Dalton, Thirsk YO7 3JH 01845 577252   Mrs. Richardson

Open Mar-Oct
3 bedrs (1 twin; 1 double; 1 family) ⟲(1)
⋔ *Listed*

Garth House Dalton, Thirsk YO7 3HY 01845 577310   Mrs. Ramshay

Open Jan-Nov
2 bedrs ⟲ ⋔*Listed*
£B&B £12-£14, WR £84, child rates.

Thornborough House Farm South Kilvington, Thirsk YO7 2NP 01845 522103   T. H. Williamson

Open Jan-Dec
3 bedrs (1 twin ba/wc; 1 double sh/wc; 1 family sh/wc) ⟲ ⋔ ⛟⛟ cc Ac Vi
£B&B £13-£17, D £8-£8.50, child rates.

YORK 11D3

Beech Tree House Farm South Holme, Slingsby, York YO6 7BA 01653 628257 Mrs. Farnell

A spacious Victorian farmhouse with a large garden on 260 acres of arable land with cattle, sheep and pigs. Home cooking, comfortable rooms with log fires, snooker/games room and a safe area for children. We are situated in a peaceful valley north east of York junction A64/B1257.

Open all year
5 bedrs (1 twin; 1 double; 1 family; 2 single) 2 ba, 2 wc ☎
£B&B £14, D £7, WR £95, WR/D £135, child rates.

Ivy House Farm Kexby, York YO4 5LQ 01904 489368
K. R. Daniel

Open Jan-Dec
4 bedrs (1 twin; 1 double; 1 family; 1 single) 1 ba, 2 wc ☎ *Listed*
£B&B £15-£18, child rates.

Sunley Court Nunnington, York YO6 5XQ 01439 748233
J. Brown

Open March-Nov
4 bedrs (1 twin sh/wc; 1 double sh/wc; 2 single) 1 ba, 1 wc ☎ 🎏 🐴 🍷🍷
£B&B £15, D £10, WR/D £140, child rates.

Treble Sykes Farm Helperby, York YO6 2SB
Mrs. Sowray

Open Mar-Oct
3 bedrs (1 twin; 2 family) 2 ba, 2 wc ☎ 🎏 🐴

SELF CATERING

INGLETON 10B3

Stacksteads Farm Tatterthorn Road, Carnforth, Ingleton LA6 3HS 01524 241386
Mr. Charlton

KIRKBY MOORSIDE 11E2

Sinnington Common Farm Kirkby Moorside YO6 6NX 01751 431719 F. M. Wiles

🐴 ☎ 🐴
£Wk £100-£180

RAVENSCAR 11E2

Church Farm Ravenscar YO13 0NA 01723 870479
Mrs. Wheeler

For full farm description see B&B Entry. Ravenscar is signposted on the A171 Scarborough to Whitby road. Enter Ravenscar, Church Farm is the 1st farm therein.

☎ 🐴
£Wk £115-£240

RIPON 11D3

Winksley Banks Farm Winksley Banks, Galphay, Ripon HG4 3NS 01765 658439
Mr. Bancroft

☎ 🐴
£Wk £155-£375

SELBY 11D3

Lund Farm Gateforth, Selby YO8 9LE 01757 228775
Mr. Middleton

For full farm description see B&B Entry. Well equipped accommodation with log fire, patio and garden. Ideal for families; washing machine, cot and high chair provided. Take A19, turn right into Brayton. The farm is then on the left 1 ½ miles up the road.

☎ 🎏
£Wk £165-£340

SKIPTON 10C3

Maypole Cottage Thorpe, Skipton BD23 6BJ 01756 720609
Mrs. Gamble

A detached stable conversion adjacent to a large garden. Parking spaces provided.

Take B6265 to Grassington at Threshfield turn R onto the B6160 towards Burnsall. 1 ½ by the railing turn R up the lane

☎ 🎏
£Wk £190-£320

THIRSK 11D2

Thornborough House Farm South Kilvington, Thirsk YO7 2NP

01845 522103   T. H. Williamson

ᕽ ⊩ cc Ac Vi

WHITBY   11E2

Blackmires Farm Danby Head, Danby, Whitby YO21 2NN 01287 660352 Mrs. Rhys

Small working farm adjacent to moors, cottage adjoins farm house, caravan nearby, private road (park at the door). Dale of outstanding natural beauty in N Yorks National Park.

A171 W about 15mls, L to Danby through village to Ainthorpe, L at school towards Botton.

ᕽ ⊩ ᵐᵐ
£Wk £150-£325

PLACES TO VISIT

HAWES

The Hawes Ropemakers
Hawes DL8 3NT 01969-667487
See how the twist is put in - watch traditional ropemaking in which many fine yarns are twisted to make a strong rope. Cattle halters, horse leading reins, bannister and barrier ropes, church bell ropes, dog leads. Note: disabled access limited on Sats.
Location: on A684 opposite children's playground.
Open: all year Mon-Fri 0900-1730, July-Oct Sats 1000-1730
Entrance: free & ⦿ WC ✗

NORTHAMPTONSHIRE

BRACKLEY   8B4

Walltree House Farm Steane, Brackley
01295 811235   Mrs. Harrison

In courtyard adjacent to farmhouse are grouped these comfortable motel-type rooms. Breakfast served in farmhouse. Arable farm in peaceful countryside & woodlands. 2 self catering cottages. County Winners of Dooker Silver Lapwing Award for Conservation. Take turn for Hinton Airfield Brackley side of Farthinghoe Garage. Follow signs to Walltree House at end of road.

Open Jan-Dec
8 bedrs (inc. 3 twin inc 2 ba/wc) 1 wc ᕽ 🏠
💥💥💥 cc Ac Vi
£B&B £19-£30, D £10-£15, child rates.

DAVENTRY   8B4

Barewell Fields Prestidge Row, Moreton Pinkney, Daventry NN11 6NJ
01295 760754   Mr. Lainchbury

Open Mar-Nov.
3 bedrs (1 twin; 1 double; 1 single) 1 ba, 2 wc ᕽ(7) 🏠 ✂ *Listed Highly Commended*

Drayton Lodge Daventry NN11 4NL
01327 702449   Ann Spicer

Drayton Lodge is a secluded 18th century farmhouse in a quiet rural location. Follow signs for A425 out of Daventry. Drayton Lodge is on left between Daventry and Staverton.

Open all year
4 bedrs (3 twin; 1 double ba/wc) ᕽ ⊩
💥💥💥
£B&B £20-£22.50, D £12-£15, child rates.

KETTERING 8C3

Dairy Farm Cranford, Kettering NN14 4AQ 01536 330273 Audrey E. Clarke

Open Jan-Dec
5 bedrs (2 twin ba/wc; 2 double ba/wc; 1 family inc 3 ba/wc) ⛺ 🏠 ♨♨♨
£B&B £18-£25, D £10-£12, child rates.

LONG BUCKBY 8B4

Murcott Mill Long Buckby NN6 7QR 01327 842236 Mrs. Hart

Beautiful Georgian Mill house on secluded rural sheep farm. All rooms well appointed and of a high standard throughout. On outskirts of Long Buckby on B5385 (road to Watford village). Very accessible to M1 & A14.

Open Jan-Dec
3 bedrs (2 twin ba/wc; 1 family ba/wc) 1 ba, 1 wc ⛺ 🏠 🐕 ♨♨
£B&B £18-£20, D £6.50-£7.50, WR £100-£120, WR/D £140-£150, child rates.

NORTHAMPTON 8B4

Wold Farm Old, Northampton NN6 9RJ 01604 781258 Mrs. Engler

Open all year
6 bedrs (1 twin sh; 3 double inc 2 sh/wc, 1 ba/wc; 2 single sh/wc) 2 wc ⛺ 🏠 🐕 ♨♨♨
£B&B £20-£22, D £12, child rates.

TOWCESTER 4B1

Manor Farm Adstone, Towcester NN12 8DT 01327 860284 Mr. Paton

Peace and quiet but plenty to see and do at this 430-acre farm. The farmhouse, built by an ancestor of George Washington in 1656, stands on the edge of a tiny village. Fun for all the family. Try our clay pigeon shooting instruction.

Open all year
6 bedrs 🐕 ♨♨ *Commended*

WELFORD 8B3

West End Farm 5 West End, Welford NN6 7HJ 01858 575226 Mrs. Bevin

Open all year
2 bedrs (1 twin; 1 double ens wc) ⛺ ✾

SELF CATERING

EAST HADDON 8B4

Rye Hill Farm Holdenby Road, East Haddon NN6 8DH 01604 770990 Mr. Widdowson

Small holding.

A428 out of Northampton. Turn off into East Haddon village, R into centre. Farm lane after last house on left hand side.

& ⛺ 🐕 ♨♨♨ cc AmEx Vi
£Wk £120-£340

NORTHUMBERLAND

ALLENDALE 10C1

Manor House Farm Ninebanks, Nr Allendale, Hexham NE4 8DA
01434 345236 Mrs. Lee

Closed Xmas
3 bedrs (1 double; 2 family) 1 ba, 1 wc ☜
🏠 🐴 ♕♕

Struthers Farm Catton, Allendale, Hexham NE47 9LP 01434 683580
Mrs. Keenleyside

Open all year

ALNMOUTH 13F3

Hipsburn Farm Lesbury, Alnwick NE66 3PY 01665 830206 Mr. Tulip

Hipsburn farm is a mixed farm with a spacious farm house. Situated ½ mile from Alnmouth overlooking Aln estuary. Rooms are centrally heated. There is a TV and tea and coffee making facilities in the bedrooms. Ideal base for golfers and birdwatchers. Situated on A1068.

Open Apr-Oct
3 bedrs (1 twin sh/wc; 2 double inc 1 ba/wc, 1 sh/wc) ☜(6) ♕
£B&B £18-£22.

All towns listed in this guide are shown on the maps at the back.

ALNWICK 13F3

Doxford Farm Embleton, Chathill, Alnwick 01665 79235 A. D. Turnbull

Georgian listed farmhouse set in 1 acre of grounds. Mixed farm, sheep and cattle, 420 acres. Follow A1 N for 5mls, turn R on B6347 and follow signs to Doxford keeping L for 3mls.

Open Jan-Dec
4 bedrs (1 twin; 2 double; 1 family sh/wc) 1 ba ☜ 🐴 ⚔ ♕♕ cc Vi
£B&B £16-£18, D £8, WR £112-£126, WR/D £168-£182, child rates.

Howick Scar Farm Craster, Alnwick NE66 3SU 01665 576665 Mrs. Curry

The farmhouse is dated 1864 and lies on the heritage coast between the villages of Craster and Howick. The farm is a working, mixed farm of 250 acres with sheep, cereals and some cattle. East from Alnwick turn right at Denwick for Longhoughton. Join coastal route towards Craster.

Open May-March

2 bedrs (2 double) 1 ba, 1 wc ੮(4)*Listed*
£B&B £14, WR £94.50, child rates.

Lumbylaw Farm Edlingham, Alnwick
NE66 2BW 01665 574277   Mrs. Lee

Friendly hospitality in a comfortable stone
farmhouse on a beef and sheep farm 6 miles
between Alnwick and Rothbury. Also 2 self-
catering farm cottages. From Alnwick on the
B6341 take road into Edlingham (not
Eglingham). Drive through the village. Farm
on the right.

Open Apr-Oct
3 bedrs (2 twin; 1 double) 1 ba, 1 wc ੮ ❦
£B&B £16.50-£17.

HALTWHISTLE   10B1

Broomhouse Farm Haltwhistle NE49
0JA 01434 321422   Mrs. Losh

This working farm with 45 suckler cows and
280 sheep is found a mile south of Haltwhistle
towards Alston. The listed Georgian farmhouse
overlooks the route of a disused railway and is
surrounded by 18th-century farm buildings.
Roman Wall 4 miles. At Haltwhistle turn south
off A69, cross river,turn right, travel ½ mile and
turn left into farm drive.

Open May-Nov
2 bedrs (2 family) 1 ba ੮ ⊬ *listed*
£B&B £14-£15, D £8.50-£9, WR £89-£95,
WR/D £142-£152, child rates.

Broomshaw Hill Farm Willia Road,
Haltwhistle NE49 9NP 01434 320866
          Mrs. Brown

Open Mar-Nov
3 bedrs (1 twin; 1 double; 1 family) ੮ ⊞ ☂
❦❦ *Highly Commended*
£B&B £32-£34, WR £110-£115, child rates.

Oaky Knowe Farm Haltwhistle NE49
9NP 01434 320648   Mrs. Murray

Open all year
3 bedrs (1 twin; 2 family) 1 ba, 1 wc ੮ ⊞

Park Burnfoot Farm Featherstone
Park, Haltwhistle NE49 0JP 01434 320378
          Mrs. Dawson

18th century, stone farmhouse on a 220 acre
family farm. Visitors are welcome to see the
cows being milked.

Open all year
2 bedrs 1 ba, 1 wc ੮ *Listed*
£B&B £14-£14.50, D £9-£10, WR £98, child
rates.

White Craig Farm Shield Hill,
Haltwhistle NE49 9NW 01434 320565
          Mrs. Laidlow

Closed Xmas and New Year
3 bedrs (1 twin ba/wc; 2 double sh/wc) ੮
⊞ ☂ ⊬ ❦❦ *Highly Commended*
£B&B £18.50-£23, WR £130-£145

HEXHAM   13E4

Gairshield Farm Whitley Chapel,
Hexham NE47 0HS 01434 673562
          Mrs. Kristensen

Gairshield is a quiet hill farm, set amidst
beautiful open countryside, in the "North
Pennine Area of Outstanding Natural Beauty"
with superb views in all directions. Whitley
Chapel is 5 miles south of Hexham.Take
turning at crossroads, road forks to right (s/p
to Gairshield).

Open all year
1 bedrs (1 family) 1 ba, 2 wc ੮ ⊞
£B&B £15, WR £95, child rates.

Rye Hill Farm Slaley, Hexham NE47 0AH 01434 673259   Mr. Courage

Come and stay in a warm and comfortable barn conversion on our small working livestock farm. Friendly atmosphere and good food. Licensed. Situated 4 miles south of Hexham on the B6306 and surrounded by miles of beautiful countryside. Hadrian's Wall 8 mile B6303 south from Hexham, after 4 miles Travellers Rest Pub on left. Take 1st turn right.

Open all year
6 bedrs (2 twin ba/wc; 2 double inc 1 ba/wc, 1 sh/wc, 2 family inc 1ba/wc, 1sh/wc) 1 ba, 1 wc ☎ ⌂ ♞ ♚♚♚
£B&B £18-£20, D £10, WR £113.40-£126, WR/D £183.40-£193, child rates.

Taylor Burn Ninebanks, Hexham NE4 78DE 01434 345343   M. A. Ostler

Taylor Burn has a large comfortable farmhouse with outstanding views. On this working hill farm in the Pennine Dales you can join in the farm's activities - free range hens, sheep and cattle. 18 miles from Hexham (A69 west, A686 south). Then signed to Ninebanks.

Open all year
3 bedrs (2 double; 1 single) 1 ba, 1 wc ☎(7) ♞ ⚹
£B&B £13.50-£16, D £9, WR £85-£100, WR/D £150-£160, child rates.

KIRKWHELPINGTON   13F3

Cornhills Kirkwhelpington NE19 2RE 01830 40232   Mrs. Thornton

Open all year
3 bedrs (2 twin; 1 family) 2 ba, 2 wc ☎
Listed
£B&B £16-£20, child rates.

MORPETH   13F3

Bickerton Cottage Farm Hepple, Rothbury, Morpeth NE65 7LW 01669 40264   Mrs. France

Open Mar-Nov
2 bedrs (1 twin; 1 double) 1 ba, 1 wc ☎ ⌂ ⚹ *Listed-Commended*

East Farm Eshott, Felton, Morpeth NE65 7LW 01670 787236   Mrs. Pickard

Open all year
2 bedrs (1 twin; 1 double) 1 ba, 2 wc ☎(12) ⌂ ♞ ⚹ *Listed*

Thistleyhaugh Farm Longhorsley, Morpeth NE65 8RG 01665 570629   Mr. Nelless

Open all year
4 bedrs (1 twin; 2 double inc 1 sh/wc, 1ba/wc; 1 single) 1 ba ☎(12) ⌂ ♚♚ *Commended*

Togston Hall Farm North Togston, Amble, Morpeth NE65 0HR 01665 712699   Mrs. Marshall

Open all year
3 bedrs ens ba/sh/wc (1 twin; 1 double; 1 family) ☎(12) ⌂ ♞ ♚♚♚

West House Farm Stannington, Morpeth NE61 6AY 01670 789576   Mrs. Smith

Open Easter-Oct
2 bedrs (1 twin; 1 double) 1ba, 1 wc ☎(5) ⚹

ROTHBURY 13F3

Thropton Demesne Thropton,
Rothbury NE65 7TL 0166 920196
Mrs. Giles

Traditional farmhouse situated in picturesque
Coquet Dale. Spectacular views, ideal for
fishing, walking, and golf. Farm is situated 2
miles west of Rothbury.

Open all year
3 bedrs (1 twin ba/wc; 1 double ba/wc; 1
family ba/wc) ☼ 🎠 ⅙ ☼☼
£B&B £18-£19, WR £126, child rates.

WOOLER 13F3

Earle Hill Head Farm Northern Berlan,
Wooler NE71 6RH 01668 281243
Mrs. Armstrong

Within the National Park. A very warm
welcome awaits you. Home away from home.
Opposite the Wheat Sheaf Hotel up Cheviot
Street, keep right all the way.

Open Jan-Dec
3 bedrs (1 twin sh/wc; 2 double) ☼(10) 🎠
Listed
£B&B £16-£20.

SELF CATERING

ALNWICK 13F3

Doxford Farm Embleton, Chathill,
Alnwick 01665 79235   A. D. Turnbull

For full farm description see B&B Entry.
Follow A1 N for 5mls, turn R on B6347 and
follow signs to Doxford keeping L for 3mls.

☼ 🐦 cc Vi
£Wk £100-£300

Lumbylaw Farm Edlingham, Alnwick
NE66 2BW 01665 574277   Mrs. Lee

For full farm description see B&B Entry. From
Alnwick on the B6341 take road into
Edlingham (not Eglingham). Drive through the
village. Farm on the right.

☼ ⅙

Titlington Hall Farm Alnwick NE66
2EB 01665 578253   Mrs. Purvis

Three lovely country cottages in a quiet and
beautiful area. All are spacious and very well
equipped with full gas central heating. All
linen included. Children and pets welcome.

A6341 out of Alnwick, 2 miles turn right 2
miles keep right at fork. 3 miles through ford,
1 mile over X-roads, 1 m on R.

& ☼ 🐦 ♨♨
£Wk £165-£285

BELFORD 13F3

Outchester and Ross Farm Cottages
Ross Farm, Belford NE70 7EN
01668 213336   Mrs. Sutherland

An 18th-century farmhouse and 11 coast-guard
and farm cottages provide a big choice of
accommodation. The farm has breeding ewes,
suckler cows with calves, and grows wheat
and barley. At Ross Farm there is 3 miles of
sandy beach.

For Ross Farm, cross A1 from Belford and
head northeast. For Outchester cross A1 from
Belford and take B1342.

♨♨♨ *Highly Commended*

BERWICK-UPON-TWEED 13F2

The Old Smithy Brackenside, Bowsden,
Berwick-upon-Tweed TD15 2TQ
01289 88293   Mary Barber

Our mixed farm comprises a suckler herd,
sheep, wheat, barley, oats, mixed woodland
and conservation area. Accommodation is
offered in the beautifully renovated Old
Smithy. Fully equipped with cot, highchair
and wood burning stove.

The farm lies south of Berwick-on-Tweed
west of the A1, near the B6525/B6353.

& ☼ 🐦

HALTWHISTLE 10B1

White Craig Farm Nr Hadrian's Wall,
Haltwhistle NE49 9NW 01434 320565
Mrs. Laidlow

See also B&B entry.

Follow signs from Haltwhistle (east) for Hadrian's Wall. Farm ½ mile on left.

& ఈ ?????
£Wk £120-£390

Kellah Cottages Kellah Farm, Haltwhistle NE49 0JL 01434 320816
A. L. Teasdale

The cottages have 2 bedrs sleeping 5.

Oaky Knowe Farm Haltwhistle NE49 9NP 01434 320648 Mrs. Murray

ఈ ʰ

Park Burnfoot Farm Featherstone Park, Haltwhistle NE49 0JP 01434 320378
Mrs. Dawson

For full farm description see B&B Entry. 2 units; each 2 bedrs ఈ ??? *Listed*

£Wk £99-£239

White Craig Farm Shield Hill, Haltwhistle NE49 9NW 01434 320565
Mrs. Laidlow

ఈ ʰ ⌖ ???? *Commended*

KIRKWHELPINGTON 13F3

Cornhills Kirkwhelpington NE19 2RE 01830 40232 Mrs. Thornton

See also B&B entry.

Newcastle airport A696 follow road N 18 miles, crossroads (Knowesgate Hotel & Garage) L 1½ miles.

ఈ ???? *Listed*
£Wk £120-£260

MORPETH 13F3

Gallowhill Farm Whalton, Morpeth 01661 881241 Mr. Coatsworth

Togston Hall Farm North Togston, Amble, Morpeth NE65 0HR 01665 712699
Mrs. Marshall

See also B&B entry. There are 2 self-catering units, each has 3 bedrooms, sleeps 6.

Northeast of Morpeth (A1/B6345)

ఈ(12) ʰ

WOOLER 13F3

Earle Hill Head Farm Northern Berlan, Wooler NE71 6RH 01668 281243
Mrs. Armstrong

For full farm description see B&B Entry. Opposite the Wheat Sheaf Hotel up Cheviot Street, keep right all the way.

ఈ(10) ???? *Listed*

Firwood Bungalow and Humphrey's House Nr Middleton Hall, Wooler NE71 6RH 01668 81243 Mrs. Armstrong

Firwood Bungalow and Humphrey's House stand in well maintained gardens at the foot of the Cheviot Hills 2 miles south of Wooler, just off A697. Both are furnished to a very high standard. Firwood sleeps 10. Humphrey's sleeps 6. You are welcome to walk the farm.

??? *Commended* ???? *Highly Commended*

NOTTINGHAMSHIRE

MANSFIELD 8B2

Blue Barn Farm Langwith, Mansfield NG20 9JD 01623 742248 Mr. Ibbotson

Welcome to our family-run 450-acre farm in peaceful surroundings on the edge of Sherwood Forest. Many interesting places catering for all tastes only a short car journey away. Excursions with qualified guide can be arranged. Cot available. 5 miles from M1 (J30) off A616.

Open all year.
3 bedrs (1 twin; 1 double; 1 family) ఈ ʰ
☙☙ *Commended*

Boon Hills Farm Nether Langwith, Mansfield NG20 9JQ 01623 743862
Mrs. Palmer

155 acre traditional family farm with cattle, sheep, goats and many pets. Large garden. Quiet, peaceful situation. A60 north to Cuckney. Left onto A632 for 2 miles. Farm on left. Sign on road side.

Open Mar-Oct
3 bedrs (1 twin; 1 double; 1 family) 1 ba, 1 wc ☻ 🐕
£B&B £14-£15, WR £84-£90, child rates.

Norton Grange Farm Norton, Cuckney, Mansfield NG20 9LP
01623 842666　　　　　　Mrs. Palmer

Open Jan-Dec
2 bedrs 1 ba, 1 wc ☻ 🐕 ♛
£B&B £15-£16, WR £90, child rates.

NEWARK　　　　　　　　　8C2

Manor Farm Laxton, Newark NG22 0NU 01777 870417　　　　P. Haigh

Open all year

2 bedrs (1 twin; 1 double) 1 ba, 1 wc ☻
Listed
£DB&B £20-£40, child rates.

New Manor Farm Greaves Lane, Edingley, Newark NG22 8BJ
01623 883044　　　　Mr. Tunnicliffe

Open all year
2 bedrs (1 twin; 1 double) 1 ba, 1 wc ☻ 🏬 🐕

WORKSOP　　　　　　　　8B1

Hazelmere Farm Creswell, Worksop S81 4HS 01909 721258　　Mr. Platts

Open all year
3 bedrs ens ba/wc (1 twin; 1 double; 1 family) 1 ba, 1 wc ☻

PLACES TO VISIT

FARNSFIELD

The White Post Modern Farm Centre
Farnsfield, Nottinghamshire NG22 8HL
01623-882977
Modern working farm with indoor and outdoor exhibitions showing over 400 animals including: chicks, piglets, cattle, deer, rabbits, owls, amphibians, reptiles, bees, snails, spiders, rheas, quails and lambs. New - Pet Learning Centre. On sale: home produce.
Location: 12 miles north of Nottingham on A614.
Open: daily 1000-1700
Entrance: adult £2.95, child £1.95, under-4s free, OAP/concessions £1.95. WC 🦽

OXFORDSHIRE

ABINGDON 4B2

Willowbrook Farm Hanney Road, Steventon, Abingdon OX13 6BE
01235 868188 Mrs. Walker

Open all year
1 bedrs (1 twin) ba/wc 1 wc 🏠

BANBURY 4B1

Agdon Farm Brailes, Banbury OX15 5JJ
01608 85226 Mrs. Cripps

Open all year

New House Farm Brailes, Banbury
OX15 5BD 01608 75239 Mrs. Taylor
500 acres sheep and arable farm situated between two villages. Beautiful views and farm walks. 18 hole golf course within walking distance. Very good eating places. Take the B4035 out of Shipston to village of Brailes. Turn right in Brailes to Sutton. 1 mile on right.

Open all year
3 bedrs (1 twin; 2 double sh/wc) 1 ba, 1 wc 🐴 🕇 👑👑
£B&B £14-£19, child rates.

CHARLBURY 4B1

Banbury Hill Farm Enstone Road, Charlbury OX7 3JH 01608 810314
Mr. Widdows

Natural Cotswold stone farmhouse commanding spectacular view, overlooking the small township of Charlbury with the ancient Wychwood Forest nestling against the River Evenlode. Large variety of animals around the farm. Friendly and peaceful atmosphere.

Open Mar-Nov.
6 bedrs 🐴 ⊁ *Applied*

CHIPPING NORTON 4B1

Bould Farm Bould, Nr Idbury, Chipping Norton OX7 6RT 01608 658850
Mrs. Meyrick

17th Century Cotswold farmhouse on 300 acre working farm set in beautiful countryside, close to Stow-on-the-Wold and Bourton-on-the-Water. Take A424 Stow-on-the-Wold Burford Rd, approx 5mls turn L to Idbury 2mls, through Idbury down hill, farm on L.

Open all year
3 bedrs (inc 1 twin ba/wc; 1 family ba/wc)
🐴 *Listed*
£B&B £20-£25, child rates.

FARINGDON 4B2

Ashen Copse Farm Coleshill, Faringdon SN6 7PU 01367 240175
Mrs. Hoddinott

Open all year
3 bedrs (1 twin; 1 family; 1 single) 1 ba, 1 wc 🐴 ⊁

Bowling Green Farm Stanford Road, Faringdon SN7 8EZ 01367 240229
Mrs. Barnard

Open all year
2 bedrs (2 family 1sh/wc, 1ba/wc) 🐴 🏠 ⊁
👑👑

HENLEY-ON-THAMES 4B2

Little Parmoor Farm Frieth, Henley-on-Thames RG9 6NL 01494 881600
Mrs. Emmett

Open all year
3 bedrs (2 twin; 1 double) 🐴
Listed Commended cc Vi
£B&B £19-£25, WR £114-£150, child rates.

MINSTER LOVELL   13A2

Hill Grove Farm Minster Lovell OX8
5NA 01993 703120   K. Brown

Open Jan-Dec
2 bedrs (1 twin ba/wc; 1 double sh/wc) ⚘
⌂ ⚹ ♨ *Highly Commended*
£B&B double £36-£44.

OXFORD   4B2

Rookery Farm Brize Norton OX18 3NL
01993 842957   Mrs. Fryer

Rookery Farm is a small holding pleasantly
situated in this small Oxfordshire village with
lovely views of surrounding countryside. We
have a variety of pets including cats, dogs,
sheep and horses. We are situated on the
edge of the Cotswolds. Oxford on A40
towards Cheltenham. Turn off A40 marked
Brize Norton, L after leaving A40, R at next
roundabout.

Open Jan-Dec
4 bedrs (1 twin; 2 double; 1 family) 2 ba ⚘
Listed
£B&B £20, D £17.50, child rates.

Earls Farm Deddington, Oxford OX15
0TH 01869 338243   Audrey Fuller

Open all year
3 bedrs (1 twin; 1 double; 1 single) 2 ba, 2
wc ⚘ ♿
£B&B £15.50-£16.50, child rates.

Mead Close Guest House Mead Close,
Forest Hill, Oxford OX33 1DY
01865 872248   Audrey Bunkley

Open all year
3 bedrs (1 twin; 1 double; 1 single) 1 ba, 1
wc ⚘ ⌂ ⚹

STEEPLE ASTON   4B1

Westfield Farm Motel *Acclaimed*
The Fenway, Steeple Aston OX5 3SS   RAC
01869 40591   Mrs. Hillier

Open all year
7 bedrs all en suite ⚘ cc Ac Vi
£B&B £32-£36.

THAME   4B2

Upper Green Farm Manor Road,
Towersey, Thame OX9 3QR
01844 212496   Mr. Aitken

Open all year
8 bedrs (2 twin inc 1ba/wc, 1 sh/wc; 5
double inc 4 ba/wc, 1sh/wc; 1 single
sh/wc) 1 ba, 2 wc ⚘(14) ⚹

WANTAGE   13A1

Lyford Manor Farm Lyford, Wantage
OX12 0EG 01235 868204   Mr. Pike

Open all year
4 bedrs (2 twin inc 1sh/wc, 1ba/wc; 1
double sh/wc; 1 single sh/wc) ⚘ ⌂ ⚹ ♨♨
Highly Commended

WOODSTOCK   4B1

Burleigh Farm Bladon Road,
Cassington, Witney, Oxford, Woodstock
OX8 1EA 01865 881352   Mrs. Cook

Open Jan-Dec
3 bedrs (1 twin ba/wc; 1 family ba/wc; 1
single ba/wc) 1 ba, 2 wc ⚘ ♞ ♨♨
£B&B £17.50-£25, WR £125-£150, child
rates.

SELF CATERING

CHIPPING NORTON   4B1

Bould Farm Bould, Nr Idbury, Chipping
Norton OX7 6RT 01608 658850
          Mrs. Meyrick

17th Century Cotswold farmhouse on 300 acre
working farm set in beautiful countryside,
close to Stow-on-the-Wold and Bourton-on-
the-Water.

Take A424 Stow-on-the-Wold Burford Rd,
approx 5mls turn L to Idbury 2mls, through
Idbury down hill, farm on L.

⚘

FARINGDON   4B2

Coxwell House Little Coxwell,
Faringdon SN7 7LP 01367 241240
          Mrs. Crossley Cooke

Superb front part 1760 Georgian farmhouse. Secluded walled garden, tennis court, indoor swimming pool. On edge of Little Coxwell, unspoilt farming village, thatched cottages, stone walls.

Follow signs to Little Coxwell S of A420 , 1ml Faringdon bypass, farm is last house on R behind large wall.

ॐ ★ ????
£Wk £350-£595

MINSTER LOVELL   13A2

Hill Grove Farm Minster Lovell OX8 5NA 01993 703120   K. Brown
ॐ

PLACES TO VISIT

WANTAGE

Ardington Pottery
15 Home Farm, School Road Ardington, Nr Wantage OX12 8PN
01235-833302
Working studio pottery with displays of handmade stoneware and porcelain ceramics which were made on the premises in the 19th century. On sale: pottery.
Location: 2 miles east of Wantage, off A417.
Open: daily, Mon-Sat 1000-1700, Sun 1130-1700.
Entrance. free WC ★ ⚓ ☙

WITNEY

Cogges Manor Farm Museum
Church Lane, Cogges, Witney OX8 6LA
01993-772602
Living museum of farming and rural Oxfordshire life set in a manor house with walled garden. Daily craft and farming demonstration, a variety of animals, nature and history trails and picnic areas.
Location: signs from A40, footpath from town centre.
Open: Apr-Oct, Tues-Fri 1030-1730, weekends 1200-1730
Entrance: adult £3.00 child/student £1.50 OAP £1.75 WC ⚓ ★ ✕ ☙

BANBURY

Waterfowl Sanctuary and Children's Farm
Wigginton Heath, Nr Hook Norton, Banbury OX15 4LB 01608-730252
Set in 22 acres of unspoilt Oxfordshire countryside, a unique collection of rare breeds of domestic fowl, poultry and farm animals. Children especially welcome and encouraged to pick up and cuddle chicks, ducklings and baby rabbits. Food on sale for larger animals. Incubation and hatching eggs on view periodically. Picnic areas. Education packs, fact sheets for teachers, souvenirs, snacks.
Location: signposted from A361 & B4035.
Open: all year, daily 1030-1930.
Entrance: adult £2.30, child £1.50, OAP £2 WC ⚓

SHROPSHIRE

BRIDGNORTH   7E3

Charlcotte Farm Cleobury North, Bridgnorth WV16 6RR 0174633 238
                                    Mrs. Green
Open all year
3 bedrs (1 twin sh/wc; 1 double sh/wc; 1 family ba/wc) 1 ba, 1 wc ॐ 👑👑
£child rates.

BUCKNELL   7D3

The Hall Bucknell SY7 0AA 015474 249
                                Christine Price
A Georgian farmhouse standing on a 200 acre mixed farm, where you can enjoy good home cooking in quiet rural surroundings. All rooms well-equipped including tea/coffee facilities and TV. On the B4367 west of Ludlow (A49/4113). At Bucknell look for church, turn R facing church clock, 100yds on R.

Open Jan-Dec
3 bedrs (1 twin sh/wc; 2 double) 1 ba, 1
wc ☻(7) ⅄ ♨♨
£B&B £16, D £8, WR £105, WR/D £156,
child rates.

CHURCH STRETTON 7D3

Batchcott Hall Farm Batchcott Hall,
Picklescott, Church Stretton SY6 6NP
01694 751234 Mr. Lambie

We have a large, 16th century farmhouse built
on an ancient site in a beautiful, rural
location. The area is mainly hill farming so is
peaceful and undisturbed. Tennis court and
lake for fishing. In Stretton turn at red phone
box, follow Rd for 2 1/2mls, R into Batchcott
Hall Dr after passing 1st farm on R.

Open Jan-Dec
2 bedrs (1 twin ba/wc; 1 double ba/wc) ☻
🏲 Listed
£B&B £17.50-£20, WR £122.50-£140, child rates.

Court Farm Acclaimed Gretton, Church
Stretton SY6 7HU   RAC
01694 771219 Mrs. Norris

Open Feb-Nov
3 bedrs (2 twin inc 1 ba/wc, 1 sh/wc)
♨♨♨ cc AmEx
£B&B £20-£24, D £12, WR £135-£140,
WR/D £214-£220.

Gilberries Farm Cottage Wall-under-
Heywood, Church Stretton SY6 7HZ
01694 771400 Mrs. Griffiths

Country cottage joining a mixed, family farm. The
cottage has a large picturesque garden with
shrubs and a pool where guests can relax in
tranquil surroundings. Take B4371 Muchwenlock
Rd on A49 into Church Stretton approx. 5 miles is
the Plough Inn, take 2nd turn L, farm 3rd on R.

Open Feb-Nov
2 bedrs (1 twin; 1 double) 1 ba, 2 wc 🏚 ♨
£B&B £16-£17, WR £112, child rates.

Glenburrell Farm Horderley, Church
Stretton SIJ Y8HP 01694 672318 S. Jones

Guests are free to wander around our stock
rearing farm, conveniently situated 3 miles
from Craven Arms on the A489 Newtown-
Welshpool road. Tea/coffee facilities and TV
provided. This is excellent walking country
near Ironbridge, Ludlow and Shrewsbury.

Open all year
☻ 2 bdrs (1twin ba/wc; 1 double ba/wc).

Rectory Farm Woolstaston,
Leebotwood, Church Stretton SY6 6QN
01694 751306 Mr. Davies

Open Feb-mid Dec
3 bedrs (2 twin ba/wc; 1 double ba/wc)
☻(12) 🏚 ⅄ ♨♨ Highly Commended

CLUN 7D3

Llanhedric Clun, Craven Arms SY7 8NG
01588 640203 Mrs. Jones

A mixed working farm, south facing, with a
characteristic old stone farmhouse, offering
beautiful panoramic views from all rooms.
Inglenook fireplace in separate sitting room. 2
miles off A488 Clun- Bishop's Castle road.
Take turning for Bicton then Mainstone.

Open Mar- Oct
2 bedrs (1 double; 1 family) 1 ba, 2 wc ☻
Listed
£B&B £14-£16, D £7.50, WR £95, WR/D
£146, child rates.

New House Farm Clun, Craven Arms
SY7 8NJ 01588 638314 Miriam Ellison

Isolated 18th century farmhouse. Hill farm, mixed
stock rearing, including an Iron-Age-Hill-Fort
called"Caer-din-ring". Take A488 Clun to Bishop's
Castle, turn L at crossroads in Colebatch, follow
road 2 miles. Turn R in Shadwell 1st L.

Open Mar- Oct.
3 bedrs (1 twin sh/wc; 1 double sh/wc; 1
family ba/wc) ☻ 🏚 🏲 ♨♨
£B&B £16.50-£18.50, D £8.50-£9.50, WR
£110-£125, WR/D £170-£175, child rates.

Springhill Farm Clun, Craven Arms
SY7 8PE 01588 640337   Mrs. Evans

Open all year
2 bedrs 1 ba, 1 wc 🛏 ⌂ 🐕 *Classified*
£B&B £16, D £6.50, child rates.

CRAVEN ARMS   7D3

Castle Farm Cheney Longville, Craven
Arms SY7 8DR 01588 673255   Mrs. Jones

Open March - November
2 bedrs (1 family) 2 wc 🛏 🐕
£B&B £14-£14.50, child rates.

Strefford Hall Strefford, Church
Stretton, Craven Arms SY7 8DE   RAC
01588 672383   Caroline Morgan

Strefford Hall is an imposing, stone-built,
Victorian farmhouse surrounded by 360 acres
of working farmland in the picturesque hamlet
of Strefford, nestling at the foot of the Wenlock
Edge. Off the A49 north of Craven Arms.

Closed Xmas and New Year
🛏(12) ⌂ 🐕

DIDDLEBURY   7D3

Glebe Farm *Acclaimed* Craven Arms,
Diddlebury SY7 9DH 01584 76221   RAC
                              Mr. Wilkes

Open Mar-Nov
3 bedrs (3 twin inc 1 ba/wc, 2 sh/wc) 🛏(8)
🐕 *Listed*
£DB&B £45-£52.

LUDLOW   7D3

Marlbrook Hall Elton, Ludlow SY8 2HR
01568 86230   Valerie Morgan

Come and savour peace and tranquility on
our family run farm. Our 18th Century
farmhouse offers comfortable accommodation
with oak beams and inglenook fire place.
Walk in quiet country lanes or foot paths.
Wigmore turn off A4110 to Ludlow, 1ml to
village of Lemthall Starkes, signpost for
Burrington 3/4ml to Marlbrook Hall.

Open Mar-Oct
2 bedrs (1 twin; 1 family) 1 ba, 1 wc 🛏(5)
👑
£B&B £15-£17, child rates.

MARKET DRAYTON   7E2

Mickley House Faulsgreen Terne Hill,
Market Drayton TS9 3QW 01630 638505
                         Paul Williamson

Enjoy traditional farmhouse hospitality on our
125-acre working farm in unspoiled, peaceful
Shropshire countryside. Relax by the
inglenook fireplace or stroll through the
garden to our fishing pools. 1 first floor, 2
luxury ground floor en suite bedrooms.

Open all year
3 bedrs (1 twin ba/wc; 2 double ba/wc) 🛏
♿ 🐕 👑👑 *Commended*

Stoke Manor Stoke-on-Tern, Market
Drayton TF9 2DU 01630 685222
                         Mrs. Thomas

Open Jan-Nov
3 bedrs (1 twin ba/wc; 1 double ba/sh/wc;
1 family ba/sh/wc) 1 wc 🛏(5) ⌂ 🍴 👑👑
Highly Commended
£B&B £20-£27.50, child rates.

OSWESTRY 7D2

Bwlch-y-Rhiw Farmhouse Llansilin, Oswestry SY10 7PT 01691 791261
Mrs. Jones

Open April-Oct
3 bedrs (1 twin ba/wc; 1 double ba/wc; 1 family sh/wc) ☎(8)
£B&B £16.50-£17.50, child rates.

SHREWSBURY 7D2

Cardeston Park Farm Ford, Shrewsbury SY5 9NH 01743 884265
Mrs. Edwards

Open all year
3 bedrs (1 twin sh/wc; 1 double sh/wc; 1 single) 1 ba ☎ ♉ ♨
£B&B £15-£18, WR £100-£105.

Grove Farm Preston Brockhurst, Shrewsbury SY4 5QA 01939 220223 Janet M. Jones

Late 17th century farmhouse on 320 acres of mixed arable. House has log fires and is centrally heated throughout. Always a warm welcome. Take A49 north, second village is Preston Brockhurst, and the house is last on left.

Open Jan-Nov
3 bedrs (1 twin; 1 double; 1 single) 1 ba, 1 wc ☎ ♨
£B&B £16.50-£18.50, child rates.

TELFORD 7E2

New Farm Muckleton, Nr Shawbury, Telford TF6 6RJ ♛ RAC
01939 250358 Mrs. Evans

New Farm is a 70 acre arable sheep farm with a modernised farm house. Follow A53 out of Shrewsbury through village of Shawbury 1ml, R for Muckleton 1ml, New Farm on L.

Open Jan-Dec
4 bedrs (1 twin sh/wc; 1 double sh/wc; 1 family sh/wc; 1 single) 1 ba, 1 wc ☎ ♨♨
cc Ac Vi
£B&B £16-£25, WR £100-£125, child rates.

Red House Farm Longdon-on-Tern, Telford TF6 6LE 01952 770245 Mrs. Jones

Red House Farm is a spacious & elegant Victorian farmhouse on a working farm with cattle, sheep & arable crops. A warm welcome awaits visitors. Home comforts and excellent breakfast. The farm is 1/4ml from the aquaduct built by Thomas Telford in 1796. From Telford leave M54 at J6, follow A442 to Whitchurch 3 1/2mls, take B5063 to Shawbury 2 1/2mls into Longdon.

Open Feb-Nov
3 bedrs (inc 1 twin ba/wc; 1 double ba/wc) 1 ba, 2 wc ☎ ♉ ♨♨
£B&B £16-£18.50, WR £105-£122.50, child rates.

WELLINGTON 7E2

Pinksmoor Farm Pinksmoor, Wellington TA21 0HD 01823 672361
Mrs. Ash

Open Jan-Dec
3 bedrs (1 twin ba/wc; 1 double sh/wc; 1 family ba/wc) ☎ ♨♨♨
£B&B £18-£21, D £11.50, WR £112-£132.50, child rates.

WEM 7D2

Lowe Hall Farm Wem SY4 5UE
01939 232236 E. A. Jones

Open Jan-Dec
3 bedrs (1 twin; 1 double; 1 family ba/wc) 1 ba, 1 wc ☎ ♨♨
£B&B £16-£17, D £8, WR £105-£112, WR/D £161-£168, child rates.

SELF CATERING

CHURCH STRETTON 7D3

Batchcott Hall Farm Batchcott Hall, Picklescott, Church Stretton SY6 6NP 01694 751234 Mr. Lambie

For full farm description see B&B Entry. In Stretton turn at red phone box, follow Rd for 2 1/2mls, R into Batchcott Hall Dr after passing 1st farm on R.

☎ ♉*Listed*
£Wk £175-£250

Court Farm Gretton, Church Stretton SY6 7HU ♛ RAC
01694 771219 Mrs. Norris

B4371 from Church Stretton 5 miles, turn left for gretton 1 mile, turn right , Farm 200 yards on right.

cc AmEx
£Wk £70-£100

DORRINGTON 7D2

Ryton Farm Ryton, Dorrington, Shrewsbury SY5 7LY 01743 718449
Mrs. Cartwright

Peacefully situated cottages and barn conversions overlooking the South Shropshire countryside, on an arable farm. Comfortable well equipped. Pets are welcome. Coarse fishing in Farm pools. Weeks or short breaks available all year.

½ mile from A49 Shrewsbury to Hereford road.

ㅎ(14) ♂ ㎡
£Wk £140-£350

LUDLOW 7D3

Brooklyn Elton, Ludlow SY8 2HR
01568 86230   Valerie Morgan

For full farm description see B&B Entry. Wigmore turn off A4110 to Ludlow, 1ml to village of Lemthall Starkes, signpost for Burrington 3/4ml to Marlbrook Hall.

ㅎ(5) ㎡
£Wk £110-£220

SHREWSBURY 7D2

Parkgate Cottages Pulverbatch, Shrewsbury SY5 8DH 01694 751303
Mrs. Hill

SOMERSET

BISHOPS LYDEARD 3D2

Slimbridge Station Farm Bishops Lydeard, Taunton TA4 3BX 01823 432223
Ann Pattemore

Closed Xmas
5 bedrs (2 twin; 2 double; 1 family) ㅎ よ ㎡ ♂
cc AmEx

BRIDGWATER 3E2

Blackmore Farm Cannington, Bridgwater TA5 2NE 01278 653442
Mrs. Dyer

Grade I listed, 14th century manor house retaining many period features, oak beams, open fireplaces and a 4 poster bed. Working arable/dairy farm. A39 from Bridgwater, by-pass Cannington (on A39) after 2nd roundabout, take 3rd turn on L (Blackmore Lane), farm 1st R.

Open Jan-Dec
3 bedrs (2 double ba/wc; 1 family sh/wc) 1 wc ㅎ ㎡ ♛♛
£B&B £18-£22, WR £113-£140, child rates.

Waterpitts Farm Broomfield, Quantock Hills, Bridgewater TA5 1AT 01823 451679
Chris Jordan

Open all year

CASTLE CARY 3E2

Orchard Farm Cockhill, Castle Cary BA7 7NY 01963 350418   Mr. Boyer

Open Jan-Dec
2 bedrs (1 double sh/wc; 1 family sh/wc)
ㅎ よ ♂ ♛♛
£B&B £15-£18, D £8.50, child rates.

CHEDDAR 3E1

Tor Farm Nyland, Cheddar BS27 3UD
01934 743710 Mrs. Ladd

Mixed farm on the beautiful Somerset levels.
Ensuite, four poster and standard rooms.
Some with private patio. Open views. Take
A371 towards Wells, after 2mls turn R
signposted Nyland. Tor Farm is 1 1/2mls on R.

Open Jan-Dec
8 bedrs (1 twin sh/wc; 5 double inc 1
ba/wc, 1 sh/wc; 1 family sh/wc; 1 single) 2
ba, 2 wc ⌘ ☺ *Highly Commended* cc Vi
£B&B £15-£21.50, WR £94.50-£135.50.

DULVERTON 3D2

Highercombe Dulverton TA22 9PT
01398 23451 Barbara Marchant

Former hunting lodge of 14th century origin
in beautiful mature gardens. Very peaceful.
Wonderful views. Wild deer often seen. From
Dulverton take B3223 signed Exford.
Highercombe is 2 ½ miles on right ¼ mile after
hairpin bend.

Open all year
4 bedrs (1 twin sh/wc; 2 double inc 1
sh/wc; 1 family sh/wc) ☺ ☻☻
£B&B £16-£19, WR/D £105-£120, child
rates.

Springfield Farm Ashwick Lane,
Dulverton TA22 9QD 01398 7236
Mrs Vellacott

Open Apr-Oct
3 bedrs (1 twin sh/wc; 1 double; 1 single) 1
ba, 1 wc ☺ ☻ ☻☻
£B&B £16-£20, D £11, WR £105-£115,
WR/D £180-£187, child rates.

EXMOOR

See entries on pg. 52

GLASTONBURY 3E2

Cradlebridge Farm Glastonbury BA16
9SD RAC
01458 831827 Mrs. Tinney

Open all year
4 bedrs (2 twin sh/wc; 2 family sh/wc) ☺
☻ ☻
£B&B £17.50-£25, WR £105-£150, child rates.

New House Farm Burtle Road,
Westhay, Glastonbury BA6 9TT
01458 860238 Mrs. Bell

Open Jan-Dec
2 bedrs; 1 ba, 1 wc ☺ ☻ ☻☻
£B&B £18-£20, D £10, WR £126-£140,
WR/D £196-£210, child rates.

HENSTRIDGE 3F2

Quiet Corner Farm Templecombe,
Henstridge BA8 0RA 01963 363045
Mrs. Partricia Thompson

This 18th century, stone farmhouse and barn
is tucked away in a conservation area in a
beautiful garden and orchard. Follow signs for
A357 (South Henstridge), take A357 south,
2nd left down Vale St., farm 150 yds on right.

Open all year
4 bedrs (1 twin; 2 double; 1 family) 1 ba, 1
wc ☺ ☻ ☻☻
£child rates.

HIGHBRIDGE 3E2

Alstone Court Farm Alstone Lane, Highbridge TA9 3DS 01278 789417
Mrs. Loud

17th century working farm. From Burnham-on-Sea take the A38 to Bridgewater on outskirt of Highbridge look for the Artillery Pub.

Open April- November
3 bedrs 3 ba, 3 wc ☃ *Listed*
£B&B £13.50-£14.50, WR £93-£100, child rates.

Laurel Farm Markcauseway, Nr Highbridge TA9 4PZ 01278 641216
Mrs. Puddy

Open all year
3 bedrs 2 ba, 3 wc ☃ ⌂
£B&B £12.50, child rates.

SHEPTON MALLET 3E2

Barrow Farm North Wootton, Shepton Mallet 01749 890245   Mrs. White

Open all year

SOMERTON 3E2

Lower Farm Kingweston, Somerton TA11 6BA 01458 223237   J. Sedgman

The attractive listed house at Lower Farm was formerly a coaching inn, and now successfully combines old world charm with modern comfort. This working farm is set in a conservation area south of Glastonbury off the A39/B3151/3. Lytes Cary 2 miles.

Open all year/
3 bedrs (1 twin sh/wc; 1 double sh/wc; 1 single sh/wc) ☃ 🕇 ⅄ ☙

STOKE-ST-GREGORY 3E2

Parsonage Farm Stoke-St-Gregory, Taunton TA3 6ET 01823 698205
Mrs. House

This lovely Victorian farmhouse, on a busy arable farm stands at the centre of a very attractive village. The house is surrounded by mature gardens with a hard tennis court & picnic table. Ample car parking space is provided.

Open all year
3 bedrs (1 twin; 2 double inc 1 ba/wc) 1 ba, 1 wc ☃ 🕇 ☙
£B&B £16-£18.

TAUNTON 3D2

Prockters Farm West Monkton, Taunton TA2 8QN 01823 412269
Mrs. Besley

Open Jan-Dec
5 bedrs (2 twin inc 1 sh/wc; 2 double inc 1 sh/wc; 1 family) 2 ba, 2 wc ☃ ⅙ ⌂ 🕇 ☙
cc AmEx
£B&B £17-£21, WR £96-£140, child rates.

WATCHET 3D2

Glasses Farm Roadwater, Watchet TA23 0QH 01984 40552   Mrs. White

This delightful thatched 16th century farmhouse is situated on the edge of Exmoor, at the foot of Brendon Hills. Ideal for seeing the many local beauty spots. We are a working farm of 220 acres, dairy and arable.

Open Jan-Nov.
6 bedrs ☃(10) 🕇 ☙

Wood Advent Farm Roadwater, Watchet TA23 0RR 01984 640920
Mrs. Brewer

Mixed - sheep and beef.

Open January to November
5 bedrs (2 twin ba/wc; 3 double sh/wc) 1 ba, 1 wc ☃ ⌂ ⅄ ☙☙☙☙
£B&B £18.50-£23.50, D £12-£15, WR/D £165-£185, child rates.

WELLS 3E2

Herons Green Farm Compton Martin, Bristol BS18 6NL 01275 333372
Mrs. Hasell

Stone built farmhouse by Chew Valley Lake. Oak beamed dining room featuring original water well. Very friendly atmosphere. West Harptree take B3114 to Chewstoke. Take 2nd R, branch L down no through road.

Open Mar-Nov
2 bedrs (1 double; 1 family) 1 ba, 1 wc
£B&B £16-£20, WR £105, child rates.

Double-Gate Farm Godney, Wells BA5 1RZ 01458 832217
H. Millard

Beautiful Georgian Farmhouse on mixed working farm. Lovely flower garden, outdoor breakfasts weather permitting. Two golden retrievers and loving moggy. From Wells take A39 (Glastonbury). At Polsham turn right. Continue 2 miles to Sheppey Inn. Farmhouse on left.

Open March-November
3 bedrs (inc 1 twin sh/wc; 1 double sh/wc)
£B&B £15-£16, WR £103-£110, child rates.

Manor Farm Old Bristol Road, Upper Milton, Wells BA5 3AH 01749 673394
Janet Gould

This listed Grade II Elizabethan manor house is superbly situated on the southern slopes of the Mendip Hills. It has a large garden within a 130-acre working farm, a mile north of Wells off the A39. Tea/Coffee facilities. A mile north of Wells off the A39.

Open all year
3 bedrs (1 twin; 1 double; 1 family) 1 ba, 2 wc *Listed*
£child rates.

Whitnell Farm Binegar, Emborough, Wells BA3 4UF 01749 840277
Mr. Rich

This manor house with unique character is set in beautiful gardens amid peaceful countryside on a mixed family farm. B3139 Wells-Bath road.

Open all year
3 bedrs (1 twin; 1 double; 1 family) 1 ba, 1 wc

WHEDDON CROSS 3D2

Cutthorne Farm Luckwell Bridge, Wheddon Cross TA24 7EW 0164 383255
Mrs. Durbin

25 acre sheep farm in the centre of Exmoor. Quiet and secluded with ensuite bathrooms and four-poster bedrooms. Log fires and candlelit dinners. A39 to Dunster. A396 to Wheddon Cross. B3224 to Luckwell Bridge.

Open Mar-Nov
3 bedrs (1 twin ba/wc; 2 double ba/wc)
£B&B £19.50-£25, D £10.50, WR £136-£189, WR/D £210-£245, child rates.

WINCANTON 3F2

Hale Farm Cucklington, Wincanton BA9 9PN 01963 33342 Mr. David

17th Century farmhouse with a wealth of beams on a mixed farm situated in the Blackmoor Vale, 2 miles from the A303. Self-catering also available in a self-contained unit sleeping four. Off A303 onto B3081 then Stoke Trister and into Cuclington, follow B & B sign.

Open May-Sep
3 bedrs (1 twin sh/wc; 1 double sh/wc; 1 family sh/wc) ⌂(6) ♉ ♨♨
£B&B £16, WR £102, child rates.

SELF CATERING

CASTLE CARY 3E2

Orchard Farm Cockhill, Castle Cary BA7 7NY 01963 350418 Mr. Boyer
⌂ ♉
£Wk £110-£340

HENSTRIDGE

Quiet Corner Farm Templecombe, Henstridge BA8 0RA 01963 363045 Mrs. Partricia Thompson

For full farm description see B&B Entry. Follow signs for A357 (South Henstridge), take A357 south, 2nd left down Vale St., farm 150 yds on right.

⌂ ⚹

MINEHEAD 3D2

Croft Cottage c/o Higher Burrow Farm, Timberscombe, Minehead TA24 7UD 01643 841427 Mr. Rusher

Double stone built cottages made into one.

Farm with suckler beef cows, oven ready ducks.

⌂ ♉ ♜♜♜
£Wk £80-£350

TAUNTON 3D2

Willow Barns Newcotts Farm, North Newton, Taunton TA7 0DQ 01278 662783 J. Day

Newcotts is a mixed stock farm with cattle, sheep and horses. Old stone barns have been delightfully converted, with lovely views over peaceful canalside farmland. The 7 cottages sleep 1-6 people and most have full wheelchair access (Access Category 2).

It lies south of Bridgwater, east off the A38.

& ♉ ♜♜♜ *Highly Commended*

WELLS 3E2

Whitnell Farm Binegar, Emborough, Wells BA3 4UF 01749 840277 Mr. Rich

For full farm description see p125. The farm has 2 holiday homes, 2-3 bedrooms, sleeping 4-8. Each has its own character and is spacious and well-equipped. Cot and highchair available. The larger unit is suitable for disabled guests.

B3139 Wells-Bath road.

& ⌂

WHEDDON CROSS 3D2

Cutthorne Farm Luckwell Bridge, Wheddon Cross TA24 7EW 0164 383255 Mrs. Durbin

For full farm description see B&B Entry. A39 to Dunster. A396 to Wheddon Cross. B3224 to Luckwell Bridge.

⌂ ♉ ♜♜♜
£Wk £200-£425

WINCANTON 3F2

Hale Farm Cucklington, Wincanton BA9 9PN 01963 33342 Mr. David

For full farm description see B&B Entry. Off A303 onto B3081 then Stoke Trister and into Cuclington, follow B & B sign.

⌂(6) ♉
£Wk £90-£200

PLACES TO VISIT

BRADFORD ON TONE

Sheppy's Cider Farm & Rural Life Museum
Three Bridges, Bradford on Tone, Taunton
01823-461233 Fax 01823-461712
Cider works and museum with a video of the cider making year. Nature walks and picnic area. Draught and bottled cider can be sampled and bought.
Location: on A38 between Taunton and Wellington.
Open: Mon-Sat all year round: 8.30-18.00 Sun (Easter to Christmas) 12.00-14.00.
Entrance: adult £1.50 child £1.00 OAP £1.25. Guided tours: adult £3.50 child £2.25 OAP £3.00 WC & ♁ ✗ ⌷

Willow & Wetlands Visitor Centre
Meare Green Court, Stoke St Gregory, Taunton TA3 6HY 01823-490249
Willow growing and basket making are traditional Somerset crafts, here all aspects of the industry can be seen from willow preparation to finished basket and other withy products. Guided tours last one hour. Historic items displayed plus RSPB exhibition of flora and fauna of surrounding wetlands.
Location: signposted at West Lyng on A361 Taunton-Glastonbury road.
Open: all year, Mon-Sat 0900-1700.
Willow tour charges: adult £2, child £1, OAP/concessions £1.50. WC & (partial access) ♁ ⌷

SOUTH YORKSHIRE

HATHERSAGE 7F1

Lane End Farm Abney, Hathersage, Hathersage S30 1AA 01433 650371
Mrs. Salisbury

A working, hill sheep farm in a small hamlet, off the beaten track. There are stunning views and many unspoilt walks from the door. Farmhouse decorated and furnished to a high standard.

Open all year
3 bedrs (1 twin; 2 double inc 1 sh/wc) 1 ba, 2 wc ♁ *Listed*
£B&B £15.50-£25, child rates.

STAFFORDSHIRE

CHEADLE 7E2

Ley Fields Farm Leek Road, Cheadle, Stoke-on-Trent ST10 2EF 01538 752875
Mrs. Clowes

Open all year
4 bedrs (1 twin sh/wc; 1 double ba/wc; 2 family sh/wc) ♁ ♛♛♛

£B&B £16-£18, D £9-£9.50, WR £110-£126, WR/D £170-£190, child rates.

LEEK 7E1

Brook House Farm Winkhill, Cheddleton, Leek ST13 7DF
01538 360296 Mrs. Winterton

Open Jan-Dec
5 bedrs (1 twin sh/wc; 2 double sh/wc; 2 family sh/wc) 🦮 ♿ 🐕 🌢🌢🌢 *Commended*
£B&B £15-£17, D £8-£9, WR £105-£119, WR/D £161-£182, child rates.

Country Cottage Back Lane Farm, Winkhill, Leek ST13 7PJ 01538 308273 Mrs. Bentley

Back Lane Farm is set in 20 acres of pastureland. The stone-built farmhouse is 18th century with original oak beams and open fires. Good breakfasts and evening meals provided. Situated off A523 5 miles southeast of Leek.

Open Jan- Dec
4 bedrs (1 twin sh/wc; 2 double sh/wc 1 single ba/wc) 1 ba, 2 wc 🦮 ♿ 🌢🌢🌢 *Highly Commended*
£B&B £17-£19, D £11-£11.50, child rates.

Micklea Farm Micklea Lane, Longsdon, Leek ST9 9QA 01538 385006 Mrs. White

17th century farmhouse with large garden, not a working farm. Follow A53 signposted Stoke for 2 ½ mls. Turn L at New Inn Pub into Denford Rd. Bear L at fork into Micklea Lane.

Open Jan-Dec
4 bedrs 2 ba, 2 wc ♿ *Listed*

All towns listed in this guide are shown on the maps at the back.

Summerhill Farm Grindon, Leek ST13 7TT 01538 304264   P. Simpson

Traditional dairy farm set in the Peak District amid rolling countryside with panoramic views. Wonderful for walkers. Tea and coffee making facilities, colour TV, clock radios. Leek - Ashbourne A523 through Onecote 1st R for Grindon 3mls up no through road.

Open Jan-Nov
3 bedrs; 1 ba 🦮 ♿ ✗ *Listed Commended*
£B&B £14-£18.50, D £6.50-£11, WR £98-£129.50, WR/D £143.50-£206, child rates.

OAKAMOOR   7F1

Ribden Farm *Acclaimed* Oakamoor ST10 3BW
01538 702830   Mrs. Shaw

Open all year
3 bedrs (1 ba/wc, 2 sh/wc) 🦮
£DB&B £32-£36.

RUGELEY   7F2

Marsh Farm Abbots Bromley, Rugeley 01283 840323   M. Whiteford

Closed Xmas
2 bedrs (1 twin sh; 1 family) 1 ba, 2 wc 🦮 🐕

STOKE-ON-TRENT   7E1

Tenement Farm Three Lows, Ribden, Nr Oakmoor, Stoke-on-Trent ST10 3BW
01538 702333   Mr. Leese

Open Mar- Nov
8 bedrs (1 twin sh/wc; 4 double inc 3 ba/wc 3 family) 1 ba, 2 wc 🦮 🌢🌢 cc Ac Vi
£B&B £17-£20, WR £120-£140, child rates.

SELF CATERING

CAULDON 7F1

Park View Farm Stoney Lane, Cauldon ST10 3EP 01538 308233 Mrs. Burndred

♞ ꝏꝏ *Highly Commended*
£Wk £140-£280

LEEK 7E1

Lower Berkhamsytch Bottom House, Nr Leek ST13 7QP 01538 308213
Mr. Mycok

2 self contained flats on dairy and pig farm. Each flat has its own private entrance and is within walking distance of 2 pubs serving meals and Little Chef restaurant.

On the A523 towards Ashbourne from Leek.

£Wk £100-£195

STOKE-ON-TRENT 7E1

Tenement Farm Three Lows, Ribden, Nr Oakmoor, Stoke-on-Trent ST10 3BW 01538 702333 Mr. Leese

cc Ac Vi
£Wk £250-£450

PLACES TO VISIT

LEEK

Blackbook World of Birds
Wink Hill, Leek 01565-873282
Fax 01538-308293
Enjoy a day with a difference amongst an amazing collection of birds in an attractive moorland setting. Cranes, owls, waterfowl, pheasants and many more. Children's farm and pets area. Gift shop with light refreshments. Picnic areas inside and out.
Open Easter-Oct, daily 1130-1730.
Entrance: adult £2.50, child £1.50, OAP/Concessions £2. WC

SUFFOLK

BECCLES 9F3

Shrublands Farm Burgh St Peter, Beccles NR34 0BB 01502 677241
RM Clarke

This attractive, homely farmhouse is peacefully situated in the Waveney Valley on the Suffolk border and surrounded by one acre of garden and lawns. The River Waveney flows through 550 acres of mixed working farmland. From Beccles take A143 to Gt Yarmouth, 1 ml from roundabout take 1st R to Burgh St Peter 2 3/4mls.

Open Jan-Dec
3 bedrs (1 twin; 1 double; 1 family) 2 ba, 2 wc (5)
£DB&B £32-£34, child rates.

BUNGAY 9F3

Park Farm Harleston Road, Earsham, Bungay 01986 892180 Mrs. Watchorn

This spacious Victorian farmhouse is set on a 600-acre mixed farm with some unusual farm animals. Excellent cooking using the farm's meat and produce. West of Bungay on A143

Open all year
3 bedrs (1 twin ba/wc; 2 double sh/wc) 1 wc *Commended*

Mundham Grange Mundham, Loddon
NR14 6EP 01508 50067   Mrs. Lord

Open Jan-Dec
2 bedrs; 1 ba, 1 wc ⚅ ⊞ ♉ ♨♨
£B&B £15-£18, D £8-£10, WR £105-£145,
WR/D £161-£185, child rates.

BURY ST EDMUNDS   9E4

Pear Tree Farm Hartest, Bury St
Edmunds IP29 4EQ 01284 830217
R. White

Open Mar-Oct
2 bedrs (1 twin sh/wc; 1 double sh/wc) ⚅
♨♨
£B&B £18-£19, child rates.

EYE   9E3

Elm Lodge Fressingfield, Eye 1P21 5SL
01379 586249   Mrs. Webster

Victorian farmhouse on 112 acre arable farm.
ETB 2 crowns commended. Follow B1116
through Weybread, Fressingfield village, 2mls
1st L to Chippenhall Green, R at T-junction,
farm 150yds.

Open Mar-Nov
3 bedrs, 2 double 1 ba, 2 wc ⚅(10) ♉ ✑
♨♨ Commended cc DC
£B&B £17-£19, D £10, WR £100, WR/D
£150, child rates.

HALESWORTH   9F3

Broad Oak Farm Bramfield, Nr
Halesworth IP19 9AB 01986 784232
Mrs. Kemsley

Open Jan-Dec
3 bedrs (2 twin inc 1 sh/wc; 1 double
ba/wc) 1 ba, 2 wc ⚅ ♉ ♨♨

£B&B £14-£16, D £8, WR £91-£98, WR/D
£147-£158, child rates.

HINTLESHAM   5E1

College Farm Hintlesham, Ipswich IP8
3NT 01473 652253   Mrs. Bryce

Open mid Jan-mid Dec
3 bedrs (1 twin; 1 double ba/wc; 1 single)
1 ba, 2 wc ⚅(5) ♨♨ Highly Commended
£B&B £16-£21, WR £105-£120, child rates.

LAVENHAM   9E4

Mount Pleasant Farm Offton,
Lavenham IP8 4RP 01473 658896
Mrs. Redman

A 16th century farmhouse on a working farm
with livestock. Specialising in evening meals.
Close to the sea with coastal walks and
fishing. Golf and sports centre near by. No
family rooms. Central heating.

Open all year
3 bedrs (1 twin; 2 double) 1ba ♨♨♨ Listed
£B&B £16.50-£28, D £8.

Weaners Farm Bears Lane, Lavenham,
Sudbury CO10 9RX 01787 247310
Mr. Rhodes

Open February to November
3 bedrs (2 twin; 1 double) 2 ba, 3 wc ⚅ ✑
£B&B £16-£17.

LOWESTOFT   9F3

Church Farm Corton, Lowestoft NR32
5HX 01502 730359   Mrs. Edwards

Church Farm is a working arable farm with a
Victorian farmhouse situated on the coast in a
quiet spot 3 miles north of Lowestoft.

Open all year
2 bedrs (2 double ba/wc) ✁ *Listed Highly Commended*

WOODBRIDGE 9F4

Grange Farm Dennington, Woodbridge
IP13 8BT 01986 798388 Elizabeth Hickson

A charming moated house dating from 14th Century in a superb spot. Set in spacious grounds with all weather tennis court. The rooms are comfortable and beautifully furnished. Set in arable land. B1116 N to Dennington, R beside church, L B1116 signed Harleston, 2 1/2mls past Dennington Bell, 1ml on R.

Open all year
4 bedrs (3 twin; 1 single) 1 ba, 2 wc ✁(12)
Listed
£B&B £18, D £10-£12.50, WR £120, WR/D £28-£30.50.

Red House Farm Maypole Green, Dennington, Woodbridge IP13 8AQ
01728 638628 Mr. Craggs

Peaceful and secluded 17th Century partly beamed farmhouse set in 4 acres of wooded grounds surrounded by farmland. Home made bread a speciality. ½ mile off A1120. Signed Maypole Green just west of Dennington village.

Open Feb-Dec
3 bedrs (2 twin inc 1 ba/wc; 1 single) 1 ba, 1 wc ✁(10)
£B&B £18.50, WR £115.

Woodlands Farm Woodbridge IP13 8PB 01379 384444 Mrs. Graham

This 6-acre smallholding with lots of farm pets, stands 6 miles north of Framlingham (B1116/B1118). The cottage-style farmhouse is

approx 200 years old and offers home cooking using fresh home produce. Snape Maltings 18 miles. Coast 20-25 miles.

Closed Xmas and New Year
3 bedrs (1 twin sh/wc; 2 double ba/wc) ✁(10) ✿✿ ✁

SELF CATERING

BRAMFIELD 9F3

Broad Oak Farm Bramfield
01986 84232 Mrs. Kemsley
✁ ✿

EYE 9E3

Elm Lodge Fressingfield, Eye 1P21 5SL
01379 586249 Mrs. Webster

For full farm description see B&B Entry. Follow B1116 through Weybread, Fressingfield village, 2mls 1st L to Chippenhall Green, R at T-junction, farm 150yds.

✁(10) ✿ *Commended* cc DC

IPSWICH 5E1

Stable Cottages and The Granary
Chattisham Place, Nr Ipswich IP8 3QD
01473 652210 Mrs. Langton

Restored stables and Tudor granary converted to 3 comfortable and well-equipped holiday cottages, one with wheelchair facilities. Situated in an SE facing courtyard with CH, fitted kitchen, colour TV.

& ✁ ✿ ♞♞♞ *Highly Commended*

LAVENHAM 9E4

Old Wetherden Hall Hitcham,
Lavenham IP7 7PZ 01449 740574
Mrs. Elsden.

Arable farm with chickens, ducks and horses. Recently restored 15th Century oak beamed moated hall, modern bathroom and kitchen. Beautiful secluded setting with large garden and an abundance of wildlife.

B1115 from Stowmarket at Hitcham White Horse, R 50 yards turn L to Kettlebaston ½ mile, 1st farm R.

✁ ♞♞♞
£Wk £100-£310

WOODBRIDGE 9F4

Woodlands Farm Woodbridge IP13 8PB 01379 384444 Mrs. Graham

PLACES TO VISIT

SUDBURY

Boyton Vineyard
Stoke-by-Clare, Sudbury CO10 8TB
01440-61893

Tour of vineyard and tastings in wine lodge. Gardens, listed 15th-century farmhouse and picnic area. On sale; estate produced wine.
Location: signposted from A1092, south of Bury St Edmunds.
Open: April-Oct, daily 1030-1800 WC 🏋
&. 🛋

SURREY

DORKING 4C3

Bulmer Farm Holmbury St Mary, Dorking RH5 6LG 01306 730210 Mrs. Hill

Open all year
8 bedrs (5 twin, inc 2 sh/wc; 3 double sh/wc) 2 ba, 2 wc 🏇(12)
🌺🌺
£B&B £18.

Crossways Farm Raikes Lane, Abinger Hammer, Nr Dorking RH5 6PZ
01306 730173 Mr. Hughes

Open all year

Sturtwood Farm Partridge Lane, Newdigate, Dorking RH5 5EE
01306 631308 Mrs. Mackinnon

Open all year
2 bedrs (1 twin sh/wc; 1 single) 1 ba, 1 wc
🏇 🌺🌺
£B&B £17.50-£22, D £8.50-£12.50, child rates.

FARNHAM 4C3

Bordefield Farm Rowledge, Farnham GU10 4EP 01252 793985 Mrs. Simpson

A working smallholding set in attractive countryside on the outskirts of the village which has two good pubs. Lounge with TV and log fire. Lovely walks. Fishing and horse riding available. Dogs and horses welcome. Camp site and caravans. Easy reach of London, New Forest and coast.

Open Feb-Nov.
3 bedrs 🏇 🏋

LINGFIELD 5D3

Stantons Hall Farm Eastbourne Road, Blindley Heath RH7 6LG 01342 832401
Vanessa Manwill

Open All year except Xmas
9 bedrs (2 twin inc 1 sh/wc; 4 double sh/wc; 2 family; 1 single) 1 ba, 1 wc 🏇 ⚔
cc DC
£B&B £16-£20, child rates.

SMALLFIELD 5D3

Chithurst Farm Chithurst Lane, Horne, Smallfield RH6 9JU 01342 842487
Mrs. Tucker

Open Feb-Nov
3 bedrs (1 double; 1 family; 1 single) 1 ba, 1 wc 🏇 ⚔ *Listed*
£B&B £14-£16.50, WR £93-£107, child rates.

PLACES TO VISIT

FARNHAM

Rural Life Centre Old Kiln Museum
Reeds Road, Tilford, Farnham GU10 2DL
01252-795571/7
Displays on all aspects of past village life, forge, wheelwright's shop, wagons, forestry etc. Arboretum, woodland walks, picnic area. On sale: crafts.
Location: off A287 Farnham-Haslemere road.
Open: Apr-Sept. Wed-Sun 1100-1800.
Entrance: adult £3, child £1.50, OAP/concessions £2.50. Rustic Sunday 30 July. WC 🏋 &. ✗ 🛋

WARWICKSHIRE

ALCESTER   8A4

Walcote Farm Walcote, Haselor,
Alcester B49 6LY 01789 488264
Mr. Finnemore

Grade II listed farmhouse on 75 acre, grass
sheep farm. Ensuite, comfortable accommodation
with lovely views in the attractive, oak-beamed,
farmhouse. Situated in a tranquil picturesque
hamlet near Stratford-upon-Avon.

Open all year
2 bedrs (1 twin sh/wc; 1 double sh/wc) ☡
🐾🐾
£B&B £18-£19, child rates.

COLESHILL   8A3

Maxstoke Hall Farm Fillongley Road,
Maxstoke, Nr Coleshill, Birmingham B46
2QT 01675 463237   Mrs. Green

Open all year
🗲

DORSINGTON   7F3

Church Farm Dorsington CV37 8AX
01789 720471   Mr. Walters

Open all year

LEAMINGTON SPA   8B4

Crandon House Avon Dassett,
Leamington Spa CV33 DAA 01295 770652
Mrs. Lea

Crandon House offers luxurious
accommodation and an especially warm
welcome. Set in a peaceful spot overlooking
traditional farmland southeast of Leamington
Spa. The farm specialises in rare breeds of
cattle, sheep and poultry.

Open Jan-Dec
3 bedrs (2 twin inc 1 ba/wc, 1 sh/wc; 1
double ba/wc) ☡(8) 🐾 🗲 🐾🐾 cc Ac Vi
Highly Commended
£B&B £17.50-£21.50, D £12.50, WR £120-
£150, WR/D £185-£260, child rates.

Hill Farm Lewis Road, Radford Semele,
Leamington Spa CV31 1UX 01926 337571
R. Gibbs

Open all year.
5 bedrs (2 twins inc 1 ba/wc, 3 double inc
2 ba/wc) 1 ba, 2wc ☡ 🗲 🐾🐾 *Approved*

Snowford Hall Snowford Hall Farm,
Hunningham, Leamington Spa CV33 9ES
01926 632297   R. Hancock

Stay in an 18th Century farmhouse on 250-
acre mixed working farm in rolling
countryside. Warm welcome amid peaceful
surroundings. Central heating and good home
cooking. A425 Southam, outside L
roundabout, L Fore Way 3mls, crossroads, turn
away from Huntington village, under bridge,
1st R.

Open Jan-Dec
3 bedrs (2 twin inc 1 sh/wc; 1 double
sh/wc) 1 ba, 2 wc ☡ 🐾🐾 *Commended*
£B&B £16-£19, child rates.

OXHILL   8A4

Nolands Farm Oxhill CV35 0RJ   RAC
01926 640309   Mrs. Hutsby

Annexed bedrooms, some in converted stable yard, mostly on ground floor, with romantic four poster beds. Peaceful and surrounded by fields. Clay pigeon shooting, fishing, and bike hire available. Situated just off the A422 Stratford to Banbury Road towards Oxhill.

Open 6 Jan-15 Dec
9 bedrs (1 twin; 6 double inc 2 ba/wc, 5 sh/wc; 1 family sh/wc; 1 single) 3 wc ⛄(7) ⌂ cc Ac Vi
£B&B £15-£20, child rates.

RUGBY   8B3

Lawford Hill Farm Lawford Heath Lane, Nr Rugby CV23 9HG 01788 542001
Mrs. Moses

This friendly Georgian farmhouse is set in a large picturesque garden on a family-run mixed farm.

Open all year-except Xmas
4 bedrs (1 twin; 2 double; 1 family) 1 ba, 1 wc ⛄ ⌂ ⋔ ✂ ♨
£B&B £15-£18, WR £105, child rates.

Manor Farm Willey, Nr Rugby CV23 0SH 01455 553143   Mrs. Sharpe

Attention to detail ensures us many repeat bookings. Being on the borders of Warwickshire, Leicestershire, Northamptonshire makes us the perfect venue for north/south travellers to NEC, NAC, etc. We offer genuine hospitality, peace and tranquility. 5 miles from Midlands motorway triangle. Convenient A5, Fosse Way.

Open all year.
6 bedrs ✂ ♨♨

SHIPSTON-ON-STOUR   7F4

Ascott House Farm Ascott, Whichford, Nr Long Compton, Shipston-on-Stour CV36 5PP 01608 684655   Mrs. Haines

Ascott House is a 500-acre arable and sheep farm. The listed two hundred year old farmhouse is built of Cotswold stone and is surrounded by an attractive garden with swimming pool. 15 acres of pasture land surround the house. A3400 towards Oxford for 4 miles, then turn left into Ascott. In Ascott, take the 1st right, then 1st drive on right.

Closed Xmas and New Year

3 bedrs (1 twin; 1 double sh/wc; 1 family sh/wc) 1 ba, 1 wc ⛄ ⋔ ♨♨
£B&B £15-£18, WR £95-£110, child rates.

STRATFORD-UPON-AVON   4A1

Cadle Pool Farm The Ridgway, Stratford-upon-Avon CV37 9RE
01789 292494   Mrs. Turney

Beautiful farm house in Warwickshire. The farm is not totally arable but we have peacocks, ducks and geese roaming freely in our extensive grounds and water gardens. Stratford take A422 to Alcester, continue for $1\frac{1}{2}$ miles at large Texaco Garage turn R onto Ridgway Rd, farm 1/2ml R.

Open Jan-Dec
3 bedrs 1 ba, 1 wc ⛄ ♨♨♨
£B&B £15-£20, WR £100-£130, child rates.

Monk's Barn Farm Shipston Road, Stratford-upon-Avon CV37 8NA
01789 293714   Mrs. Meadows

Open all year
5 bedrs (1 twin sh/wc; 2 double inc 1 sh/wc; 1 family inc 1 single inc 1 sh/wc) 2 ba, 2 wc ⛄ ⋔ cc Vi
£B&B £14-£16.50, WR £85-£100, child rates.

All towns listed in this guide are shown on the maps at the back.

Thornton Manor Ettington, Stratford-upon-Avon CV37 7PN 01789 740210
Mrs. Hutsby

16th century stonebuilt manor house overlooking fields and woodland with sheep and cattle. There is fishing and a grass tennis court. Riding about 5 miles away. Take A422 Banbury road from Stratford. At first roundabout take A429 Warwick road. We are ¾ mile on the right.

Open March-Nov
3 bedrs 1 ba ☼(7) ♕♕
£B&B £17-£19.50, WR £110-£125, child rates.

Whitchurch Farm Wimpstone, Stratford-upon-Avon CV37 8NS
01789 450275   Mrs. James

Lovely Georgian farmhouse set in park like surroundings, 4.5 miles from Stratford on the edge of the Cotswolds, ideal for touring holiday. The farm is on 220 acres arable land with beef and sheep. Take A3400 towards Oxford in 4 miles turn R for Wimpstone, turn L at telephone box, keep straight to farm.

Open all year
3 bedrs (1 twin sh/wc; 2 double sh/wc) ☼ ♕♕
£B&B £15-£17, D £9.50, child rates.

WARWICK 8B4

Lower Watchbury Farm Wasperton Lane, Barford CV35 8DH 01926 624772
Mrs. Eykyn

Situated in 50 acres with outstanding views, our beautifully refurbished accommodation offers a warm welcome. Large garden. Excellent farmhouse breakfast. Take A429 to Stowe through Barford. Left opposite Granville Arms pub. 2nd farm on left.

Open all year
4 bedrs (2 twin inc 1 ba/wc, 1 sh/wc; 1 double sh/wc; 1 family ba/wc) ☼ ⊞ ♞ ♕♕
£B&B £18.50-£21.50, WR £120-£140.

Redlands Farm Banbury Road, Lighthorne, Nr Warwick CV35 0AH
01926 651241   Mrs. Stanton

Open Mar-Sep
3 bedrs (1 double ba/wc; 1 family; 1 single) 1 ba ☼
£B&B £15-£18.50, child rates.

Little Hill Farm Wellesbourne, Warwick CV35 9EB 01789 40261   Mrs. Hutsby

Set in 700 acres of beef and arable farmland, our rambling William & Mary farmhouse offers a warm, friendly relaxed atmosphere, with antiques and beams throughout the house. Each bedroom has private bathroom. Drawing room with colour TV. The farm is situated on A492 Warwick Road from Wellesbourne.

Open all year
6 bedrs all en suite ☼ ♞ ♕♕

Shrewley Pools Farm Haseley, Warwick CV35 7HB 01926 484315
C. W. Dodd

Beautiful 17th Century farmhouse with beamed ceilings, oak floors and open fireplaces set in stunning 1 acre garden. Traditional mixed farm with sheep, cows, pigs and poultry. Take A4177 from Warwick. At Fiveways roundabout take Shrewley Rd. Farm is located ¾ ml on L.

Open Jan-Dec
2 bedrs (1 twin; 1 family ba/wc) 1 ba, 2 wc
🐕 🏠 ⅃ *Listed*
£B&B £18-£24, D £5-£8, WR £120-£16, WR/D £155-£200, child rates.

The Croft Guesthouse Haseley Knob, Warwick CV35 7NL   RAC
01926 484447   Mr. Clapp

Open Jan-Dec
5 bedrs inc (1 twin sh/wc; 1 double sh/wc; 1 single ba/wc) 2 ba 🐕 🐎 ⅃ 👑👑
£B&B £18.50-£30, D £9.50, child rates.

WOOTTON WAWEN

Wootton Park Farm Wootton Wawen, Solihull, Stratford-upon-Avon B95 6HJ
01564 792673   Mrs. McCall

Delightful 16th century half timbered farmhouse, standing in 340 acres of farmland. We have a working dairy farm and guests are welcome to enjoy the friendly atmosphere and the beautiful surroundings. Take the B4089 in the middle of the village, turn over railway, ½ mile on R, go up the long farm drive.

Open all year
3 bedrs (1 double ba/wc; 2 family) 🐕 👑👑
£B&B £18-£22, WR £108-£132, child rates.

SELF CATERING

LEAMINGTON SPA   8B4

Snowford Hall Snowford Hall Farm, Hunningham, Leamington Spa CV33 9ES
01926 632297   R. Hancock

For full farm description see B&B Entry. A425 Southam, outside L roundabout, L Fore Way 3mls, crossroads, turn away from Huntington village, under bridge, 1st R.

🐕 ⅃ 🏠
£Wk £110-£260

WEST MIDLANDS

COVENTRY   8B3

Camp Farm Hob Lane, Balsall Common, West Midlands, Coventry CV7 7GX 01676 533804   Sandra A. Evans

Camp Farm is a mixed farm 7 miles from M6 Jn 4. The farmhouse is about 200 years old and gets its name from when Cromwell used the site for a camp when besieging nearby Kenilworth. Cot and highchair provided. Berkswell Mill, 1826 nearby. From Coventry centre go to Tile Hill and further to Cremwell Lane. Continue driving to Hob Lane.

Open all year
5 bedrs (1 twin; 2 double; 1 family; 1 single) 1 ba, 2 wc 🐕 🏠 🐎
£B&B £14.50-£18.10, D £8, WR £101.50-£126.70, WR/D £157.50-£182.70, child rates.

Mill Farmhouse Mill Lane, Fillongley, Coventry CV7 8EE 01676 541898
                          Mrs. Chamberlain

Beautiful counrty guest house offering peace

and tranquility. Luxury en suite, rooms with colour TV. At junction 9 off ring road take A51 to Tamworth via Radford, follow B4098 to Fillongley, 2nd L crossroads into Mill Ln.

Open Jan-Dec
5 bedrs (2 twin ba/wc, sh/wc; 1 double sh/wc; 2 single ba/wc, sh/wc) 1 ba, 1 wc
🐕(5) 🏠 ⅃ 👑👑👑
£B&B £20-£30, D £8-£10, child rates.

The Byre Lords Hill Farm, Coalpit Lane, Wolston, Coventry CV8 3GB
01203 542098   Mrs. Betty Gibbs

Open all year
3 bedrs (inc 1 twin sh/wc) 1 ba 🐕(5)
👑*Listed*
£B&B £15-£20, WR £100-£130.

SOLIHULL   8A3

Irelands Farm Irelands Lane, Henley-in-Arden, Solihull B95 5SA 01564 792476
RAC
                          Mr. Shaw

Open all year
3 beds (1 twin sh/wc; 2 double ba/wc)

Yew Tree Farm Wootton Wawen,
Solihull B95 6BY 01564 792701
Mrs. Haimes

Open all year

WOLVERHAMPTON 8A3

Moors Farm & Country Restaurant
Chillington Lane, Nr Wolverhampton,
Codsall WV8 1QF   RAC
01902 842330   Mrs. Moreton

100 acre mixed working farm. 200 years old
farmhouse with modern additions situated in a
pretty valley 1 mile from village of Codsall.
Farmhouse is well furnished with some
antiques & oak beams & lovely views from the
windows. Take road from Codsall to Codsall
Wood Village. At 40mph signs turn R into
Chillington Lane. Turn R and 1st R to farm.

Open all year

6 bedrs (2 twin; 3 double inc 2 sh/wc; 1
family sh/wc) 2 ba, 4 wc ☎(4) 🏠 👑👑👑
£B&B £20-£29, D £9-£15, WR £126-£190,
WR/D £186-£250, child rates.

PLACES TO VISIT

DUDLEY

Dudley Canal Trust
Unit 44 High Street, Tipton, Dudley
01121-5205321
Narrow boat trips into Dudley Canal
Tunnel and Singing Cavern limestone
mine. Audio-visual display. Refreshments
only on pre-booked evening trips. On
sale: souvenirs at towpath shop.
Location: signposted off A4123
Birmingham to Wolverhampton road.
Open: Mar-Nov, daily 1000-1700.
Entrance: adults £1.90, child £1.50,
OAP/concessions £1.50 🐕 ♿ 🎒

WEST SUSSEX

HENFIELD 4C4

Great Wapses Farm Henfield
01273 492544   Mrs. Wilkin

Part Tudor, part Georgian farmhouse in
peaceful surroundings with horses. Four
poster bed and tennis court available. On
B2116 Henfield /Albourne Road.

Open all year
5 bedrs (1 twin sh/wc; 3 double inc 2

ba/wc, 1 sh/wc; 1 family sh/wc) ☎ 🐴 cc
AmEx
£B&B £17.50-£22, D £7.50, child rates.

Sparright Farm Rackam, Pulborough,
Henfield RH20 2EY 01798 872132
Mrs. West

This 17th century farmhouse, complete with
inglenook fireplace, makes an ideal base for
touring. Tea/coffee facilities. Surrounded by
peaceful woods, it is located west of the A283
between Pulborough and Storrington.

Closed Xmas and New Year
2 bedrs (1 double; 1 family) 1 ba, 2 wc ☎
🐴 ✕
cc AmEx

HORSHAM 4C3

Black Cottage c/o Newells Farm,
Newells Lane, Lower Beeding, Horsham
RH13 6LN 01403 891326   Mr. Storey

Open all year

Swallows Farm Dial Post, Horsham
RH13 8NN 01403 710385   Bette Sawyer

Swallows Farm has been in the family for over
60 years. It is a 210-acre mixed farm of beef,
sheep, horses and arable crops. Good home
cooking. The farm is just off the A24 at Dial Post.

Open Mar-Nov
3 bedrs (1 twin; 2 double) 1 ba, 2 wc ♿
♨♨

WEST CHILTINGTON   6B2

New House Farm Broadford Bridge
Road, West Chiltington, Pulborough RH20
2LA 01798 812215   Mrs. Steele

Open all year
3 bedrs (2 twin inc 1 ba/wc, 1 sh/wc; 1
double) ♿(10)
£B&B £20-£25, WR £120-£150, child rates.

SELF CATERING

HENFIELD   4C4

Sparright Farm Rackam, Pulborough,
Henfield RH20 2EY 01798 872132
                              Mrs. West

♿ 🐕 cc AmEx

PLACES TO VISIT

PULBOROUGH

Pulborough Brooks
Uppertons Barn Visitor Centre,
Wiggonholt, Pulborough RH20 2EL
01798-875851
A major wetland reserve with impressive
wintering and breeding wildfowl and
waders. In spring, the surrounding
wooded slopes and hedgerows abound
with flowers and songbirds.
Location: on the A283 Pulborough-
Storrington road.
Open: daily 1000-1700.
Entrance: adult £2.50, child 50p
OAP/concession £1.50. WC ♿ ✗ 🦽

WEST YORKSHIRE

BINGLEY

March Cote Farm Cottingley, Bingley
BD16 1UB 01274 487433   L. Jean Warin

Self-catering available in Thimble Cottage,
sleeps 4/5. A605 Bredford- Keighley road , at

Cottergley Bow traffic lights turn right up
B6146 then 1 mile to farm.

Open all year
3 bedrs (1 twin sh; 1 double ba/wc; 1
family) 1 ba, 1 wc ♿ 🏠*Listed*
£B&B £16-£18, D £7-£9, WR £112-£126,
WR/D £161-£189, child rates.

WILTSHIRE

CHIPPENHAM 3F1

Oakfield Farm Easton Piercy Lane, Yatton Keynell, Chippenham SN14 6JU
01249 782355 Mrs. Read

Open Mar-Nov
3 bedrs (1 twin; 1 double; 1 family) 🎠
Listed Commended

CORSHAM 3F1

Boyds Farm Gastard, Corsham SN13 9PT 01249 713146 Mrs. Robinson

This arable working farm lies in the peaceful rural setting of Gastard. The attractive farmhouse is 16th-century with a welcoming atmosphere. Babysitting is offered, and cot and highchair provided. Good pub food close by.

Open all year
3 bedrs (1 twin; 1 double; 1 family) 2 ba, 2 wc 🎠 🏠 ✄

Hatt Farm Old Jockey Box, Corsham SN14 9DJ 01225 742989 Carol Pope

The Pope family warmly invite you to enjoy the peace and comfort of their home. Hatt Farm was built in the 18th century and overlooks the magnificient Wiltshire countryside. It is ideally placed for visiting the many National Trust properties in the area. Situated only 6 miles northeast of the Georgian city of Bath, off the A356/B3109 junction.

Open Jan-Nov
2 bedrs (1 twin ba/wc; 1 family ba/wc) 🎠
👑 *Commended*

Pickwick Lodge Farm Corsham SN13 0PS 01249 712207 Mrs. Gill Stafford

This Grade II listed farmhouse is just 8 miles northeast of Bath. The rooms are spacious, well furnished and fully equipped with all modern conveniences. Guests are welcome to relax in the large garden. Delicious home cooking. Highchair available. Take A4 towards Bath go through Pickwick turn left into Guyers Lane, farm at the bottom on right hand side.

Open Jan-Nov
3 bedrs (1 twin ba/wc; 2 double inc 1 ba/wc, 1 sh/wc) 🎠(5) 🏠 🐕 *Listed*
£B&B £17-£20, WR £119-£140, child rates.

Saltbox Farm Drewetts Mill, Box, Corsham SN14 9PT 01225 742608 M. M. Gregory

Open all year
2 bedrs (1 double; 1 family) 1 ba, 2 wc 🎠
🐕 ✄ 👑 *Commended*
£B&B £14-£16, WR £90, child rates.

DEVIZES 4A3

Lower Foxhanger Farm Rowde, Devizes SN10 1SS 01380 828254 Mrs. Fletcher

This early 18th-century farmhouse is in a quiet, calm setting by the Kennet and Avon Canal. It is 300 yards from the A361, 2 miles west of Devizes. The Caen Hill flight of locks (29) is the longest in the country, (200 yds from the farm).

Open Easter-Oct
3 bedrs (1 twin sh/wc; 1 double, 1 family)
🎠 🐕 👑👑👑

Longwater Farm Erlestoke, Nr Devizes
SN10 5UE 01380 830095   Mrs. Hampton

Open all year
5 bedrs (2 twin ba/wc; 2 double ba/wc; 1
family ba/wc) ☺(7) ⌂ ♉ ♨♨♨
£B&B £20-£25, D £11, WR £140-£165,
WR/D £210-£235, child rates.

MALMESBURY   4A2

Angrove Farm Rodbourne, Malmesbury
SN16 0ET 01666 822982   Mrs. Parfitt

Peacefully situated beef farm. Personal
attention, choice of breakfast menu. TV
lounge for guests, available at any time. Tea &
coffee facilities in all rooms. Each room has
basin & either private or en suite facilities.
A429 to Chippenham Rd, L into Grange Ln 1
1/2mls, L into Angrove Ln, farmhouse at end
of lane.

Open Feb-Nov
3 bedrs (1 twin sh/wc; 2 double sh/wc) ☺ ✂
£B&B £15-£17, WR £91-£105.

Manor Farm Corston, Malmesbury SN16
0HF 01666 822148   Mrs. Eavis

Open Jan-Dec
5 bedrs; (2 twin inc 1 ba/wc; 1 double; 1
family; 1 single) 1 ba, 2 wc ☺ ♨♨
Commended cc Ac Vi
£B&B £16-£22, child rates.

Oakwood Farm Upper Minety,
Malmesbury SN16 9PY 01666 860286

A friendly farming couple welcome you to
their working dairy farm close to the quiet
village of Minety and overlooking the church.
A429 to Credwell.

Open All year, including Xmas.
3 bedrs (1 twin, 2 double) 1 ba, 2 wc ☺ ♉

Listed Commended
£B&B £14.

Stonehill Farm Charlton, Malmesbury
SN16 9DY 01666 823310   Mrs. Edwards

500 year old house on dairy farm. Guests are
welcome to watch the milking and walk the
fields. Self catering in converted barn. Take
B4040 Cricklade Road through village of
Charlton 1 mile on, half way up hill on left.

Open Jan-Dec
3 bedrs (1 twin; 2 double inc 1 sh/wc) 1
ba, 1 wc ☺ ♉ *Listed* cc Ac AmEx Vi
£B&B £14-£20.

Widleys Farm Sherston, Malmesbury
SN16 0PY 01666 840213   Mrs. Hibbard

200 year old Cotswold stone farmhouse on
300-acre mixed working farm. Very peaceful
and quiet but within easy driving of Bath,
Berkeley Castle, Arboretum etc. Sherston turn
opposite Church, R bottom of hill, bear ¾ way
up hill over crossroads taking Alderton Rd, 1st
farm on R.

Open Jan-Dec
3 bedrs (1 twin; 1 double; 1 family) ☺ ⌂
♨
  cc Ac AmEx Vi £B&B £15, D £8, WR £120,
child rates.

MELKSHAM   4A3

Frying Pan Farm Broughton Gifford
Road, Melksham SN12 8LL 01225 702343
B. Pullen

17th Century farmhouse with large garden on
stock rearing farm. Melksham take B3107
Bradford on Avon Rd for 1/3ml, turn R for
Broughton Gifford, go 1/2ml, farm on left
hand side.

Open Jan-Dec
2 bedrs (1 twin; 1 double ba/wc) 2 ba, 2
wc ⚡ 👑👑
£B&B £16-£17.50.

SALISBURY   3F2

Newton Farmhouse Southampton
Road (A 36), Whiteparish, Salisbury SP5
2QL 01794 884416   J. W. Lanham

Open all year
8 bedrs all en suite (6 twin; 2 double) 🐂 ⌂
⚡
£B&B £17.50-£20, D £14.

Templeman Old Farmhouse
Redlynch, Salisbury SP5 2JS 01725 510331
June Dabell

Open Apr-Oct
3 bedrs (1 twin, 1 double, 1 single) 1 ba, 2
wc 🐂(5) ⌂
£B&B £17-£19.

WESTBURY   4A3

Hillside Farmhouse Edington,
Westbury BA13 4PG 01380 830437
C. Mussell

Small working beef farm. Farmhouse in lovely
position with superb views from conservatory

and gardens. Very comfortable rooms. From
Westbury take B3098 to village.

Open Feb-Dec
2 bedrs (1 twin; 1 double) 1 ba, 2 wc 🐂 👑
£B&B £15-£17, child rates.

WOOTTON BASSETT   3F1

Little Cotmarsh Farm Broad Town,
Wootton Bassett, Swindon SN4 7RA
01793 731322   Mrs. Richards

Open all year
3 bedrs (1 twin; 1 double; 1 family sh/wc)
1 ba, 1 wc 🐂
£B&B £15-£18, WR £98-£112, child rates.

SELF CATERING

DEVIZES   4A3

Longwater Farm Erlestoke, Nr Devizes
SN10 5UE 01380 830095   Mrs. Hampton

🐂(7) 🐂
£Wk £180-£375

MALMESBURY   4A2

Stonehill Farm Charlton, Malmesbury
SN16 9DY 01666 823310   Mrs. Edwards

For full farm description see B&B Entry. Take
B4040 Cricklade Road through village of
Charlton 1 mile on, half way up hill on left.

🐂 🐂 ⚏ cc Ac AmEx Vi
£Wk £130-£210

SCOTLAND

BORDERS

GALASHIELS 13E3

Overlangshaw Farm Langshaw, Galashiels TD1 2PE 01896 860244 Sheila Bergius

Traditional whitewashed dairy farm with most comfortable rooms and family atmosphere. Quiet walks through the fields. Southern Upland Way nearby. Sheep and other livestock kept on the farm. A7 1ml N of Galashiels past Golf Course, R at Langshaw sign, 2 mls on then R at T-junction, L at Earlston sign farm 1ml

Open Jan-Dec
3 bedrs (1 twin; 1 double sh/wc; 1 family ba/wc)
£B&B £16-£18, child rates.

HAWICK 15E3

Wiltonburn Farm Hawick
01450 372414 Sheila Shell

A friendly welcome awaits all at this charming farmhouse situated in the peaceful and beautiful surroundings of a 400 acre mixed hill farm at the end of a sheltered valley. A7 from Hawick for 1 ml. R to B711 Roberton Rd, R over bridge. L round corner & 'No Through Road' sign, then end of road

Open Jan-Dec
3 bedrs (1 twin; 1 double; 1 family ba/wc, sh/wc) 2 ba
£B&B £14-£15, D £7.50-£8.50, WR £95-£105, WR/D £50-£55, child rates.

KELSO 13E3

Cliftonhill Farm Ednam, Kelso TD5 7QE 01573 225028 Mrs. Stewart

Cliftonhill is a mixed working farm with cows, sheep, hens, geese and arable. The spacious farmhouse is set amid breathtaking scenery. Full and continental breakfasts are available. The farm lies 2 miles north of Kelso (B6461).

Open all year
3 bedrs (2 twin; 1 family ba/wc) 1 ba, 1 wc

NEWCASTLETON 13E3

Bailey Mill Bailey, Newcastleton TD9 0TR 016977 48617 Mr. Copeland

A small friendly holiday complex in an extended and converted 18th Century grain mill, providing self catering in courtyard

apartments and pony trekking centre. Full
board available in farmhouse for riders and
non riders. Home away from home
atmosphere. Leave M6 at junction 44, A7 to
Longtown, R Bush Hotel, R Bridge Inn T-
junction, follow 6mls until Crossroads, L, 2nd
R.

Open Jan-Dec
4 bedrs (2 twin sh/wc; 2 double sh/wc) ⟡
🐴
£B&B £12-£18, D £6-£8, WR £98-£120,
WR/D £120-£180, child rates.

PEEBLES   13D2

Traquair Bank Innerleithen
01896 830425   Mrs. Caird

The attractive farmhouse of Traquair Bank has
a mellow friendly atmosphere. Children are
made particularly welcome with toys, a safe
garden and the family pets to play with. Cots
and highchairs provided. Good home
cooking.

Open all year
3 bedrs (1 twin, 1 double, 1 family) 2 ba, 2
wc
⟡ 🐴

Langhaugh Kirkton Manor, Peebles
01721 740226   Mrs. Campbell

Open Jan-Dec
3 bedrs (inc 2 twin inc 1 sh/wc) 1 ba ⟡ ⊞
🐴
£B&B £20-£22, D £12-£15, WR £120-£135,
WR/D £190-£225, child rates.

Lyne Farm Peebles EH45 8NR
01721 740255   Arran Waddell

Tastefully decorated Georgian farmhouse
situated on a 1300 acre mixed farm. Tea and
coffee facilities. Also available spacious four
bedroom cottage, sleeps 8. 4 miles west of
Peebles on A72.

Open Jan-Dec
3 bedrs (1 twin; 2 double) 1 ba ⟡ ⊞ 🐴
♨ ♨ ♨ ♨
£B&B £14-£16, WR £90-£105, child rates.

Hamilton Hall West Linton EH46 7DB
01968 60347   Mrs. Dickson

This traditional, sandstone farmhouse was
built in 1886, and stands in 7 acres of
peaceful countryside. There are horses, sheep,
goats and hens. Home-made preserves and
free-range eggs make breakfast special. To
find the farm take the A702/B7059

Open Apr-Oct
2 bedrs (1 double; 1 family) 1 ba ⟡ ⊞ 🐴

SELF CATERING

HAWICK   15E3

Wiltonburn Farm Hawick
01450 372414   Sheila Shell

For full farm description see B&B Entry. A7
from Hawick for 1 ml. R to B711 Roberton Rd,
R over bridge. L round corner & 'No Through
Road' sign, then end of road

£Wk £65-£220

KELSO   13E3

Cliftonhill Farm Ednam, Kelso TD5
7QE 01573 225028   Mrs. Stewart
⟡ 🐴

NEWCASTLETON   13E3

Bailey Mill Bailey, Newcastleton TD9
0TR 016977 48617   Mr. Copeland

For full farm description see B&B Entry. Leave
M6 at junction 44, A7 to Longtown, R Bush
Hotel, R Bridge Inn T-junction, follow 6mls
until Crossroads, L, 2nd R

♿ ⟡ 🐴 ⬚
£Wk £78-£398

PEEBLES 13D2

Lyne Farm Peebles EH45 8NR
01721 740255 Arran Waddell

For full farm description see B&B Entry. 4 miles west of Peebles on A72.

🏕 📞 ⚹

£Wk £170-£300

CENTRAL

CUMBERNAULD 12C2

Bandominie Walton Road, Castlecary, Bonnybridge, Cumbernauld FK4 2HP
01324 840284 Mrs. Forrester

This working farm rears a beef suckler herd. Cots and highchairs provided. The farm lies 2 miles east of Cumbernauld. Antonine Wall 2 miles, Stirling Castle and Wallace's Monument 12 miles.

Open all year
3 bedrs (1 twin; 1 double; 1 single) 1 ba 🏕

DENNY 12C2

Topps Farm Fintry Road, Denny FK6 5JF
RAC
01324 822471 Jennifer Steel

This "chalet-style" farmhouse is set on a beautiful hillside with stunning panoramic views. It is a working sheep and cashmere goat farm. Licenced with superb food. Stirling Castle is 10 miles, Edinburgh 36.

Open all year
8 bedrs (3 twin sh/wc; 4 double inc 1 ba/wc, 3 sh/wc; 1 family sh/wc) 🏕 📞

DUNBLANE 12C1

Inverardoch Mains Farm Dunblane, Doune FK15 9NZ 01786 841268
Mrs. Anderson

Open Mar-Oct
3 bedrs 1 ba 🏕 📞
£B&B £14-£16, child rates.

LINLITHGOW 13D2

Woodcockdale Farm Lanark Road, Linlithgow EH49 6QE 01506 842088
Mrs. Erskine

Open Jan-Dec
4 bedrs (1 twin; 2 double; 1 family) 🏕 📞
£B&B £16, WR £108, child rates.

PORT OF MENTEITH 12C2

Inchie Farm Stirling, Port of Menteith FK8 3JZ 01877 385233 Norma Erskine

Open Apr-Oct
2 bedrs (1 twin; 1 family) 🏕 ⚹ 🐝
£B&B £13-£14, D £8, child rates.

STIRLING 12C2

Lochend Farm Near Stirling, Denny FK6 5JJ 01324 822778 Jean Morton

750 acre upland sheep & suckler farm. Centrally heated, 18th Century farmhouse with tasteful furnishings. Situated overlooking Loch Coulter with panoramic views over unspoilt countryside, yet only 5 miles from M9 jn 9. Junction 9 of M9/M80 take A8708 Stirling, 1st L at Pirnhall, to end of road L follow signs to

Carronbridge, 4mls site L.

Open Mar-Oct
2 bedrs (2 twin) 1 ba ⚡ ♨♨ *Commended*
£B&B £16, child rates.

West Plean Denny Road, Stirling
01786 812208   Moira Johnston

Enjoy warm Scottish farming hospitality in an oasis of peace, with sweeping lawns, walled garden, extensive woodland walks, surrounded by our mixed farm. We offer quality food, spacious comfort, bedrooms en-suite and attentive hosts. Located on the A872 Denny road. 2 minutes from M9/M80 (junction 9).

Open Feb-Nov
6 bedrs ➤ ♨♨ *Commended*

DUMFRIES & GALLOWAY

CASTLE DOUGLAS   12C4

Airds Farm Grossmichael,
Kirkcudbrightshire, Castle Douglas DG7
3BG 01556 670418   Barbara McBride

Open all year

Balannan Farm Ringford, Castle
Douglas DG1, 2AF 0155722 283 Mrs. Millar

Balannan is a beef and sheep farm. Visitors are welcome to walk over the farm and watch farm activities. Leave Castle Douglas by A75 Stanway Rd, drive over River Dee Bridge past the A711 Kirkcudbright Rd, farm sign on right.

Open Jan-Dec
2 bedrs (1 double; 1 family ba/wc) 1 wc ➤
🏠 ➤ ⚡

Craig of Balmaghie Farm Laurieston,
Castle Douglas DG7 2NA 016445 287
Mr. Gordon

Open Mar-Oct
3 bedrs (2 twin inc 1 ba/wc; 1 double ba/wc) 1 ba, 2 wc 🏠
£B&B £14-£18, D £7, WR £91-£112, WR/D £140-£161, child rates.

High Park Balmaclellan, Castle Douglas
DG7 3PT 01644 2298   Jessie E. Shan

Open all year
3 bedrs; 1 ba, 1 wc ➤ ⚡ ♞
£B&B £14, D £7, WR £90, WR/D £140, child rates.

LOCKERBIE   13D4

Nether Boreland Boreland, Lockerbie
DG11 2LL 01576 610248   Mrs. Rae

Nether Boreland is a 200-acre sheep and cattle farm situated in a quiet unspoilt village nestling in the Boreland Hills. Here you will find warm hospitality and country cooking. With over 20 golf courses in the region and fishing available. B723 north of Lockerbie.

Open all year
3 bedrs (1 twin sh/wc; 2 double inc 1 sh/wc) 1 ba, 1 wc ♨♨ *Highly Commended*

MOFFAT   13D3

Ramlodge Guest House High Street,
Moffat DG10 9RU 01683 20594 Mr. Murray

Open all year
5 bedrs; 1 ba ♞
£B&B £14.50-£15.

NEWTON STEWART   12C4

Auchenleck Farm Minnigaff, Newton
Stewart DG8 7AA 01671 402035
Mrs. Hewitson

Open Easter-Oct
3 bedrs (1 twin ba/wc; 2 double inc 1 ba/wc, 1 sh/wc) ➤ 🏠 ♨♨
£B&B £17.50-£18, WR £119-£122.50, child rates.

WHITHORN 12C4

Baltier Farm Whithorn DG8 8HA
01988 600241 Mrs. Forsyth

Open Feb-Nov
3 bedrs (1 twin; 2 double) 1 ba, 2 wc
☎Listed
£B&B £14-£15, child rates.

SELF CATERING

CASTLE DOUGLAS 12C4

Balannan Farm Ringford, Castle
Douglas DG1 2AF 0155722 283
Mrs. Millar

Balannan is a beef and sheep farm. Visitors
are welcome to walk over the farm and watch
farm activities.

Leave Castle Douglas by A75 Stanway Rd,
drive over River Dee Bridge past the A711
Kirkcudbright Rd, farm sign on right.

☎ ♞
£Wk £130-£310

KIRKCUDBRIGHT 12C4

High Kirkland Cottages Cannee Farm,
Kirkcudbright DG6 4XD 01557 330684
Mrs. Dunlop

☎ ♞
£Wk £110-£270

FIFE

AUCHTERMUCHTY 13D1

Ardchoille Farmhouse *Highly Acclaimed*
Dunshalt, Auchtermuchty KY14 7ER RAC
01337 828414 Mr. Steven

Open Jan-Dec
3 bedrs (3 twin inc 1 ba/wc, 2 sh/wc) ☎
🌢🌢🌢 cc Ac Vi
£B&B £25-£35, D £20.

ST ANDREWS 13E1

Spinkstown Farmhouse St Andrews
KY16 8PN 01334 473475 Mrs. Duncan

A uniquely designed farmhouse with views of
the sea and surrounding countryside. Bright
and spacious with tastefully decorated rooms
with ensuite facilities. Dining room & lounge
with TV. 2 miles from St Andrews on A917
Coast Road to Crail, 3rd farmhouse on right,
name at bottom of drive.

Open Jan-Dec
3 bedrs (1 twin ba/wc, 2 double ba/wc,
sh/wc) 1 wc ☎
£B&B £17-£18, D £10-£12, child rates.

GRAMPIAN

BANFF 15F3

Bankhead Croft Gamrie, Banff AB45 3HN 01261 851584 Mrs. Smith

Delightful modern country cottage with ensuite facilities.Tea facilities and home cooking. House on one level with disabled facilities. From Banff take A88 Fraserburgh Road for 6 miles, sign for Bankhead Croft is on the right.

Open Jan-Dec
4 bedrs (2 twin; 1 double; 1 family) 1 ba, 2 wc ᗾ ᵺ ᵺ ᴥ *Commended*
£B&B £14, D £7, WR £93, WR/D £136, child rates.

Clayfolds Farm Alvah, Banff AB45 3UD 01261 821288 Mrs. Addison

Open Mar-Oct
3 bedrs (1 twin; 1 double; 1 family) 1 ba, 1 wc ᗾ ᵺ ⚘
£B&B £15, WR/D £100, child rates.

The Palace Farm Banff AB45 3HS 01261 851261 Mrs. Duncan

18th century farmhouse, on family run mixed arable farm. Beautiful rugged clifftop coast. Off the A98 Fraserburgh- Banff road.

Open March- November
3 bedrs (1 twin; 1 double; 1 family) ᗾ ᵺ
£B&B £15-£17, D £9-£11, WR £98-£119, WR/D £161-£196, child rates.

INVERURIE 15F3

Earlsfield Kennethmont, Insch AB52 6YQ 014643 473 Mrs. Grant

Open Jan-Dec
3 bedrs (1 twin; 1 family; 1 single) 2 ba ᗾ ᵺ ᵺ
£B&B £14-£16, WR £14-£16, child rates.

KEITH 15E3

The Haughs Farm Keith AB55 3QN 01542 882238 Mrs. Jackson

Open Apr-Oct
4 bedrs (1 twin sh/wc; 2 double inc 1 ba/wc, 1 sh/wc; 1 family) ᗾ(1) ᵺ ᵺ ᵺ *Commended*
£B&B £15-£18, D £10-£11, child rates.

SELF CATERING

HUNTLY 15E3

Monedie Aberchirder, By Huntly AB54 5PL 01466 780287 Shena Bowle
ᗾ ᵺ
£Wk £120-£200

PLACES TO VISIT

CRIMOND

Loch of Strathbeg RSPB Nature Reserve
Starnafin, Crimond, Fraserburgh AB43 4YN 01346-532017
A large shallow loch separated from the sea by wide sand dunes and bordered by freshwater fen, salt marsh and woodland. Location: off the A952 Crimond, 30 miles north of Aberdeen.
Open: dawn to dusk.
Entrance: £1, RSPB members free. WC

HIGHLAND

BEAULY   15D3

Rheindown Farm Beauly IV4 7AB
01463 782461   Mrs. Ritchie
Open Apr-Oct
2 bedrs (1 twin; 1 family) 1 ba, 1 wc ☾ ♉
☙ *Commended*

FORT AUGUSTUS   14C4

The Old Pier Fort Augustus H32 4BX
01320 6418   Mrs. Mackenzie
This charming farmhouse was built over 100
years ago, but has recently been modernised
and extended. It lies half a mile north of Fort
Augustus on a private road alongside Loch
Ness.

Open Mar-Nov
3 bedrs (1twin sh/wc; 1 double sh/wc; 1
family ba/wc) 1ba, 1wc ☾ ✗ ☙☙☙
Commended

GAIRLOCH   14B2

Duisary Strath, Gairloch 01445 2252
M. Mackenzie

This is a modernised croft house which has
exellent views of the sea and hills, looking
over Loch Gairloch. The croft is mostly used
for grazing cattle and sheep. Gairloch is on
the A832, 60 miles west of Dingwall.

Open Apr-Oct
3 bedrs (1 twin; 1 double; 1 family) 2 ba, 3
wc ☾ ♉ ☙☙ *Commended*

INVERNESS   15D3

Balaggan Farm Culloden Moor,
Inverness IV1 2EL 01463 790213
                               Phyllis Alexander

This comfortable farmhouse set in quiet,
peaceful countryside, close to Clava Cairns
and standing stones. 1 family and 1 twin
bedroom. Relax in front of open peat fire in
sitting room with colour TV. Sample the warm
hospitality and the good home cooking.

Open Apr - Oct
2 bedrs (1 twin; 1 family) ☾ ♉

Borlum Farmhouse Drumnadrochit,
Inverness IV3 6XN 01456 450358
                             Duncan McDonald-Haig

This traditional farmhouse commands a
spectacular view over Loch Ness. Borlum with
its friendly atmosphere is a working hill farm
stocking sheep and suckler cows, with its own
BHS approved riding centre, making it the
ideal place for a riding holiday.

Open all year.
15 bedrs ☾ ♉ ✗ ☙☙ *Commended*

Daviot Mains Farm Daviot, Inverness
IV1 2ER 01463 772215
                              Margaret Hutchison

Open all year
3 bedrs (1 twin sh/wc; 1 double sh/wc, 1
family) 1 ba, 1 wc
£B&B £16-£21, D £10.

Woodside of Culloden Westhill,
Inverness IV1 2BP 01463 790242
                               Margaret Maclean

Open May-Oct
3 bedrs (2 twin sh/wc; 1 double sh/wc) 1
ba ☾ ☙☙☙ *Highly Commended*

MUIR-OF-ORD   15D3

Gilchrist Farm Muir-of-Ord IV6 7RS
Ann B.G. Fraser

Open all year
✗

ISLE OF SKYE   14A3

Cnoc Preasach Snizort, Isle of Skye
IV51 01470 42406   Mr. Nicolson

This 100-acre sheep farm is set in peaceful
countryside 12 miles north of Portree on the
A856.

Open Mar-Oct
3 bedrs (1 twin; 1 double; 1 family) 1 ba, 1
wc ☼ ♠ ♔

LATHERON   15E1

Upper Latheron Farm Caithness,
Latheron KW5 6DT 015934 224
                        Camilla Sinclair

Oustanding views of the coast can be found
at a farm which is surrounded by a wealth of
animal life. The farm is an excellent base for
touring the Highlands. 20 miles South of Wick
on the A9

Open all year
3 bedrs (1 twin; 1 double; 1 family) 1 ba, 2
wc ☼ ⌸ *Highly Commended*

PLOCKTON   14B3

Achnahenich Farm Plockton IV52 8TY
0159984 238   Mrs. Townend

The croft house was built in 1900 and has
been comfortably modernised. Situated in a
secluded glen, this is a friendly working farm
with beef cattle and sheep.

Open all year
3 bedrs (2 twin; 1 family sh/wc) 1 ba ☼
£child rates.

Craig Highland Farm Plockton, Ross-
shire IV52 8UB 01599 544205

Mrs. Heaviside

This converted croft house is an open rare
breeds farm where you can feed sheep, goats,
pigs, poultry, waterfowl and even a llama.
There are wonderful views over Loch Carron
and a private coral beach. Children's games,
toys and cot available. The farm is midway
between Plockton and Stromeferry on the
shore road west of the A890.

Open all year
3 bedrs (1 twin; 1 double; 1 family) 1 ba, 1
wc ☼ ♠ ♔♔♔ *Commended*
£B&B £14-£15, child rates.

SPEAN BRIDGE   14C4

Old Pines Gairlochy Road, Spean Bridge
PH34 4EG 01397 712324   B. & S. Barber

This is a scandanavian-style log house quietly
set in 30 acres with breathtaking views to Ben
Nevis. All bedrooms are on the ground floor,
3 are specially equipped for wheelchairs.
Holiday Care Award – best small hotel in
Britain 1994. Old Pines is a paradise for
children. Friendly atmosphere with good food
– represented Scotland in regional cuisine
competition. One mile north of Spean Bridge
(B8004/ A82)

Open all year
8 bedrs (2 twin sh/wc; 2 double sh/wc; 2
family sh/wc; 2 single sh/wc) 1 ba ☼ ⚅ ♠
⚡ ♔♔♔
£child rates.

ULLAPOOL   14C2

Clisham Rhue, Ullapool IV26 2TJ
01854 612498   Mrs. Campbell

The croft house stands on 10 acres of arable
land, 3 miles northwest of Ullapool. The local

area has boat trips, fishing, an interesting museum and many pleasant walks. 3 miles northwest of Ullapool (A835).

Open May-Oct
2 bedrs (2 family) 1 ba, 1 wc ☎(3) ♕ £child rates.

SELF CATERING

KINGUSSIE 15D4

Alvie Holiday Cottages Alvie Estate Office, Kingussie PH21 1NE
01540 651255 David Kinnear

Open all year

LATHERON 15E1

Upper Latheron Farm Caithness, Latheron KW5 6DT 015934 224
Camilla Sinclair

For full farm description see B&B Entry. 20 miles South of Wick on the A9

☎ ⊬

PLACES TO VISIT

BOAT OF GARTEN

RSPB Abernethy Forest Reserve
Loch Garten, Nr Boat of Garten
One of the finest areas of Caledonian pinewood left in Scotland. Crested tits, crossbills, red squirrels and ospreys. Location: off the Boat of Garten-Nethybridge road.
Open: reserve at all times. Osprey centre and shop open Apr-Aug, daily 1000-2000. Entrance: adult £2 child 50p
OAP/concession £1. ⅙ ☎

LOTHIAN

EAST CALDER 13D2

Ashcroft Farmhouse Ashcroft Farm, East Calder EH53 0ET 01506 881810
Elizabeth Scott

Open all year

EDINBURGH 13D2

Dunsyre Mains Dunsyre, Carnwath, Lanark ML11 8NG 0189981 251
Mr. Armstrong

Open Jan-Dec
3 bedrs (1 twin; 1 double; 1 family) 1 ba, 1 wc ☎ ⌂ ♘
£B&B £14, D £9, WR £98, WR/D £160, child rates.

HADDINGTON 13E2

Barney Mains Farm Haddington EH41 3SA 01620 880310 Mrs. Kerr

Beautiful farmhouse, tastefully decorated, comfortably furnished with large, spacious rooms. Spectacular views. Mixed farm of 580 acres. ½ mile east of Haddington sign posted ¾ mile off A1.

Open Mar-Nov
3 bedrs (2 twin; 1 double) 2 ba, 2 wc ☎ ⌂
£B&B £15-£20, WR £103-£140, child rates.

Eaglescairnie Mains Gifford, Haddington EH41 4HN 01620 810491
Mrs. Williams

Open Jan-Dec
4 bedrs (1 twin; 2 double ba/wc; 1 single) 1 ba, 3 wc ☎ ⌂ ♘ ♕♕
£B&B £16-£20, child rates.

STRATHCLYDE

AIRDRIE 12C2

Easter Glentore Farm Greengairs, Airdrie ML6 7TJ 01236 830243
Mrs. Hunter

This early 18th century, single storey, farmhouse is set on a 245-acre stock farm with panoramic views. The tasteful, comfortable rooms have tea/coffee facilities. Homemade shortbread and home baking are offered in the lounge in the evenings.

Open all year
3 bedrs (3 double inc 1 sh/wc) 1 ba ⌂
♚♚ *Highly Commended*

AYR 12C3

Fisherton Farm Dunure, Ayr KA7 4LF
01292 500223
Maureen Wilcox

A traditional Scottish farmhouse set on a working dairy, beef and arable farm with lovely sea views. Cot and ground floor bedrooms available. 5 miles south of Ayr (A719)

Open Mar-Nov
2 bedrs (2 twin ba/wc) ⌂ ⋔ ♚

Meikle Auchengree Glengarnock, Beith, Ayr KA14 3BU 01294 832205
Mrs. Workman

This is a 250-acre dairy farm with a large farmhouse in a lovely setting with views of the loch. There is a big games room with indoor bowling mat, pool table and table tennis. Cot and ground floor bedrooms provided. The farm is north of A737 Beith-Dalry

Open all year
3 bedrs (1 twin; 2 double inc 1 sh/wc) 1 ba, 2 wc ⌂ ⌂ ⋔ ♚♚

BARRHEAD 12C2

East Uplaw Uplawmoor, Barrhead
01505 850383
Mrs. McLeod
Open all year

4 bedrs (1 twin; 2 double; 1 family) 2 ba ⌂ ⌂ ⋔ *Commended*

BIGGAR 13D3

Howburn Farm Elsrickle, Biggar ML12 6QZ 01899 81276
A. Barrie

This traditional 18th-century farmhouse has a warm and friendly atmosphere. The farm covers 830 acres, comprising mainly beef cattle and sheep, and is located 5 miles north east of Biggar on the A721.

Open all year
2 bedrs (1 twin; 1 double) 1 ba, 1 wc ⌂ ⌂
⋔ ⌤

South Mains Farm Skirling, Biggar ML12 6HF 01899 6226
R. Harper

A working, family farm with beef cattle and sheep. Good views of the surrounding countryside. Centrally heated and well furnished farmhouse. On B7016 between Biggar and Broughton

Open Jan-Dec
3 bedrs (2 double, 1 single) 2 ba, 2 wc ⌂ ⌂ ⋔
£B&B £11-£12.50, child rates.

CAMPBELTOWN 12B3

Mains Farm Carradale, Campbeltown
PA28 6QG 01563 3216   Mrs. MacCormick

Open Apr-Oct
3 bedrs (1 double; 1 family; 1 single) 1 ba
🛇 🏋
£B&B £13.50, D £5.50, WR £94.50, WR/D
£133, child rates.

DALMALLY 12B1

Rockhill Farm and Guest House
Ardbrecknish, Argyll, Dalmally PA33 1BH
018663 218   Mrs. Whalley

Rockhill is a 200-acre Hanoverian horse stud
and sheep farm with a long shoreline on the
south side of Loch Awe. On the loch there is
free fishing, boating and bathing. The farm
has show mares and foals, a miniature
Shetland pony and donkey. Licensed. B&B,
off the A819 south of Dalmally.

Open mid May-Sept
5 bedrs (1 twin ba/wc; 1 double ba/wc; 3
family ba/wc) 🛇(12) 🏠 🏋 🐾

DUMBARTON 12C2

Lea Farm Cardross, Dumbarton G82
5EW 01389 63035   Mrs. Russell

Open Apr-Oct
2 bedrs (1 twin; 1 family) 1 ba, 1 wc 🛇

GARTOCHARN 12C2

Mardella Farmhouse Old School Road,
Gartocharn GS3 8SO   RAC
01389 830428   Mrs. Sally MacDonell

Open all year
3 bedrs; 1 ba 🛇 🏋
£B&B £16.50-£40.

GIRVAN 12B3

Blair Farm Barrhill, Ayrshir, Girvan
01465 82247   Mrs. Hughes

A family-run, beef and sheep farm of 180
acres ideally situated for touring south west
Scotland. Situated 12 miles south east of
Girvan on the A714. Spacious rooms, tasteful
decor and good home cooking. Fishing

available on the farm.

Open Apr-Oct
2 bedrs (1 double; 1 family) 1 ba 🛇 🏠 🏋
🐾🐾 *Commended*
£B&B £14, D £8, WR £91, WR/D £133,
child rates.

Glengennet Farm Barr, Girvan KA26
9TY 01465 86220   Vera Dunlop

Former shooting lodge now a comfortable
farmhouse with lovely views in a quiet
location. Barr signposted from A77
roundabout, north end from Barr take
Glenginnet Road 1 ½ miles left, 100 yards left.

Open May-Oct
2 bedrs (1 twin ba/wc; 1 double) 🛇 🏠
🐾🐾 *Commended*
£B&B £17, WR £119, child rates.

Hawkhill Farm Old Dailly, Girvan
KA26 9RD 01465 871232   Mrs. Kyle

Open Mar-Oct
3 bedrs (1 twin ba/wc; 2 double sh/wc) 🛇
🏋 🐾🐾 *Highly Commended*
£B&B £17.50-£18, D £8-£10.50, WR £119,
child rates.

Maxwelston Farm Dailly, Girvan KA26
9RH 01465 81210   Mrs. Whiteford

Our 200 year old, listed farmhouse has been tastefully decorated and offers a peaceful lounge with coal fire, separate dining room and a large garden in which to relax. Take B734 at Girvan A77 roundabout, keep on road for 5 miles, farm is right of main road.

Open April-Oct
2 bedrs (1 twin; 1 double) ☎ 🏠 🐾 ⅏ ♨
£B&B £14, D £8, child rates.

ISLE OF ARRAN 12B2

Rosebank Farm Corriecravie, Isle of Arran KA27 8PD 01770 870228
Mrs. Manson

Open Jan-Dec
3 bedrs (2 double; 1 single) 1 ba, 2 wc ☎ 🏠 ♨♨ *Commended*
£B&B £15-£17, WR £100-£125, child rates.

KILBARCHAN 12C2

Pannell Farm Kilbarchan Road, Bridge of Weir, Kilbarchan PA11 3RN
01505 612480 Mrs. McIntyre

Milking can be viewed twice daily on this working dairy and sheep farm. There are also calves and lambs. The comfortable house was built in 1826. Cots, highchairs and games provided. The farm is 10 miles from Glasgow, M8 J29/A761 via Kilbarchan.

Open all year
3 bedrs (1 double; 1 family sh/wc; 1 single) 3 ba, 1 wc ☎ 🐾
£child rates.

KILMARNOCK 12C3

Hillhouse Farm Grassyards Road, Kilmarnock 01563 23370 M. Howie

Spacious, very comfortable house on a working dairy farm with central heating, large bedrooms, lounge and dining room. From A77 (Glasgow to Ayr Rd) take B7082 for Kilmarnock and at top head towards country. Site is ½ mile on right.

Open Jan-Dec
3 bedrs (1 twin; 2 family inc 1 sh/wc) ☎ 🐾 ♨♨
£B&B £13-£16, child rates.

Laigh Todhill Farm Rowallan Castle Estate, Fenwick, Kilmarnock KA3 2LW
01563 40354 Lenice Bell

Laigh Todhill is a working farm with many rare breeds, horses, sheep and pigs. The period farmhouse offers panoramic views. The farm is 3 miles north of Kilmarnock, A77/B751.

Open Mar- Oct
3 bedrs (1 twin; 1 double; 1 family) 2 ba, 2 wc ☎ 🐾 ♨♨ *Commended*

LANARK 13D2

Craighead Farm Abington, Biggar ML12 6SQ 01864 502356 Mrs. Hodge

Open May-Nov
2 bedrs (1 twin; 1 double) 2 ba, 1 wc ☎ 🏠 ♨
£B&B £15-£16, D £6.50-£7.50, child rates.

Hillhouse Farm Sandilands, Lanark
01555 88661 J. Lamb

This 17th-century farmhouse has a warm and comfortable atmosphere. Hillhouse is a working farm, mainly beef and sheep. The farm also has a stud of Clydesdale horses. Cot and highchair available Situated south of Lanark off the A70 near Douglas Water.

Open all year
2 bedrs (1 double; 1 family) 1 ba, 1 wc ☎ 🐾

LARGS 12B2

South Whittlieburn Farm Brisbane Glen, Largs KA30 8SN 01475 675881
Mary Watson

Attractive working sheep farm in peaceful Brisbane Glen. Lovely walks along the river, or get spectacular scenic views from hillside.

Turn R off A78 in Largs just past swimming pool, at signpost for Brisbane Glen road, for 2 miles. 2nd farm on left.

Open all year
3 bedrs (1 twin; 1 double ba/wc; 1 family)
2 ba ⛺ 🏠 ♨️♨️ *Commended*
£B&B £15.50, child rates.

MAYBOLE 12C3

Three Thorns Farm Straiton, Nr Maybole KA19 7QR 01655 7221
H. R. Henry

Open all year
4 bedrs (1 twin sh; 1 double sh/wc; 1 family sh/wc; 1 single sh) 1 ba, 2 wc ⛺ 🐕 ♨️♨️

SELF CATERING

AYR 12C3

Fisherton Farm Dunure, Ayr KA7 4LF
01292 500223 Maureen Wilcox

One 3 Bedroom unit, sleeps 6-8.

5 miles south of Ayr (A719)

⛺ 🐕

Gadgirth Cottages Gadgirth Mains Farm, Nr Annbank, Ayr KA6 5AJ
01292 520721 Mr. Hendry

Four cottages gathered around a cobbled courtyard have been imaginatively converted from barns, stables and haylofts. The cottages have 1-2 bedrooms, sleeping 2-4. Gadgirth Mains is 6 miles from Ayr (A70/B742). Championship golf course nearby.

♿ ⛺ 🐕
£Wk £100-£380

BIGGAR 13D3

Carmichael Home Farm Carmichael, Biggar ML12 6PG 01899 3336
Mr. Carmichael

A unique time capsule of integrated land stewardship. This estate combines agriculture and forestry with deer, sheep and cattle, a barley malting and timber mill. There are 10 cottages with 1-4 bedrooms, sleeping 2-9. The farm is 6 miles west of Biggar.

DALMALLY 12B1

Rockhill Farm and Guest House
Ardbrecknish, Argyll, Dalmally PA33 1BH
018663 218 Mrs. Whalley

A cottage and a bungalow are offered for self-catering holidays. The cottage is a traditional stone built building, and the bungalow is a capacious cedarwood bungalow. Both sleep up to 6.

B840, off the A819 south of Dalmally.

GIRVAN 12B3

Glengennet Farm Barr, Girvan KA26 9TY 01465 86220 Vera Dunlop

For full farm description see B&B Entry. Barr signposted from A77 roundabout, north end from Barr take Glenginnet Road 1 ½ miles left, 100 yards left.

£Wk £105-£280

ISLE OF MULL 12A1

Croig Dervaig, Isle of Mull PA75 6QS
01926 400219 Mrs. Galbraith

This stone-built croft house is on a beef and sheep stock farm which overlooks a tiny harbour off the B8073 between Dervaig and Tobermory. There are 3 bedrooms, sleeps 6. Ideal base for hill walking and nature watching.

KILMARNOCK 12C3

Hillhouse Farm Grassyards Road, Kilmarnock 01563 23370 M. Howie

For full farm description see B&B Entry. From A77 (Glasgow to Ayr Rd) take B7082 for Kilmarnock and at top head towards country. Site is ½ mile on right.

£Wk £120-£295

PLACES TO VISIT

KINROSS

Vane Farm RSPB Nature Reserve
Loch Leven, Kinross 01577-862355
Farmland with wet grasslands and pools, scrub and woodland plus open hills with spectacular views of Loch Leven. Location: on south side of Loch Leven on B9097 2 miles east of M90.
Open: reserve at all times. Shop and centre open Apr-Dec 1000-1700, Jan-Mar 1000-1600.
Entrance: adult £2 child 50p OAP/Concessions £1. WC ♿ ⚒

TAYSIDE

BRECHIN   15F4

Blibberhill Farm Brechin DD9 6TH
01304 830225   Mrs. Stewart

18th Century farmhouse on a 300 acre beef/arable farm in peaceful, rural surroundings with a conservatory, dining room and lounge. Clock radio, TV's, electric blankets, tea & coffee facilities in rooms. Take B9134 for about 4 miles, after passing Netherton Garage take 1st left (signed Melgund), then 1st left again.

Open Jan-Dec
3 bedrs (2 twin sh/wc; 1 double ba/wc) 1 ba ✠ ♨♨♨
£B&B £14.50, D £8.50.

Tillygloom Farm Brechin DD9 7PE
01356 622953   Lorna Watson

Tillygloom is a traditional stone-built house on 80 acres of mixed arable farm with soft fruit, potatoes and cereals. Set in a large, peaceful garden, the house is 1.5 miles north of Brechin. Country walks, local golf course and Steam Railway.

Open Apr-Oct
2 bedrs (1 twin ba/wc; 1 family ba/wc) 1 ba, 1 wc ♨ ▦ *Listed Commended*
£B&B £13, D £6.50, WR £130.

Wood of Auldbar Farmhouse
Aberlemno, Brechin DD9 6SZ
01307 830218   Jean Stewart

Arable/mixed farm of 187 acres with a well-appointed farmhouse in a peaceful location. All home cooking, baking and preserves. Tea facilities and smoke alarms.. From Brechin take B9134 drive 1 ½ mls, fork left to Pitkennedy, drive 3 mls, farm sits on right.

Open Jan-Dec
3 bedrs (1 twin; 1 family; 1 single) ♨ ▦ ✠
Listed Commended
£B&B £14.50, D £9, child rates.

CLEISH   13D1

Ardgairney Farm Kinros, Cleish
01577 850233   Mr. Lawrie

Open all year
3 bedrs (1 twin; 2 double inc 1 ba/wc) 1 ba
☼ ⌂ ♄

CRIEFF   13D1

Concraig Farm Crieff PH7 4HH
01764 653237   Mrs. Scott

Comfortable farmhouse with large rooms on
an arable farm. Peacefully situated in a lovely
garden. 1 ½ miles south of Crieff on A822.
Farm is on right with 2 white stones at
entrance.

Open Apr-Oct
3 bedrs (1 twin; 2 double; 1 family) 1 ba ☼
£B&B £14.50-£16, WR £90-£100, child rates.

DUNKELD   13D1

Scotson Trochry, Dunkeld PH8 0ED
01350 725225   Marcia Lash

Open all year
2 bedrs (1 double; 1 family sh/wc) 1 ba, 1
wc ⌂ ♄

Stralochy Farm Spittalfield, By Murthly,
Dunkeld PH1 4LQ 01738 71447 Agnes W.
Smith

Stralochy is situated in an elevated postion
with beautiful views. Located 4 miles east of
Dunkeld off the A984. Malting barley,
potatoes and sheep are produced. Fishing on
the River Tay in close proximity.

Open Apr-Oct
3 bedrs (1 twin, 1 double, 1 family) 2 ba ☼
⌂ ♄

Tirchardie Farm Glen Quaich,
Amulree, Dunkeld PH8 0DE
01350 725266   Christine Simpkins

This is an old-fashioned farmhouse with
sheep, hens and ducks. Cots, highchairs,
ground floor bedrooms and a play area are
provided. The farm offers lovely walks. Water
sports at Loch Tay and Kenmore 6 miles. A822
Crieff-Aberfeldy road.

Open all year
4 bedrs (1 twin; 1 double; 1 family; 1
single) 2 ba, 2 wc ☼ ⌂ ♄

FORFAR   13E1

Wemyss Farm Montrose Road, Forfar,
Forfar DD8 2TB 01307 462887
Mrs. Lindsay

Open Jan-Dec
2 bedrs (1 double; 1 family) 2 ba, 2 wc ☼
⌂ ♄ cc Ac Vi
£B&B £14, D £8, child rates.

West Mains of Turin Farmhouse
Rescobie, Forfar, DD8 2TE 01307 830229
Mrs. Jolly

This is a family-run stock farm with panoramic
views over Rescobie Loch. The farmhouse is
warm and welcoming, with croquet in the
large garden and snooker available. Excellent
home cooking, cots and children's games
provided. B9113 Montrose road, approx. 4
miles. 2nd farm on left after Rescobie Church
and Loch.

Open Mar-Oct
3 bedrs (1 double sh/wc; 1 family sh/wc; 1
single) 1 ba, 1 wc ☼ ♨♨ *Commended*
£B&B £14-£16, D £7-£8, WR £91-£105,
WR/D £140-£160, child rates.

KIRRIEMUIR   15E4

Purgavie Farm Lintrathen, Kirriemuir
01575 560213   Moira Clark

Open Jan-Dec
3 bedrs (1 twin ba/wc; 1 double; 1 family)
☼ ⌂ ♄ ♨♨♨ *Highly Commended*
£B&B £14-£16, D £8-£10, WR £98-£112,
WR/D £154-£182, child rates.

PERTH   13D1

Fingask Farm Rhynd, Perth PH2 8QF
01738 812220   Mrs. Stirrat

Open Feb-Nov
3 bedrs (1 twin; 1 double; 1 single) 2 ba, 2
wc ☟ *Listed*
£B&B £15, D £4.50-£9, child rates.

Stanley Farm Stanley, by Perth PH1
4QQ 01738 828334   Mrs. Howden

This 200-acre farm is mixed arable, sheep and
cattle. There is a play area for children and a
separate dining room and lounge. Tea/coffee
facilities.

Open Apr-Oct
2 bedrs (1 double; 1 family) 2 ba, 2 wc ☟
⅄ *Listed Commended*
£B&B £13-£15, D £8-£10, WR £85-£95,
WR/D £130-£160, child rates.

SELF CATERING

BLAIRGOWRIE   13D1

Fyal Farm Clunie, Alyth, Blairgowrie
PH11 8LE 01828 32997   Mrs. Ferguson
& ☟ ♞
2 units; 4 bedrs
£Wk £100-£200

BRECHIN   15F4

Tillygloom Farm Brechin DD9 7PE
01356 622953   Lorna Watson

Tillygloom is a traditional stone-built house on
80 acres of mixed arable farm with soft fruit,
potatoes and cereals. Country walks, local
Golf course and Steam Railway.

☟

KIRRIEMUIR   15E4

Purgavie Farm Lintrathen, Kirriemuir
01575 560213   Moira Clark

£Wk £150-£350

WALES

CLYWYD

DENBIGH 6C1

Ty Coch Farm Llangynhafal, Denbigh
LL16 4LN 01824 790423 A. Lloyd Richards

Closed Xmas
2 bedrs (1 twin; 1 family) 1 ba, 1 wc ☼ ⌂
⚥ ♚
£child rates.

HOLYWELL 7D1

Greenhill Farm Holywell CH8 7QF ⛨
01352 713270 Mrs. Jones

This beautifully modernised 16th-century
farmhouse stands on 120 acres of mixed
farmland with milking and pedigree herds,
and some barley. The house looks over the
Dee estuary and can be found just outside the
small town of Holywell. Tea/coffee facilities

Open Mar-Nov
3 bedrs (3 double inc 1 ba/wc) 2 ba ☼ ⌂
£DB&B £32.

MOLD 7D1

Plas Penucha Caerwys, Mold CH7 5BH
01352 720210 Mrs. Price

Small working farm. The farmhouse is in parts
500 years old and has many associations with

Welsh literature and politics. Fine views. A541
towards Denbigh. After 8 miles turn right to
Caerwys.Take road to Pen-y-Cefn for 1
mile.Turn left to Tremmeirchion.

Open all year
4 bedrs (2 twin inc 1 sh/wc; 2 double inc 1
sh/wc) 1 ba, 2 wc ☼ ⌂ ♞ ⚥ ♚♚ *Highly
Commended*
£B&B £16.50, D £10, WR £105, WR/D £150,
child rates.

RUTHIN 7D1

Llanbenwch Farm Llanfair DC, Ruthin
01824 702340 Mrs. Jones

This 13th-century farmhouse has all modern
comforts as well as its period charm. It stands
on a mixed farm of 40 acres. Tea/coffee
facilities and TV. The 40-acre mixed farm is
set in superb scenery and convenient to all
beauty spots. On A525- 3 miles south of
Ruthin.

Open Mar-Oct
3 bedrs (1 twin; 1 double, 1 family) 1 ba, 2
wc ☼(5) ♚ *Highly Commended*
£B&B £13, D £5, WR £85, WR/D £115,
child rates.

ST ASAPH 6C1

Bach-y-Graig *Acclaimed* Tremeirchion,
St Asaph LL17 0UH ⛨
01745 730627 Mr. Roberts

Bach-y-Graig is a 200-acre farm with a variety
of animals. The large 16th-century listed
farmhouse nestles at the foot of the Clwydian
Range with wonderful views over the
surrounding countryside. The farm is off the
A541 from Trefnant (A525).

Open all year
☼ ⌂ ⚥ ♚♚♚ *Highly Commended*

DYFED

ABERPORTH 6B3

Penbontbren Farm Hotel Glynarthen,
Cardigan, Aberporth SA44 6PE   **RAC**
01239 810248   Mr. Humphries

Open all year
10 bedrs all en suite ❄ ⌂ ♞ cc Ac AmEx Vi
£B&B
£35-£68, D £13, WR/D £290-£301.

ABERYSTWYTH 6B3

Erwbarfe Farmhouse Devil's Bridge,
Aberystwyth SY23 3JR 01970 890251
Mrs. Lewis

400 mixed hill farm. Spectacular views. Old
stone farmhouse, fresh home cooking, warm
& friendly welcome. Take the A44 to
Ponterwyd then the A4120 to Devil's Bridge.
Farm 2 miles on left.

Open April-Sept
2 bedrs (1 double; 1 family) 1 ba, 1 wc ❄
♨
£B&B £16-£18, D £6-£8, WR £110-£120,
WR/D £150-£200, child rates.

CARDIGAN 6B4

Croft Farm Guesthouse & Cottages
Llantood, Cardigan SA43 3NT
01239 615179   Andy & Sylvie Gow

We are a small holding with a variety of farm
animals to help feed. The farmhouse has been
converted to guesthouse with emphasis on
home-away-from-home feel. Take A487
towards Fishguard. 3 miles out of Cardigan
there is a crossroads. Take the 1st right . We
are on the right.

Open all year
3 bedrs (1 twin sh/wc; 2 double inc 1
ba/wc, 1 sh/wc) ❄ ♞
£B&B £14-£17, D £6.50, WR £95-£115,
WR/D £127.50-£147.50, child rates.

CARMARTHEN 6B4

Glog Llangain, Carmarthen SA33 5AY
01267 83271   C. A. Gribble

Glog is a 40-acre working farm with a beef
suckler herd and horses, situated off the
B4312, south of Carmarthen standing 5 miles
equidistant between the busy market town
and the quiet beach and historic castle at
Llanstephan. Comfortable accommodation.

Open all year
❄ ♞

Pantgwyn Farm Whitemill, Carmarthen
SA32 7ES 01267 290247   T. F. Gluss

Pantgwyn Farm, Whitemill Oct 1990

200 year old farmhouse offering very
comfortable accommodation. Sheep and cattle
on farm, donkey and Shetland pony available
for children's rides. Peaceful location. Take
A40 from Carmarthen towards Llandeilo. After

1 mile turn left to Whitemill, take 1st left sign to chapel, turn left.

Open all year
7 bedrs (2 twin inc 1 ba/wc, 1 sh/wc; 3 double inc 2 ba/wc, 1 sh/wc; 2 family inc 1 ba/wc, 1 sh/wc) 🏖 & 🏇 ♨♨♨
£B&B £19-£28, D £14.50, WR £120-£176, WR/D £212-£268, child rates.

CROESGOCH   6A4

Bank House Croesgoch SA62 6X2
01348 831305   Mrs. Lloyd

Open Feb-Oct
2 bedrs (1 twin; 1 double) 1 ba, 1 wc 🏖

GWAUN VALLEY   6A4

Tregynon Country Farmhouse Hotel
Gwaun Valley, Fishguard SA65 9TU   RAC
01239 820531   Mr. Herd

Open all year
8 bedrs (4 double inc 3 ba/wc, 1 sh/wc; 4 family inc 2 ba/wc, 2 sh/wc) 2 wc 🏖 🏛
♨♨♨ cc Vi
£B&B £23-£64, D £14.75-£19.95, WR £248.75-£310.50, WR/D £248.75-£316, child rates.

HAVERFORDWEST   6A4

Cuckoo Mill St. Davids Road, Pelcomb Bridge, Haverfordwest SA62 6EA
01437 762139   Mrs. Davies

Open all year
4 bedrs (1 twin; 2 double; 1 family) 2ba, 2wc 🏖 🏇 *Listed*
£B&B £14-£16, D £7.50, WR £90-£100, WR/D £130-£140, child rates.

Lower Haythog Spittal, Haverfordwest
SA62 5QL 01437 731279   Mrs. Thomas

Working farm, mainly dairy - trout fishing. Pony rides for children. From Haverfordwest take B4329, 4 miles - farm sign on right side of road .

Open All year
4 bedrs (1 twin ba/wc; 2 double inc 1 ba/wc, 1 sh/wc; 1 family ba/wc) 🏖 🏛 🏇
♨♨♨
£B&B £17.50-£20, D £9.50-£11, WR £125-£140, WR/D £185-£200, child rates.

Spittal Cross Farm Spittal,
Haverfordwest SA62 5DB 01437 87206
Mrs. Evans

Family run dairy farm, offering breakfasts and traditional home cooked dinners. Comfort, cleanliness and personal attention assured. Take A40 Haverfordwest to Fishguard Rd . Turn off right (Village of Spittal), one mile to the farm.

Open April - Oct.
2 bedrs (1 twin; 1 double) 1 ba, 1 wc 🏖 🏛
🏇 ♨
£B&B £14.50-£15, D £8, WR £101.50, WR/D £157.50, child rates.

The Bower Farm Little Haven,
Haverfordwest SA62 3TY 01437 781554
Mrs. Birt-Llewellin

Open all year
5 bedrs 🏖 🏇
£B&B £18-£23, D £12.50-£15, WR £116-£150, WR/D £195-£250, child rates.

LAMPETER   6B4

Bryncastell Farm Llanfair Road,
Lampeter SA48 8JY 01570 422447
Mr. Davies

Open all year
3 bedrs 🏖 & 🏛 ♨♨
£B&B £16-£18.50, D £10-£12, WR £105-£110, WR/D £155-£165, child rates.

Nantymedd Farm Llanfair Clydogau,
Lampeter SA48 8JZ 01570 45208
Mrs. Evans

Traditional Welsh Longhouse Farmhouse. Working dairy and sheep farm, free salmon trout fishing on the farm river. Take A482 into Lampeter, then take the unclassified road by side of Pioneer Store. We are 3 miles along the road.

Open Jan-Dec
4 bedrs (1 twin; 2 double; 1 family) 1 ba ☎
🐕 ♨
£B&B £12-£15, D £8-£10, WR £84-£105,
WR/D £140-£175, child rates.

LLANDELOY   6A4

Upper Vanley Farm Nr Solva,
Llandeloy SA62 6LJ   ᴿᴬᴄ
01348 831418   Ms Shales

Open all year

PEMBROKE   2B1

Chapel Farm Castlemartin, Pembroke
SA71 5HW 01646 661312   Mrs. Smith

Open all year
2 bedrs (1 twin; 1 family) 1 ba ☎ 🏬 🐕
£child rates.

SOLVA   6A4

Llanddinog Old Farmhouse Solva,
Haverfordwest SA62 6NA 01348 831224
Mrs. Griffiths

Open all year
2 bedrs (1 double ba/wc; 1 family sh/wc)
☎ 🏬 🐕 ♨♨♨
£B&B £16, D £8, WR £112, WR/D £168,
child rates.

Lochmeyler Farm Highly Acclaimed

Pen-y-Cwm, Llandeloy, Solva,
Haverfordwest SA62 6LL   ᴿᴬᴄ
01348 837724   M. Jones

Lochmeyler is a 220-acre dairy farm set 3
miles inland in the centre of St David's
Peninsula off the A487 Haverfordwest-St
David's road. The 16th-century farmhouse has

been renovated without losing its character.
Comfortable, well-equipped rooms.

Open all year
10 bedrs all en suite; 1 ba ☎(10) 🏬 🐕
♨♨♨♨ cc Ac Vi
£B&B £20-£30, WR/D £200.

TREGARON   6C3

Neuaddlas Guest House Tregaron
SA25 6LJ 01974 298905   Mrs. Cutter

Open all year
6 bedrs (2 twin inc 1 ba/wc; 1 double
ba/wc; 3 family) ☎ 🏬 🐕 ♨♨♨
£B&B £16.50-£19.50, D £8, WR £115.50-
£136.50, WR/D £171.50-£192.50, child rates.

WHITLAND   6B4

Brunant Farm Whitland SA34 0LX
01994 240421   Mrs. Ebsworth

200 acre old farmhouse, set in attractive
grounds. Peaceful, rural setting central for
sightseeing, beaches, walking. Spacious
bedrooms with TV and tea/coffee making
facilities. A477 from St Clears, turn R at
Llanddowror. Continue for 1.5 miles turn R,
2nd entrance on R.

Open Apr- Oct
4 bedrs (2 twin ba/wc, sh/wc; 2 double
sh/wc) ☎ 🏬 ♨♨♨
£B&B £16-£20, D £10-£12, child rates.

Maencochyrwyn Farm Login,
Whitland SA34 0TN 01994 419283
                         Brenda Worthing

An ideal place for a peaceful holiday. The
farm, an 80 acre working dairy farm, is
situated just over 2 miles from the village of
Llanboidy. The farmhouse has every modern

amenity and offers good home cooking. Cot
and highchair provided.

Open all year
3 bedrs (1 twin; 1 family; 1 single) 1 ba, 1
wc ⮜ 🐴
£child rates.

SELF CATERING

CARDIGAN   6B4

Croft Farm Guesthouse & Cottages
Llantood, Cardigan SA43 3NT
01239 615179   Andy & Sylvie Gow

For full farm description see B&B Entry. Take
A487 towards Fishguard. 3 miles out of
Cardigan there is a crossroads. Take the 1st
right . We are on the right.

£Wk £105-£375

CARMARTHEN   6B4

Cwmdwyfran Farm Cottages
Cwmdwyfran, Bronwydd Arms,
Carmarthen SA33 6JF 01267 281419
Mrs. Brandrick

These two superb holiday cottages have
been converted from a stone farm building
and are equipped to a high standard.
Bordering the farmyard, each has a south
facing verandah with beautiful views, sleeps
4/5 people.

Take A484 Cardigan Road, after approx. 3
miles Cwmdwyfran village (name sign on
right).Take 2nd left after sign.

⮜ 🐴

Pantgwyn Farm Whitemill, Carmarthen
SA32 7ES 01267 290247   T. F. Gluss

For full farm description see B&B Entry.
Taking A40 from Carmarthen towards
Llandeilo. After 1 mile turn left to Whitemill,
take 1st left sign to chapel, turn left.

£Wk £120-£290

HAVERFORDWEST   6A4

Lower Haythog Spittal, Haverfordwest
SA62 5QL 01437 731279   Mrs. Thomas

For full farm description see B&B Entry. From
Haverfordwest take B4329, 4 miles - farm sign
on right side of road .

£Wk £150-£400

SOLVA   6A4

Llanddinog Old Farmhouse Solva,
Haverfordwest SA62 6NA 01348 831224
Mrs. Griffiths

£Wk £100-£450

WHITLAND   6B4

Brunant Farm Whitland SA34 0LX
01994 240421   Mrs. Ebsworth

For full farm description see B&B Entry. A477
from St Clears, turn R at Llanddowror.
Continue for 1.5 miles turn R, 2nd entrance on
R.

PLACES TO VISIT

CAREW

Carew Castle and Tidal Mill
Nr Tenby, Carew
01646-651782
The magnificent Norman castle which
later became an Elizabethan residence
traces its royal links back to Henry
Tudor. Also a tidal mill.
Location: 5 miles east of Pembroke just
off A477.
Open: Easter-Oct, daily 1000-1700.
Entrance: adult £2.00 child £1.20 (under 6
free) OAP/concession £1.20 WC 🐴 ⮜

PEMBROKE

Pembroke Castle
Pembroke SA71 4LA 01646-681510
A Norman castle with a magnificent early
13th century Keep.
Location: west end of main street in
Pembroke.
Open: daily, April- Sep 0930-1800; Mar &
Oct 1000-1700, Nov-Feb 1000-1600.
Entrance: adult £2.20 OAP/child £1.40
Family Ticket £6.00. WC ⮜

LLANDYSUL

Museum of the Welsh Woollen Industry
Dre-fach Felindre, Llandysul SA44 5UP
01559-370929
Working museum shows the history of the woollen industry and its people, with regular demonstrations of the skilled process of turning fleece into fabric. Located alongside a working woollen mill and craft shops. On sale: crafts, souvenirs. Location: on A484 Carmarthen-Lampeter road, 4 miles east of Newcastle Emlyn. Open: April-Sept Mon-Sat, Oct-Mar Mon-Fri, 1000-1700
Entrance: adult £1, child 50p, OAP/concessions 75p WC ♿ (partial access) ✕ ⌺

Rock-Mill Woollen & Water Mill
Rock-Mill, Capel-Dewi, Llandysul SA44 4PH 01559-362256
This water-powered woollen mill was built in 1890 by the great-grandfather of the present owner. One of the few remaining working woollen mills where the complete process from raw wool to finished cloth can be seen. The shop sells pure new wool and finished articles e.g. bedspreads, rugs, scarves. Location: off the B4459 in Capel-Dewi village. Open: Sat 1000-1300 (April-Sept) Mon-Fri 1000-1700 (All year) WC ♿ ✖(restricted) ⌺

GWENT

ABERGAVENNY
7D4

Chapel Farm Nr Coalbrookvale, Abergavanny, Blaina NP3 3DJ
01495 290888   Mrs. Betty Hancocks

Tastefully renovated 15th century farmhouse, farming Welsh mountain sheep. Panoramic views, home cooking. All assured a warm welcome. From Brynmawr take A467 road, travel about 1 mile, turn right into Coalbrookvale. Newport- A467- to Coalbrookvale.

Open all year
2 bedrs (2 family inc 1 sh/wc) 1 ba, 2 wc
🛏 ⌸ ♨ *Commended*
£B&B £16-£18, D £6-£9.50, child rates.

CHEPSTOW
3E1

Parsons Grove Earls Wood, Chepstow
NP6 6RD 01291 641382   Gloria Powell

Country house with small vineyard. Magnificient views. Totally peaceful. Heated swimming pool, sunbeds etc. All rooms en-suite, colour TV, radios, beverage trays. Also cottages to let. Take A48 towards Caerwent (3 miles) turn right. Straight through village (1 ml) First left, follow farm signs.

Open all year
2 bedrs (2 family inc 1 ba/wc, 1 sh/wc) 🛏 🐴 ♨
£B&B £17-£19, WR £105-£114, child rates.

MONMOUTH
7D4

Lower Pen-y-Clawdd Farm
Dingestow, Monmouth NP5 4BG
01600 83223   Mrs. Bayriss

Open all year
3 bedrs (1 twin; 1 double; 1 family) 2 ba, 2 wc 🛏 🐴 ♨
£B&B £15-£16, child rates.

NEWPORT
3E1

Pentre-Tai Farm Rhiwderin, Newport
NP1 9RQ 01633 893284   Mr. Proctor

A warm welcome awaits you at our peaceful sheep farm. We have ensuite facilities and all rooms have colour TV and tea/coffee making facilities. Pub with excellent food nearby. 3 miles from junction 28 M4 motorway.

Open Feb- Nov
3 bedrs (1 twin sh/wc; 1 double; 1 family ba/wc) ☎ 🐾🐾
£B&B £16-£19, child rates.

PONTYPOOL   3E1

Pentwyn Farm Little Mill, Pontypool NP4 0HQ 01495 785249   Mrs. Bradley

Open Feb-Nov
3 bedrs; (2 twin inc 1 sh/wc; 1 double inc 1 sh/wc) 1 ba, 2 wc ☎ 🐾🐾🐾
£B&B £14-£18, D £10, WR £91-£119, WR/D £151-£178, child rates.

Ty'Ry-Ywen Farm Lasgarn Lane, Trevethin, Pontypool NP4 8TT
01495 785200   Mrs. Armitage

25 acre hill farm in Brecon Beacons National Park with marvellous views down the Usk Valley. The 16th century house is spacious and well-appointed, four-poster bed and jacuzzi in one room.

Open all year
3 bedrs (1 twin ba/wc, sh/wc; 2 double ba/wc, sh/wc) 🐓 ✂ cc Ac Vi 🐾🐾🐾
£B&B £19-£35.

TINTERN   3E1

Parva Farmhouse *Highly Acclaimed* Nr

Chepstow, Tintern NP6 6SQ   🅁🅰🅲
01291 689411   Mr. Stubbs

Open all year
9 bedrs all en suite; 1 ba ☎ 🐓
cc Ac Vi £B&B £39-£60, D £16.50, WR/D £225-£250.

USK   3E1

Ty Gwyn Farm Gwehelog, Usk NP5 1RT 01291 672878   Mr. Arnett

Open all year
3 bedrs (2 twin ba/wc; 1 double sh/wc) ☎(5) 🏠 🐾🐾🐾
£B&B £33-£35, D £10, WR £210, WR/D £330, child rates.

SELF CATERING

CHEPSTOW   3E1

Parsons Grove Earls Wood, Chepstow NP6 6RD 01291 641382   Gloria Powell

For full farm description see B&B Entry. Take A48 towards Caerwent (3 miles) turn right. Straight through village (1 ml) First left, follow farm signs.

£Wk £100-£340

PONTYPOOL   3E1

Pentwyn Farm Little Mill, Pontypool NP4 0HQ 01495 785249   Mrs. Bradley
☎
£Wk £160-£230

GWYNEDD

ABERGYNOLWYN   6C2

Tan y Coed Ucha Abergynolwyn, Tywyn LL36 9UP 01654 782228 Mrs. Pugh

This is a mixed farm with cattle and sheep. The farmhouse is over 100 years old, but has been well modernised for comfort and convenience. The atmosphere is welcoming and homely. From Tywyn take A493 for 2 miles.Then take B4405 for approx. 3 miles. Our farm is between Dolgoch Falls and Abergynolwyn

Open Mar-Nov
2 bedrs (1 twin; 1 single) 1 ba, 1 wc ⚘ ⌂
⌁ *Listed*
£B&B £13.50-£14.50, D £6-£7.50, WR
£94.50-£101.50, WR/D £136.50-£154, child
rates.

BALA 6C2

Erw Feurig Farm Guest House Cefn-
ddwysarn, Bala LL23 7LL 01678 530262
Mrs. Jones

Open all year
5 bedrs (1 twin; 2 double sh/wc; 1 family;1
single) 1 ba, 1 wc ⚘ ⌂ ⚘⚘ *Highly
Commended*
£B&B £13-£16, D £7.50, WR £90-£110,
WR/D £150-£160, child rates.

Rhyd Y Defaid Farm Frongoch, Bala
LL23 7NT 01678 520456 Mr. Olwen Davies

Traditional Welsh stone farmhouse on 100-
acre working farm. Inglenook fireplace,
exposed beams. Quiet and comfortable.
Take A4212 road from Bala for 3 miles. Turn
left in Frongoch Village and follow signs to
farm.

Open all year
3 bedrs (1 twin; 1 family sh/wc; 1 single) 1
ba ⚘ ⌂ ⌁ *Listed Highly Commended*
£B&B £14-£17.50, child rates.

Talybont Isa Rhyduchaf, Bala LL23 7SD
01678 520234 Mrs. Ann Skinner

Open Jan-Oct
3 bedrs (1 twin inc 1 sh/wc; 1 double; 1
family) 2 ba, 2 wc ⚘ ⌁ ⚘
£B&B £13-£14.50, D £6-£7, WR £90-£95,
WR/D £125-£140, child rates.

BETWS-Y-COED 6C1

Maesgwyn Pentre Foelas, Betws-y-Coed
LL24 0LR 01690 770668
Mrs. Florence Jones

Open April-Nov
2 bedrs (1 double; 1 family) 1 ba, 1 wc ⚘
⌁
£B&B £13-£14, WR £88-£91, child rates.

BANGOR 6B1

Goetre Isaf Farmhouse Caernarfon
Road, Bangor LL57 4DB 01248 364541
Mr. Whowell

Although isolated, Goetre Isaf is only 2 miles
from Bangor mainline station. Ideal touring
centre for the mountains of Snowdonia, Isle of
Anglesey, and the beaches of the Lleyn
Peninsula. Imaginative farmhouse cooking.
Special diets accommodated. 2 miles west of
Bangor on Caernarfon road A4087.

Open all year
3 bedrs (2 twin inc 1 ba/wc; 1 double
sh/wc) 2 ba, 2 wc ⚘ ⌂ ⌁
£B&B £13-£18, D £5.50-£8, WR £91-£126,
WR/D £129.50-£182, child rates.

BEAUMARIS 6C1

Plas Cichle Beaumaris LL58 8PS
01248 810488 Mrs. Roberts

Open Feb-Nov
3 bedrs (2 double inc 1 ba/wc, 1 sh/wc; 1
family sh/wc) ⚘(6) ⌂ ⌁

BLAENAU FFESTINIOG 6C1

Bryn Celynog Farm Cwm Prysor,
Trawsfynydd, Blaenau Ffestiniog LL41
4TR 01766 540378
Mrs. Gwladys E. Hughes

Mixed beef and sheep farm (working) 200-
acre. Comfortable modernised farm house,
with a reputation for good food and
friendliness. Relaxed atmosphere. Tea and
coffee making facilities in all bedrooms. A4212
from Bala. Dolgellau A470 to Trawsfynydd.
Turn right on to A4212, 15 miles from Bala.
Farm 3 ml from turning.

Open all year
3 bedrs (1 twin sh/wc; 1 double sh/wc; 1
family) ⊃ 🏠 🐎 🍲🍲
£B&B £16-£18.50, D £9.50, WR £105-£125,
WR/D £160-£180, child rates.

CAERNARFON 6B1

Pengwern Farm Llangrug, Saron,
Llanwnda, Caernarfon LL54 5UH
01286 830717 Mr. Gwyndaf Rowlands

This charming, spacious farmhouse is
beautifully situated between mountains and
sea, with unobstructed views of Snowdonia,
The farm covers 130 acres which run down to
Foryd Bay, noted for its birdlife. Meals are
cooked to a professional standard. Take A487
south from Caernarfon, as you leave, hospital
left, over bridge, first right , after Saron on
right.

Open Feb-Nov
4 bedrs (1 twin sh/wc; 2 double ba/wc, 1
family ba/wc, sh/wc) ⊃ 🏠 🍴 🍲🍲🍲
£B&B £19-£22, D £10-£12, WR £126-£154,
WR/D £196-£224, child rates.

Ty Mawr Farmhouse Saron, Llanwnda,
Caernarfon LL54 5UH 01286 830091
Ruth Evans

This charming award-winning farmhouse, part
of which dates from the 1600s, is to be found
3 miles south of Caernarfon off the A487.
Furnished with antiques, the farmhouse offers
splendid breakfasts including British grill,
wholefood and vegetarian.

Open Apr-Oct
3 bedrs (1 twin sh/wc; 1 double ba/wc; 1
family sh/wc) 1 wc ⊃(2) 🏠 🍴 🍲🍲🍲
Highly Commended

DOLGELLAU 6C2

Fronoleu Farm Hotel Tabor, Dolgellau
LL40 2PS 🛈 RAC
01341 422361 Mr. Jones

Open all year
10 bedrs 6 en suite; 2 ba ⊃ ⅊ 🐎
£B&B £17.50-£40, child rates.

Glyn Farm Dolgellau LL40 17A
01341 422286 E. Wyn Price

This 300-year old farmhouse sits on a hill with
all windows facing the picturesque Mawddach
estuary. The farm lies close to the A493, just
west of Dolgellau. The warm and well-
equipped accommodation assures a pleasant
stay. Cot and highchair available.

Open all year
4 bedrs (1 twin; 3 double inc 1 sh/wc) 1
ba, 2 wc ⊃ 🐎 🍲

LLANDUDNO 6C1

Tyddyn Du Farm Gellilydan,
Llandudno LL41 4RB 01766 590281
Paula Williams

Our 17th century farmhouse has a relaxed friendly atmosphere, inglenook fireplace. Most bedrooms ensuite. One superb private cottage suite. Candle-light dinners with excellent farmhouse cuisine. Working farm with ducks, bottle-fed lambs and ponies. Just off the A470 near the A487 junction at the village of Gellilydan.

Open all year
4 bedrs (1 twin ba/wc; 2 double ba/wc; 1 family ba/wc) 1 ba, 1 wc ⛺ 🐴 ♛♛♛
£B&B £16-£19, D £8.50-£9, WR £102-£127, WR/D £150-£175, child rates.

LLANERCHYMEDD   6B1

Drws y Coed Llanerchymedd LL71 8AD
01248 470473   Jane Bown

This beautifully appointed award-winning farmhouse is set on a 550-acre working farm of beef, sheep and arable surrounded by peaceful wooded countryside, with panoramic views of Snowdonia. The farm lies between the B5111 and B5108, east of Llannerch-y-Medd.

Open Jan-Nov
3 bedrs (1 twin ba/wc; 1 double ba/wc; 1 family ba/wc) ⛺ 🏠 🐴
£B&B £16-£18, D £10, WR £112-£170, child rates.

LLANFAIRPWLLGWYNGYLL   6B1

Bryntirion Open Farm Dwyran, Llanfairpwllgwyngyll LL61 6BQ
01248 430232   Mrs. Naylor

Open Mar-Oct
3 bedrs (2 double; 1 family) 1 ba, 2 wc ⛺ ♛
£B&B £12.50-£14, WR £84, child rates.

Llwydiarth Fawr Llanfairpwllgwyngyll
LL71 8DF 01248 470321   Mrs. Hugh

Open all year
4 bedrs (1 twin ba/wc; 1 double ba/wc; 1 family ba/wc; 1 single sh/wc) 1 ba, 1 wc ⛺

Plas Trefarthen Brynsiencyn, Llanfairpwllgwyngyll LL61 6SZ
01248 430379   Mr. Roberts

Open all year

PWLLHELI   6B2

Mathan Uchaf Farm Boduan, Pwllheli
LL53 8TU 01758 720487   Mrs. Coker

Open Mar-Oct
3 bedrs (1 twin; 1 double, 1 family) 1 ba, 2 wc ⛺ 🐴
£B&B £15-£17, D £8-£10, WR £100-£110, WR/D £160-£165, child rates.

Pen-y-Bryn Chwilog, Pwllheli LL53 6SH
01766 810208   Mrs. Edwards

Open all year
2 bedrs (2 twin inc 1 ba/wc) 1 ba, 1 wc ⛺ 🐴
£B&B £12.50-£15, D £6.50-£8, child rates.

TRAWSFYNYDD   6C2

Old Mill Farmhouse Fronoleu Farm, Trawsfynydd LL41 4TR 01766 87397
Mrs. Bain

Open all year
7 bedrs (2 twin sh/wc; 3 double inc 1 ba/wc, 2 sh/wc; 2 family inc 1 ba/wc, 1 sh/wc) ⛺ ♿ 🏠 🐴 ♛
£B&B £17.50-£19, D £8.50-£9.50, WR £115-£125, WR/D £165-£180, child rates.

TYWYN 6B2

Dolffanog Fach Talyllyn, Tywyn LL36
9AJ 01654 761235 Mrs. Pughe

Open all year
3 bedrs (1 twin; 1 family; 1 double
ba/sh/wc) 1 ba, 2 wc 🛏 🏠 ♛♛
£B&B £15.00-£18, D £8-£9, WR £100-£110,
WR/D £150-£165, child rates.

SELF CATERING

ABERSOCH 6B2

Ty'n Don LLanengan, Abersoch, Pwllheli
LL53 7LG Elisabeth Evans

£Wk £99-£390

BALA 6C2

Talybont Isa Rhyduchaf, Bala LL23 7SD
01678 520234 Mrs. Ann Skinner

£Wk £100

DOLGELLAU 6C2

Glyn Farm Dolgellau LL40 17A
01341 422286 E. Wyn Price

For full farm description see p166. An old
farm cottage and converted wing are available
for self-catering. Low doorways and inglenook
fireplace. there are 2 and 3 bedrooms,
sleeping 4 and 7.

DYFFRYN ARDUDWY 6B2

Ynys Ystumgwern Hall Farm Dyffryn
Ardudwy LL44 2DD 01341 247249 Jane
Williams

16th century farmhouse and barn conversions
on 1,000 acre working farm. Luxury
accommodation in one of the most beautiful
parts of Wales.

Travel north on the A496, go through the
village of Dyffryn. The sign for Ystumgwern is
on your left.

£Wk £140-£420

LLANFAIRPWLLGWYNGYLL 6B1

Llwydiarth Fawr Llanfairpwllgwyngyll
LL71 8DF 01248 470321

LLWYNGWRIL 6B2

Carn y Gadell Uchaf c/o Henblas,
Llwyngwril LL37 2QA 01341 250350
Mrs. Pugh

£Wk £100-£385

PWLLHELI 6B2

Pen-y-Bryn Chwilog, Pwllheli LL53 6SH
01766 810208 Mrs. Edwards

£Wk £100-£425

POWYS

BRECON 7D4

Caebetran Farm Felinfach, Brecon LD3
0UL 01874 754460 Mrs. Davies

Open All year
3 bedrs (1 twin sh/wc; 2 double inc 1
ba/wc, 1 sh/wc) 🛏(10) 🏠 🐕
£B&B £17-£25, D £10, child rates.

Trehenry Farm Felinfach, Brecon LD3
0UN 🔛
01874 754312 Mrs. Theresa Jones

Enjoy the beauty of the Welsh countryside at
our spacious 18th century farmhouse on a

200-acre farm with sheep, cattle and cereals.
Good home cooking. The Brecon Beacons
and Black Mountains make this a paradise for

walkers. Also locally fishing, riding. Take A470
Hereford road to Felinfach, second turning on
left, second turning on right. Approx 1.75
miles along road.

Open all year
3 bedrs (1 twin sh/wc; 1 double sh/wc; 1
family ba/wc) ♿ ♘ ♨♨♨
£B&B £18-£19, D £9-£10, WR £126-£130,
WR/D £185-£190, child rates.

BUILTH WELLS   6C3

Cae Pandy Farm Gorth Road, Builth
Wells 01982 553793   Z. E. Hope

Open all year
3 bedrs (1 twin; 2 double) 1 ba, 1 wc ♿ ♨
♘ ♨
£child rates.

Disserth Mill Builth Wells 01982 553217
Mr. Worts

Open Mar-Oct
3 bedrs (1 twin; 2 double) 1 ba, 1 wc ♿ ♨
♘ ✂

New Hall Llandewircwm, Builth Wells
LD2 3RX 01982 552483 Mrs. Iris M. James

17yh century farmhouse overlooking Wye
Valley and Aberedw Hills. B4520 Upper
Chapel Brecon road

Open all year
5 bedrs (1 twin ba/wc, sh/wc; 3 double inc
1 ba/wc, 2 sh/wc; 1 family ba/wc, sh/wc)
♿ ♨ ✂ ♨♨♨
£B&B £14-£18, D £7.50, WR £98-£126,
WR/D £140.50-£178.50, child rates.

HAY-ON-WYE   7D4

Lower Rhydness Bungalow Llyswen,

Brecon LD3 0AZ 01874 754264
Mrs. Williams

Open all year
2 bedrs (1 family; 1 single) 1 ba, 1 wc ♿ ♘
£B&B £13.50, D £7, WR £13, WR/D
£136.50, child rates.

LLANDRINDOD WELLS   6C3

Brynhir Farm Chapel Road, Howey,
Llandrindod Wells LD1 5PB 01597 822425
Mrs. Nixon

Open Mar-Nov
8 bedrs (4 twin inc 2 ba/wc, 2 sh/wc; 2
double ba/wc; 1 family sh/wc; 1 single) ♿
♨ ♘ ♨♨♨ *Highly Commended*
£B&B £16.50-£17.50, D £7-£8, WR £110-
£115, WR/D £155-£165, child rates.

Holly Farm Howey, Llandrindod Wells
LD1 5PP 01597 822402   Ruth Jones

Open April-Nov
3 bedrs (1 twin ba/wc; 1 double ba/wc; 1
family sh/wc) ♿ ♨ ♨♨
£B&B £16-£18, D £7-£8, WR £112-£126,
WR/D £155-£160, child rates.

Three Wells Farm *Highly Acclaimed*
Chapel Road, Howey, Llandrindod wells
LD1 5PB   **RAC**
01597 822484   Mrs Bufton

Three Wells Farm is a licensed farm guest
house and working farm overlooking a fishing
lake in beautiful countryside. Good food,
spacious dining room, sun lounge, TV room
and two bars. 1 mile south of Llandrindod
Wells on A483 turn into Village of Howey.
Follow up Chapel Road, ½ mile to farm.

Open all year
15 bedrs (6 twin inc 5 ba/wc, 1 sh/wc; 7

double inc 5 ba/wc, 2 sh/wc; 1 family
ba/wc; 1 single sh/wc) 2 wc ☎(8) ⌂ ♞
♨♨♨♨
£B&B £17-£22, D £8.50-£9.50, WR £110-
£145, WR/D £165-£200, child rates.

LLANIDLOES 6C3

Dol-Llys Farm Llanidloes SY18 6JA
01686 412694 Olwen Evans

Open all year
3 bedrs (1 twin sh/wc; 2 double ba/wc,
sh/wc) ☎ ♨♨ *Commended*
£B&B £15-£17, WR £105-£119, child rates.

MACHYNLLETH 6C2

Bryn Sion Farm Cwm Cywarch, Dinas
Mawddwy, Machynlleth 01650 531251
Mrs. none

This old stone farmhouse is set in the
picturesque valley of Cywarch, 10 miles
northeast of Machynlleth off A489/470. The
farm is mostly sheep, 700 ewes, but some
Welsh Black cattle are also kept. Fishing,
shooting and hill walking available on the
farm.

Open all year
2 bedrs (2 double) 1 ba, 1 wc ☎ ⌂ ♞
£child rates.

Gogarth Hall Farm Pennal,
Machynlleth 01654 791235
Deilwen Breese

Built around 1700, the farm has magnificent
views overlooking the Dove Estuary. There
are also 3 self-catering units in a converted
coach house, farmhouse and caravan, with 2-3
bedrooms, sleeping 4-6. Situated on the A493,
6 miles west from Machynlleth past Pennal.

Open all year
2 bedrs (1 double sh/wc; 1 family sh/wc) 2
ba, 2 wc ☎ ⌂ ♞ ♨♨♨
£child rates.

MONTGOMERY 7D3

The Drewin Farm Church Stoke,
Montgomery 01588 620325
Ceinwen Richards

Offa's Dyke footpath runs through this mixed
working farm of sheep, cattle and corn. There

are panoramic views from the 17th-century
farmhouse where you can enjoy good home
cooking. The games room has a snooker
table. Located off the B4385 west of Church
Stoke (A489).

Open April-Nov
2 bedrs (2 family inc 1 sh/wc) 1 ba, 2 wc
☎ ♞ ♨♨♨♨ *Highly Commended*
£child rates.

NEWTOWN 7D3

Dyffryn Aberhafesp, Newtown SY16
3JD 01686 688817 Sue Jones

Luxury converted barn on working sheep and
beef farm. Farm is situated next to a number
of lakes and hills. All rooms are ensuite, food
provided is delicious farmhouse fare. Take
B4568, turn right to Bulchyffridd, branch left,
and left again to Bethel. Right at crossroads,
farm is on right.

Open all year
3 bedrs (1 twin ba/wc; 1 double ba/wc; 1
family ba/wc) 1 wc ☎ ⌂ ♨♨♨
£B&B £20-£23, D £10-£12, WR £140-£160,
WR/D £210-£230.

RHAYADER 6C3

Beili Neuadd Farmhouse Rhayader
LD6 5NS 01597 810211 Mrs. Edwards

The farm is set amidst glorious countryside in
a secluded position beside a trout pool. Good,
imaginative meals are served using farm and
garden produce. This is a Wales Farmhouse
Award winner. Located just off the A44.

Open all year
3 bedrs (1 twin sh/wc; 2 double inc 1
ba/wc, 1 sh/wc) ☎ ♞ ♨♨♨ *Highly
Commended*
£B&B £17-£18, D £10.50, child rates.

SENNYBRIDGE 6C4

Brynfedwen Farm Trallong Common, Sennybridge, Brecon LD3 8HW
01874 636505 Mrs. Mary C. Adams

Family run sheep farm set high above the River Usk Valley, overlooking the Brecon Beacons. Traditional stone farmhouse, centrally heated, lounge with log fire. Enjoy good home cooking. From Brecon take A40 towards Llandovery. After 7 miles, take 2nd right (Trallong) Over at top of hill onto farm road.

Open all year
3 bedrs (1 twin sh/wc; 2 double inc 1 ba/wc, 1 sh/wc)
£B&B £16, D £9, WR £112, WR/D £175, child rates.

Cwmcamlais Uchaf Farm
Cwmcamlais, Sennybridge, Brecon LD3 8TD 01874 636376 Mrs. Phillips

Open all year

Llwynneath Farm Sennybridge, Brecon LD3 8HN 01874 636641 Mr. Val Williams

Open all year
2 bedrs (1 double ba/wc; 1 family sh/wc)
£B&B £16, WR £105, child rates.

TALGARTH 7D4

Lodge Farm Talgarth, LD3 0DP
01874 711244 Mrs. Marion Meredith

Warm welcome with quality accommodation and "Real Food", are of prime importance at this 18th century farmhouse, situated between Brecon and Black Mountains within National Park. From Talgarth take street named "The Bank". At junction bear right, passing church on left, 2nd left along country road.

Open all year
3 bedrs (1 twin ba/wc; 1 double sh/wc; 1 family sh/wc)
£B&B £16-£18, D £9.50.

WELSHPOOL 7D2

Cwmllwynog Llanfair Caereinion, Welshpool SY21 0HFE 01938 810791
Mrs. Cornes

17th century traditional Welsh longhouse farmhouse. Working dairy farm. Warm welcome. Good home cooking using local produce. Take A458 from Welshpool towards Dolgellau.Turn left into Llanfair Caereinion past church. Farm sign 1 ½ miles on left.

Open April- Oct
2 bedrs (inc 1 twin ba/wc) 1 ba
£B&B £15-£18, D £8, child rates.

Moat Farm Welshpool SY21 8SE
01938 553179 Mrs. Jones

Moat Farm is a 250-acre dairy farm. Good home cooking is served in the fine timbered dining room. Guests will appreciate the pool table and tennis lawn. Off the A483, 3 miles

south of Welshpool.

Open April- Oct
3 bedrs (1 twin ba/wc; 2 double sh/wc; 1
family ba/wc) 1 wc 🐾 ⌗ 🌺🌺
£B&B £18-£19, D £10-£12, WR £126-£133,
WR/D £190-£200, child rates.

Trefant Hall Farm *Acclaimed* Berriew,
Welshpool SY21 8AS 01686 640262

Closed winter exc bookings
3 bedrs (2 ba/wc, 1sh/wc) ✄
£B&B £20

Tynllwyn Farm Welshpool SY21 9BW

01938 553175   Mrs. Emberton
Open all year
6 bedrs; 2 ba, 3 wc 🐾 🐂
£B&B £14.50-£15, D £8-£8.50, WR £140,
WR/D £22.50-£23.50, child rates.

SELF CATERING

BRECON   7D4

Trehenry Farm Felinfach, Brecon LD3
0UN   RAC
01874 754312   Mrs. Theresa Jones

For full farm description see B&B Entry. Take
A470 Hereford road to Felinfach, second
turning on left, second turning on right.
Approx 1.75 miles along road.
£Wk £280-£380

CAERSWS   6C3

Red House Trefeglwys, Caersws SY17
5PN 01551 6285   Mr. Williams

RHAYADER   6C3

Beili Neuadd Farmhouse Rhayader
LD6 5NS 01597 810211   Mrs. Edwards

SENNYBRIDGE   6C4

Brynfedwen Farm Trallong Common,
Sennybridge, Brecon LD3 8HW
01874 636505   Mrs. Mary C. Adams

For full farm description see B&B Entry. From
Brecon take A40 towards Llandovery. After 7

miles, take 2nd right (Trallong) Over at top of
hill onto farm road.
£Wk £150

WELSHPOOL   7D2

Cwmllwynog Llanfair Caereinion,
Welshpool SY21 0HFE 01938 810791
Mrs. Cornes

For full farm description see B&B Entry. Take
A458 from Welshpool towards Dolgellau.Turn
left into Llanfair Caereinion past church.Farm
sign 1 ½ miles on left.

PLACES TO VISIT

LLANFAIR CAEREINION

Welshpool and Llanfair Railway
The Station, Llanfair Caereinion
01938-810441
A turn of the century narrow gauge
railway built to serve a farming
community. Now the home of a
collection of trains from local railways all
around the world. Steam operated.
Location: both terminal stations are
alongside the A458.
Open: Apr-Oct and Dec, all weekends,
mid June-mid July Tues-Thurs,; daily mid
July- early Sept. First train 1030, last train
1715. Return fares: adult £6.50 child £3.00
OAP/concession £5.00. WC craft 🐂 ✗

MACHYNLLETH

Ynys-Hir Nature Reserve
Eglwysfach, Machynlleth
01654-781265
Wonderful variety of habitats from river
saltings and freshwater marsh to oak
woodlands and open hillside.
Location: signposted off A487 in the
village.
Open daily 0900-2100
Entrance: adults £3 child 50p
OAP/concession £1.50 WC 🦽 🐂

LLANWDDYN

Lake Vyrnwy RSPB Nature Reserve
Llanwddyn, Oswestry 0169 173-278
A man-made reservoir flanked by conifer

plantations and broad-leaved woodlands of oak and birch with rolling heather moorlands.

Location: B4393 to Llanwddyn from Llanfylin. Open: at all times. Entrance free. WC ♿ 🐾

WEST GLAMORGAN

SWANSEA   2C1

Coynant & Ganol Farm Guest House
Felindre, Swansea SA5 7PU   RAC
01269 595640   Mrs. Jones

200 acre livestock farm surrounded by open common with views to sea and Black Mountain. Absolute peace, beautiful setting.

Lakes, woods, streams and hills. Leave M4 Jn46 right onto A48 First right Felindre 2 ½ miles to village. Right at mill, farm 2 ½ miles on right.

Open all year
5 bedrs 3 en suite ⟳ 🏠 ♔♔♔
£B&B £18, D £22.50-£23.50, WR £126, WR/D £157.50-£164.50, child rates.

CHANNEL ISLANDS

PLACES TO VISIT

ST LAWRENCE

Hamptonne - Country Life Museum
Rue de la Patente, St Lawrence
01534-863955
Attractions include a medieval dwelling, a 17th century home, an early 19th century

farmhouse and a host of Victorian outbuildings, a working cider press and picnic area. Daily demonstrations.
Location: St Lawrence road, signposted at Three Oaks.
Open April-Oct daily 1000-1700.
Entrance: adult £2.90, under 10s free, OAP/concessions £1.90 WC ♿ ✗ 🐾

NORTHERN IRELAND

CO. ANTRIM

BUSHMILLS 17E1

Carnside Farm Guest House 23
Causeway Road, Giant's Causeway,
Bushmills BT57 8SU 01265 731337
Mr. Lynch

Open Jan-Nov
6 bedrs (2 twin; 4 double) 3 ba, 3 wc ♿ 🐾
Listed
£B&B £14-£17, D £9-£10, child rates.

CARRICKFERGUS 17F2

Beech Grove 412 Upper Road, Troopers
Lane, Carrickfergus BT38-8PW
01960 363304 Mr. Barrow

Open all year
6 bedrs (1 twin inc 1 ba/wc; 2 double; 2
family; 1 single) 1 ba 2 wc ♿ 🐾 🐴
£B&B £14-£16, D £6-£8, WR £98-£112,
WR/D £140-£168, child rates.

PORTGLENONE 17E2

Sprucebank 41 Ballymacombs Road,
Portglenone BT44 8NR 01266 822150
T. Sibbett

Inviting old traditionally furnished farmhouse
on mixed farm. Hospitality trays in bedrooms.
Sprucebank is on A54, 1.5 miles south of town.

Open all year
4 bedrs (1 twin; 2 double inc 1 sh/wc; 1
family) 1 ba ♿ 🐾
£B&B £14-£16, D £10, WR £95-£100, child
rates.

PORTRUSH 17E1

Maddybenny Farm House 18
Maddybenny Park, Lougestown Road,
Portrush BT52 2PT 01265 823394
Mrs. White

Open Jan-Nov
3 bedrs (1 double ba/wc; 1 family ba/wc; 1
single ba/wc) 1 ba, 1 wc ♿ 🚭 *Approved*

SELF CATERING

PORTRUSH 17E1

Maddybenny Farm House 18
Maddybenny Park, Lougestown Road,
Portrush BT52 2PT 01265 823394
Mrs. White

See also B&B Entry.

PLACES TO VISIT

BALLYMONEY

Heritage Park Farm
Leslie Hill, Ballymoney BT53 6QL
0126 56-66803
Idyllic setting with old farm buildings,
large collection of horse drawn machines,
farm animals, poultry, pets, carriages,
museums, lakes, walks, trap rides,
adventure playground and walled garden.
On sale: home produce: eggs, jams,
plants plus crafts.
Location: signposted from A26
(Ballymoney bypass) roundabout.
Open: Easter-Jun & Sept Sat, Sun & Bank
hols 1400-1800, Jul-Aug Mon-Sat 1100-
1800, Sun 1400-1800
Entrance: adults £1.90, child £1.30.
OAP/Concessions £1.30 WC ♿ (partial
access) ✗ 🦽

CO. DOWN

DOWNPATRICK 17F3

Hillhouse 53 Killyleagh Road, Downpatrick BT30 9EE 01396 830792 Mr. Davison

Secluded Georgian house (listed) close to scenic sites of Strangford, Mournes and St Patrick's Country. Spacious rooms with all comforts- shower, TV etc. Separate dining room and TV lounge. Stabling facilities. Take A7 from Belfast, Saintfield or Downpatrick, to Crossgar roundabout then take B7 to

Killyleagh. House approx 1 ml R.

Open all year
6 bedrs ☼ ♂ ♞

SELF CATERING

NEWTOWNARDS 17F2

Ballycastle House 20 Mountstewart Road, Newtownards BT22 2AL 012477 88357 Mr. Deering
☼ ⚑

CO. FERMANAGH

ENNISKILLEN 17D3

Riverside Farm Guesthouse Gortadrehid, Culkey P.O., Enniskillen 01365 322725 Mrs. Fawcett

This modern farmhouse is situated on a working beef farm in a peaceful rural setting, 2 miles west of Enniskillen. Cot/ highchair,

playroom and games available. Facilities for disabled. There is also a 3-bedroom self-catering unit available, sleeps 6. 2 miles west of Enniskillen (A4/A509).

Open all year
6 bedrs (3 twin; 1 double; 2 family) 1 ba, 3 wc ☼ ⚑
cc Vi

REPUBLIC OF IRELAND

CO. CARLOW

BALLON 19E2

Sherwood Park House Kilbride, Ballon 0503 59117 Maureen Owens

Timeless elegance and a warm welcome await you at Sherwood. Our early Georgian house is on 100 acre mixed farm set in rolling parklands and tranquil countryside, just off N80 midway Dublin/Rosslare. Open fires,

romantic bedrooms with brass & canopy beds. Continue on N81 till you meet junction of N80, signposted from this junction.

Open all year
5 bedrs (2 double; 3 family ba/wc) 1 ba, 2 wc ☼ ⚑
£B&B £16-£20, D £15, WR £110-£135, WR/D £200-£225, child rates.

CO. CLARE

BALLYVAUGHAN 18C1

Rocky View Farmhouse Coast Road, Fanore, Ballyvaughan 065 76103
Teresa Linnane

A comfortable modern bungalow style house on the coast overlooking Aran Islands. The farm rears a suckling herd and is an ideal spot for a quiet relaxing holiday. On the coast road by Blackhead on Galway Bay, 13 km from Ballyvaughan.

Open 21 Apr-Oct
5 bedrs (2 twin ba/wc; 2 double ba/wc; 1 family ba/wc) 1 wc ⛄(10) 🏠 ⊁
£child rates.

DOOLIN 18B1

Horseshoe Farmhouse Fisher Street, Doolin 065 74006   Josephine Moloney

This spacious bungalow is set on a dairy farm overlooking Doolin, a village famous for traditional Irish music. Well-equipped rooms, cot available. Licensed. Tennis court. The farm lies west of N67 Ennistymon-Ballyvaughan road.

Open Jan-Oct
6 bedrs (2 twin sh/wc; 4 double sh/wc) 1 ba, 2 wc ⛄

LISDOONVARNA 18B1

Benrue Farmhouse Lisdoonvarna
065 74059   Mrs. Casey

This modern farmhouse is set on a farm rearing a suckling herd, 6km from Lisdoonvarna. Tea/coffee facilities in bedrooms. Excellent home cooking includes fresh sea food and organic farm produce. Ideal for walkers. Daily boat trips to the Aran Islands.

Open Easter-15 Oct
6 bedrs (1 twin; 2 double inc 1 sh/wc; 3 family sh/wc) 2 ba, 2 wc ⛄ 🏠 🐕

Slieve Elva Farm Kilmoon, Lisdoonvarna 065 74318
Teresa Donnellan

This modern farmhouse in the Burren region is located 2km north of Lisdoonvarna on N67 (T69). The farm has a suckling herd. Scenic country for walks, cycling, mountain climbing, pony trekking and angling.

Open Mar-Nov
4 bedrs (2 twin inc 1 sh/wc; 1 double; 1 family sh/wc) 1 ba, 1 wc ⛄ 🏠 🐕 ⊁

SELF CATERING

DOOLIN 18B1

Horseshoe Farmhouse Fisher Street, Doolin 065 74006   Josephine Moloney

This spacious bungalow is set on a dairy farm overlooking Doolin, a village famous for traditional Irish music. Well-equipped rooms, cot available. Licensed. Tennis court. The farm lies west of N67 Ennistymon-Ballyvaughan road. Good base for touring the Burren.

⛄

LISDOONVARNA 18B1

Benrue Farmhouse Lisdoonvarna
065 74059   Mrs. Casey

This modern farmhouse is set on a farm rearing a suckling herd, 6km from Lisdoonvarna. ⛄ 🐕

Slieve Elva Farm Kilmoon, Lisdoonvarna 065 74318
Donnellan

Farm in the Burren region located 2km north of Lisdoonvarna on N67 (T69). The farm has a suckling herd. Scenic country for walks, cycling, mountain climbing, pony trekking and angling.

♿ ⛄ 🐕

CO. CORK

BLARNEY 18C3

Green Grove Stone View, Blarney
021 385167 Mrs. Quill

This comfortable modern farmhouse overlooks Blarney Castle and is set on a tillage and vegetable farm. It is under 2 miles from Blarney. There is an 18-hole pitch and putt (mini golf) course on the farm. Cork city 5 miles.

Open Feb-Nov
3 bedrs (1 double; 1 family sh/wc; 1 single) 1 ba, 1 wc ❄ 🏠

CLONAKILTY 18C4

An Garran Coir Castlefreke, Clonakilty
023 48236 Mrs. Calnan

Modern split-level farmhouse with panoramic views of peaceful picturesque valley situated on the coastline of sandy beaches. Dairy farm with pony rides, childrens games & playhouse. Tennis court, croquet lawn, home baking & gourmet food. Signposted on Clonakilty/Rosscarbery N71 Road beyond Lisavaird village.

Open Jan-Dec
7 bedrs (3 twin inc 1 ba/wc, 2 sh/wc; 2 double sh/wc; 2 family sh/wc) 1 ba, 1 wc ❄ 🏠 ✈ ✂
£B&B £14-£15, D £9-£12; WR £95-£100, WR/D £170-£175, child rates.

Ard Na Greine Ballinascarty, Clonakilty
023 39104 Mrs. Walsh

At this warm modern farmhouse near Ballinascarty village (N71 north of Clonakilty)

the emphasis is strongly on Norma Walsh's delicious home cooking and baking with wholesome fresh food. A 5-course dinner or a la carte menu is offered.

Open all year
6 bedrs (3 twin inc 2 sh/wc; 1 double; 2 family sh/wc) 2 ba ❄ 🏠 ✈

Hillside Farm Kilgarriffe, Clonakilty
023 33139 Bella Helen

Open Mar-Sept
4 bedrs (3 twin inc 2 sh/wc; 1 double) 1 ba, 2 wc ❄ 🏠 ✈

Liscubba House Rossmore, Clonakilty
023 38679 Mrs. Beechinor

Open all year
6 bedrs (1 twin; 2 double; 2 family; 1 single) 2 ba, 4 wc ❄ 🏠 ✈
cc Ac Vi

GLANDORE 18B4

Kilfinnan Farm Glandore 028 33233
Margaret Mehigan

The large modernised farmhouse overlooks Glandore Harbour. Glandore is on the R597, off the N71 Skinnereen-Clonakilty road. An ideal location for fishing, country walks and water sports, with sandy beaches and Drombeg Stone Circle close by.

Open all year
4 bedrs (1 twin; 2 double inc 1 sh/wc; 1 family sh/wc) 2 ba, 2 wc ❄ 🏠

INNISHANNON 18C4

Ballymountain House Innishannon
021 775366 Mrs. Cummins

The 200-year-old country house is on a cattle and sheep farm, off the N71 midway between Cork and Clonakilty, 3km from Bandon. Home cooking is a speciality, with full breakfasts and a 5-course dinner served. Cot available.

Open March-mid Nov
8 bedrs (4 twin; 2 double; 2 family) 3 ba, 3 wc ❄ ✈

CO. DONEGAL

LIFFORD 17D1

The Hall Greene Porthall, Lifford
074 41318 Mrs. McKean

The farmhouse, built circa 1611, complete with antique furnishings, overlooks the River Foyle and the Sperrin Mountains with an uninterrupted view for miles. Hall Greene is signposted 3km from Lifford (N14). This working farm has beef, sheep, pigs.

Open all year

4 bedrs (1 double; 3 family inc 2 sh/wc) 1 ba, 2 wc ⛨ 🛏 ⅄
cc Ac Vi

The Haw Lodge The Haw, Lifford
074 41397 Eileen Patterson

Open Mar-Oct
4 bedrs (1 twin sh; 2 double inc 1 sh/wc; 1 family ba/wc) 1 ba, 2 wc ⛨ ♈ ⅄ *Approved*
cc Ac Vi
£B&B £13.50-£15, D £11, WR/D £160.

CO. GALWAY

CASHEL 16A4

Ardmayle House Cashel 01504 42399
Annette V. Hunt

Open all year
⅄

OUGHTERARD 16B4

Cashel Rock Farmhouse Raha,
Oughterard 091 80213 Sheila Walsh

Open Easter-Oct
5 bedrs (2 twin sh/wc; 1 double sh/wc; 1 family sh/wc; 1 single sh/wc) ⛨
♈*Approved*
cc Ac Vi

SELF CATERING

CONNEMARA 18C1

High Trees Farmhouse Errigsbeg,
Roundstone, Connemara 095 35881 Marie King

4th generation farmhouse in secluded wooded setting in 40 acre sheep farm. Situated at food of Errisbeg Mountain (private path). Own

spring water supply, barn for bicycles, clothes line, peaceful walks, close to sandy beaches.

From Galway through Roundstone village, 1 mile on the main Coast road to Clifden, right hand side.

⛨(5)
£Wk £160-£230

ORANMORE 18C1

Cartroon Farm Coast Road, Oranmore
091 94345 Mrs. Cannon

This modern farmhouse is set on a dairy farm which also keeps ponies and a donkey. It is a mile west of Oranmore along the Galway city coast road. Ideal base for touring Connemara, the Burren and the Cliffs of Moher. Golf, swimming, sailing and horse riding

⛨ ♈

OUGHTERARD 16B4

Cashel Rock Farmhouse Raha,
Oughterard 091 80213 Sheila Walsh

⛨ ♈*Approved* cc Ac Vi

CO. KERRY

KILLARNEY 18B3

Glebe Farmhouse (off) Tralee Road,
Killarney 064 32179   Betty O'Connor

Open April-mid Dec
9 bedrs (3 twin inc 1 ba/wc, 1 sh/wc; 3
double inc 2 sh/wc; 3 family inc 2 sh/wc)
♿ 🏠 🐴
cc Ac AmEx Vi

KILLORGLIN 18B3

Hillview Farm Tralee Road, Milltown,
Killorglin 066 67117   Dorothy Stephens

This modern farm bungalow is on the main
N70 between Killorglin and Milltown,
overlooking the Slieve Mish Mountains and
the hills of Kilderry. Hillview is a family-run
dairy and sheep farm with ducks, hens, pony,
donkey, pet rabbits, fish, dogs and cats.

Open 17 Mar-Oct
6 bedrs (2 twin sh/wc; 2 double sh/wc; 1
family sh/wc; 1 single) 1 ba, 1 wc ♿ 🏠 🐴

CO. KILDARE

CASTLEDERMOT 19E2

Kilkea Lodge Farm Casteldermot
0503 45112   Godfrey D. Greene

Open all year
6 bedrs (1 twin; 3 double inc 2 ba/wc; 1
family sh/wc; 1 single) 1 ba, 3 wc
♿(12)*Approved*
£child rates.

CO. LAOIS

DONAGHMORE 19D2

Castletown House and Open Farm
Castletown House, Donaghmore
01505 46415   Mrs. Phelan

Early 19th century award- winning farm
guesthouse on a 200 acre beef and sheep
farm. River Erkina and remains of Norman
Castle on farm. Beautiful view of Slieve Bloom
Mountains. Recommended by Frommers,
Dillard and Causin - Travel writers. Signposted
from Borris-in-Ossory on N7, also from
Donaghmore village.

Open Mar-Dec
4 bedrs ♿ ♿ 🏠 🐴 ⚜ cc Ac Vi
£B&B £13.50, D £12, WR £90, WR/D £170,
child rates.

CO. LEITRIM

BALLINAMORE 17D3

Riversdale Farmhouse *Acclaimed*
Ballinamore   RAC
078 44122   Mr. Thomas

The spacious residence includes an indoor
heated swimming pool, sauna, squash court
and games room. The cuisine is excellent,
licensed. Beautiful scenery of lakes and
mountains. Ballinamore is south of Enniskillen
(A32/R202).

Open all year
9 bedrs (1 twin ba/wc; 4 double inc 1
ba/wc; 4 family inc 2 ba/wc) 1 ba, 4 wc ♿
🏠 *Approved* cc Ac Vi
£B&B £20-£24, D £10, WR £110, WR/D
£170, child rates.

CO. LIMERICK

ADARE 18C2

Hollywood House Adare, Croagh
061 396237   P. O'Shaughnessy

This 300-year-old farmhouse is set in peaceful rural parkland surrounded by a natural game sanctuary. The rooms are spacious and beautifully furnished, log fires in the drawing room and library. Cot available. The house is 5km from Adare (N20 south of Limerick) and signposted from the village hall.

Open May-Sept
4 bedrs (2 double sh/wc; 2 family ba/wc)
☎ ⚥ *Approved*
£child rates.

BRUFF 18C2

Bridge House Farm Grange, Bruff
061 390195   Patricia Barry

Open Apr-Oct
5 bedrs (1 twin; 1 double sh/wc; 1 family sh/wc; 2 single inc 1 sh/wc) 1 ba, 2 wc ☎
⌂ *Approved*
£B&B £14-£16, D £12, WR £90, child rates.

CROOM 18C2

Cronin Farmhouse Ballymacamore,
Croom 061 97497   Mary B. Cronin

Open all year
3 bedrs (1 treble, 2 family inc 1 sh/wc) 1 ba, 3 wc ☎ ⚥ ♞
£child rates.

KILMALLOCK 18C3

Flemingstown House Kilmallock
063 98093   Mrs. Sheedy-King

Flemingstown House is a listed 18th-century farmhouse set on a dairy farm. Located 4km from R515 Rock-of-Cashel-Tipperary-Killarney road, at the intersection of 3 counties: Limerick, Cork and Tipperary, making it ideal for touring.

Open Mar-Oct
6 bedrs (2 twin sh/wc; 1 double sh/wc; 2 family sh/wc; 1 single) 2 ba, 2 wc ☎ ♞

SELF CATERING

KILMALLOCK

Flemingstown House Kilmallock
063 98093   Mrs. Sheedy-King

CO. LONGFORD

GRANARD 17D4

Toberphelim House Granard
043 86568   Mary Smyth

This Georgian farmhouse with period furniture is set on a 200 acre family run cattle and sheep farm. For childen there are swings, climbing frame, highchair and playroom. The house is on the Castlepollard road 2km from Granard.

Open May-Sept
3 bedrs (1 twin; 2 family) 1 wc ☎ *Approved*
cc Ac Vi

CO. MAYO

LOUISBURGH 16A4

Cuaneen House Carramore, Louisburgh
098 66460   Teresa Sammon

Open April-Oct.

5 bedrs (2 twin; 2 double inc 1 sh/wc; 1 single) 3 ba, 4 wc ☎

NEWPORT 16A3

Youngwoods Farm Whitehouse Road, Porchfield, Newport PO30 4LJ

01983 522170 Mrs. Shanks
Open all year
☎(8) ♉ cc Ac Vi

CO. MEATH

DUNSHAUGHLIN 17E4

Gaulstown House Dunshaughlin
01825 9147 Kathryn Delany

Open Apr-Oct
3 bedrs (1 twin; 1 double; 1 family sh/wc)
1 ba, 2 wc ☎(10) ⌗ ✂
£child rates.

CO. SLIGO

KNOCKNAREA 16C3

Primrose Grange House Knocknarea
071 62005 Maisie Carter

Built in 1723, the farmhouse stands 350ft up the southern slope of Knocknarea mountain with stunning views of Ballisodare Bay. The 55-acre dairy farm rears pedigree shorthorns. 4 miles west of Sligo.

Open Feb-Nov
9 bedrs (4 twin inc 3 ba/wc, 1 sh/wc; 3 double inc 2 ba/wc, 1 sh/wc; 2 family ba/wc) 3 ba, 3 wc ☎ ⌗
£child rates.

SLIGO 16C3

Hillside Farm Kilseligh, Sligo 071 42808
Elma Stewart

This large farmhouse is on a dairy and beef farm close to Glencar Lake, waterfall and safe sandy beaches. On the N16 Enniskillen road just northeast of Sligo.

Open Apr-Nov
4 bedrs (4 family inc 2 sh/wc) 1 ba, 3 wc
☎ ♉

CO. TIPPERARY

CLONMEL 19D3

Nire Valley Farmhouse Ballymacarbry, Clonmel 052 36149 Mary Doocey

This award winning farmhouse lies 9 km south of Clonmel on the R671. It is set on a beef and sheep farm overlooking the scenic Nire Valley. Excellent home cooking. Trout fishing on the farm; large mature gardens.

Open all year
4 bedrs (1 twin sh/wc; 1 double sh/wc; 1 family sh/wc; 1 single) 1 ba, 2 wc ✂

TIPPERARY 18A3

Homeleigh Farmhouse Ballinacourty, Glen of Aherlow, Tipperary 062 56228
John Frewen

Homeleigh is a 50-acre working farm with some sheep in a beautiful position between the Galtee Mountains and Slievenamuck. The modern bungalow is very comfortable with all bedrooms on the ground floor. Good country cooking. Off the N24 south of Tipperary.

Open all year
5 bedrs (2 twin sh/wc; 2 double; 1 single sh/wc) 2 ba, 2 wc ☎ ♿ ♉
£child rates.

CO. WATERFORD

CAPPOQUIN   19D3

Aglish House Aglish, Cappoquin   **RAC**
024 9619   T. Moore

A 17th century farmhouse on dairy farm.

Open all year
4 bedrs all en suite sh/wc

DUNGARVAN   19D3

Ballyguiry Farm Dungarvan 058 41194
Mrs. Kiely

The farmhouse was built in 1833 and is part
of a mixed farm situated south of Dungarvan
off the N25. Children are particularly welcome
with a pony to ride, playground and hard
tennis court. Cot and highchair also provided.
Open Mar-Nov

6 bedrs (2 double inc 1 sh/wc; 3 family
sh/wc; 1 single) 1 ba, 2 wc ☙ ♞

The Castle Cappagh Farm Millstreet,
Cappagh, Dungarvan 058 68049
Mrs. Nugent

This farmhouse is in the restored wing of a
15th-century castle. It stands in a beautiful
valley on a 120-acre dairy farm, signposted off
the N72 Dungarvan-Cappoquin road. Wine
licence. For children, a playroom, playground,
swings, slide, and pony rides.

Open Mar-Oct
5 bedrs (2 twin sh/wc; 2 double sh/wc; 1
family sh/wc) 1 wc ☙ 🌐 ♞
   cc Ac Vi

YOUGHAL   19D3

Cuilin Farm Shanacoole, Kinsalebeg,
Youghal 024 92537   Mrs. Collender

This 200-year-old farmhouse has all modern
conveniences and stands in beautiful
countryside overlooking Youghal Bay. Cuilin
Farm is on N25, under 6km north of Youghal.
The mixed farm has some tillage, beef cattle,
a mare, a donkey and poultry.

Open Apr-Oct
6 bedrs (2 twin; 2 double; 2 family inc 1
sh/wc) 2 ba, 3 wc ☙ 🌐 ✂

CO. WESTMEATH

MULLINGAR   17D4

Annascanan House Killucan, Kinegad,
Mullingar 044 74130   Pamela Cooney

The Royal Canal flows through the grounds of
this lovely old house. The farm, 350 acres of
cows, cattle, sheep and tillage, is to be found
3.3km off the N4 at Kinnegad, southwest of
Mullingar.

Open Apr-Oct
3 bedrs (1 twin; 1 double; 1 family) 3 ba, 3
wc ☙ 🌐 ♞

CO. WEXFORD

DRINAGH   19E3

Killiane Castle Farmhouse Drinagh
053 58885   Kathleen Mernagh

Open Mar-Nov
8 bedrs (3 twin sh/wc; 3 double sh/wc; 2
family sh/wc) 2 wc ☙ ✂
£B&B £16, D £13, WR £112, WR/D £190,
child rates.

ENNISCORTHY   19F2

Clone House Ferns, Enniscorthy
054 66113   Mrs. Breen

This award-winning farmhouse is 3km
southwest of Ferns off the N11 Enniscorthy-
Gorey road. The farmhouse dates back to
1600 and is set in lovely gardens with the
ruins of a 12th-century church and the River

Bann on the farm. Fishing, shooting, and hunting.

Open Mar-Oct
5 bedrs (1 twin; 1 double ba/wc; 3 family inc 1 ba/wc, 1 sh/wc) 1 wc ⋊ ♠ ⊬

Ballyorley House Boolavogue, Ferns, Enniscorthy 054 66287   Margaret Gough

Open all year
4 bedrs (4 double inc 2 ba/wc) 2 ba, 2 wc
⋊ ♠*Approved*
£child rates.

CO. WICKLOW

ASHFORD   19F1

Ballyknockan House Glenealy,
Ashford 44614   Mrs. Byrne

Open all year
7 bedrs (4 twin sh/wc; 2 double sh/wc; 1 single sh/wc) 1 ba, 1 wc ⋊ ⊞
£B&B £15, D £8, WR/D £165-£175, child rates.

CLONEGAL   19F2

Park Lodge Farmhouse Clonegal
055 29140

Park Lodge is a charming 18th-century farmhouse set in peaceful surroundings of a 200-acre farm. Cot and highchair available. Off the R725 Gorey-Carlow road, between the N11 and N81.

Open all year
4 bedrs (4 twin inc 3 ba/wc, 1 sh/wc) 2 ba, 2 wc ⋊ ⊞ cc Ac Vi
£child rates.

INDEX OF TOWNS

ENGLAND

SCOTLAND

WALES

NORTHERN IRELAND

REPUBLIC OF IRELAND

KEY TO MAPS

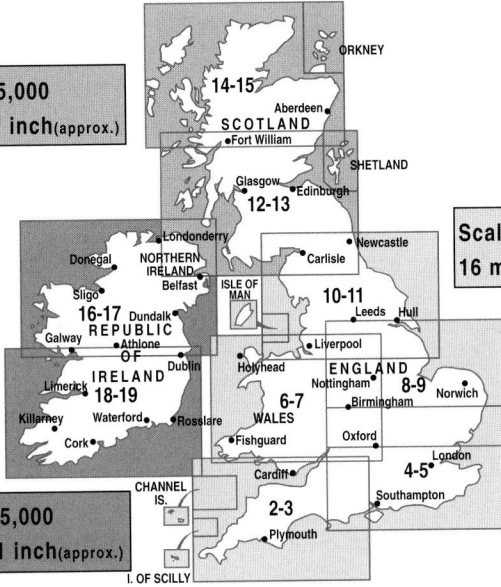

Scale 1:1,185,000
19 miles to 1 inch(approx.)

ORKNEY

14-15
Aberdeen
SCOTLAND
Fort William

SHETLAND

Glasgow Edinburgh
12-13

Scale 1:1,050,000
16 miles to 1 inch(approx.)

Londonderry
Donegal   NORTHERN
IRELAND
Belfast   ISLE OF
MAN

Newcastle
Carlisle

10-11
Leeds Hull

Sligo
16-17 Dundalk
Galway   REPUBLIC
OF
Athlone
IRELAND
Limerick   18-19   Dublin   Holyhead
Killarney   Waterford   Rosslare
Cork   Fishguard
6-7

Liverpool
ENGLAND
Nottingham   8-9
Birmingham   Norwich

WALES
Oxford

CHANNEL
IS.
2-3
Cardiff
Plymouth
Southampton
4-5
London

Scale 1:1,135,000
18 miles to 1 inch(approx.)

I. OF SCILLY

LEGEND

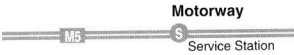

Motorway
Service Station

Junction

Primary Route
Dual Carriageway

Primary Route

A697   A38   'A' Road
(Dual Carriageway)

B3166   'B' Road

Ferry Route

⊕ Airport

EXMOOR   National Park

◉Salisbury   Farm Location

•••••••••••••••••••   National Boundary

·······················   County Boundary

Bay
Broad Haven
Haverfordwest
Narberth
B4314
A40
A4076
Milford Haven
Skomer I.
St. Ann's Head
Dale
A4075
Neyland
Pembroke
Dock
Pembroke
Tenby
Caldey I.
St. Govan Head
PEMBROKESHIRE COAST
NATIONAL PARK
6
B4777
Saundersfoot
Pendine
Laugharne
Kidwelly
A484
A40
A48
A483
Ammanford
Pontardulais
Pon
Neat
Burry
Port
Llanelli
SWANSEA
The Mumbles
Port
Talbot
Mumbles
Head
Port Eynon
A4118
Carmarthen
Bay

A
B
C

1
To Torquay
Alderney
To Plymouth, Weymouth and Poole
To Cork
B r i s t o l   Ch

St. Sampson
Herm
St. Peter
Port
Guernsey
Sark
2
C h a n n e l
I s l a n d s
Jersey
Rozel
St. Ouen
St. Helier
St. Brelade
Gorey
St.
Aubin

Lundy
Lynmouth
Lynton
Ilfracombe
Lee
Combe
Martin
Woolacombe
A361
Croyde
Braunton
Barnstaple
Barnstaple
or
Bideford Bay
Hartland Point
Westward Ho!
A39
Bideford
A361
South
Molton
Hartland
Clovelly
A386
B322
Chulmleigh
Parkham
A388
B3227
Torridge
Torrington
A386
A377
DE

3
es of Scilly
St. Mary's
St. Mary's
Trevose Head
Port Issac
Padstow
A389

Stratton
Bude
A3072
Holsworthy
A3072
Hatherleigh
A386
A3072
Marhamchurch
A39
A388
Tamar
B3218
Okehampton
A382
Boscastle
Tintagel
A395
Launceston
Laneast
A388
Lydford
Chagford
Camelford
Lifton
A30
DARTMOOR NATIONAL PARK
BODMIN
MOOR
A388
DARTMOOR
Widecombe-in-
the-Moor
A388
Two Bridges
Ashburton
Wadebridge
Bodmin
Liskeard
Taviotook
A386
A38
Buckfastleigh
A30
Tregaswith
St. Columb Major
A390
A38
Callington
A386
A38
Newquay
A3059
A30
A391
Lostwithiel
Landrake
Ivybridge
Ugborough
Perranporth
A3075
A392
Polbathic
Saltash
Torpoint
Ivybridge
Modbury
St. Agnes
A3058
A387
A374
Woodleigh
4
St. Ives
Bay
Redruth
A390
A3078
A39
A390
St. Blazey
Par
A3082
Looe
Polperro
PLYMOUTH
A379
Aveton Gifford
Loddiswell
Kingsbridge
St. Just
Penzance
A3071
Marazion
Breage
Cambourne
Troon
A394
A30
A393
A3078
Truro
St. Austell
Trenarren
Mevagissey
Bay
A381
St. Just in Roseland
St. Just
St. Mawes
Fowey
Mevagissey
Salcombe
Bolt Head
Helston
Falmouth
Falmouth
Bay
Hayle
Penryn
St. Ives
A30
St. Just
nd's
nd
St. Mary's
Mount's
Bay
B3293
St. Keverne
B3083
Mullion
Lizard
Lizard Point

A
B
C

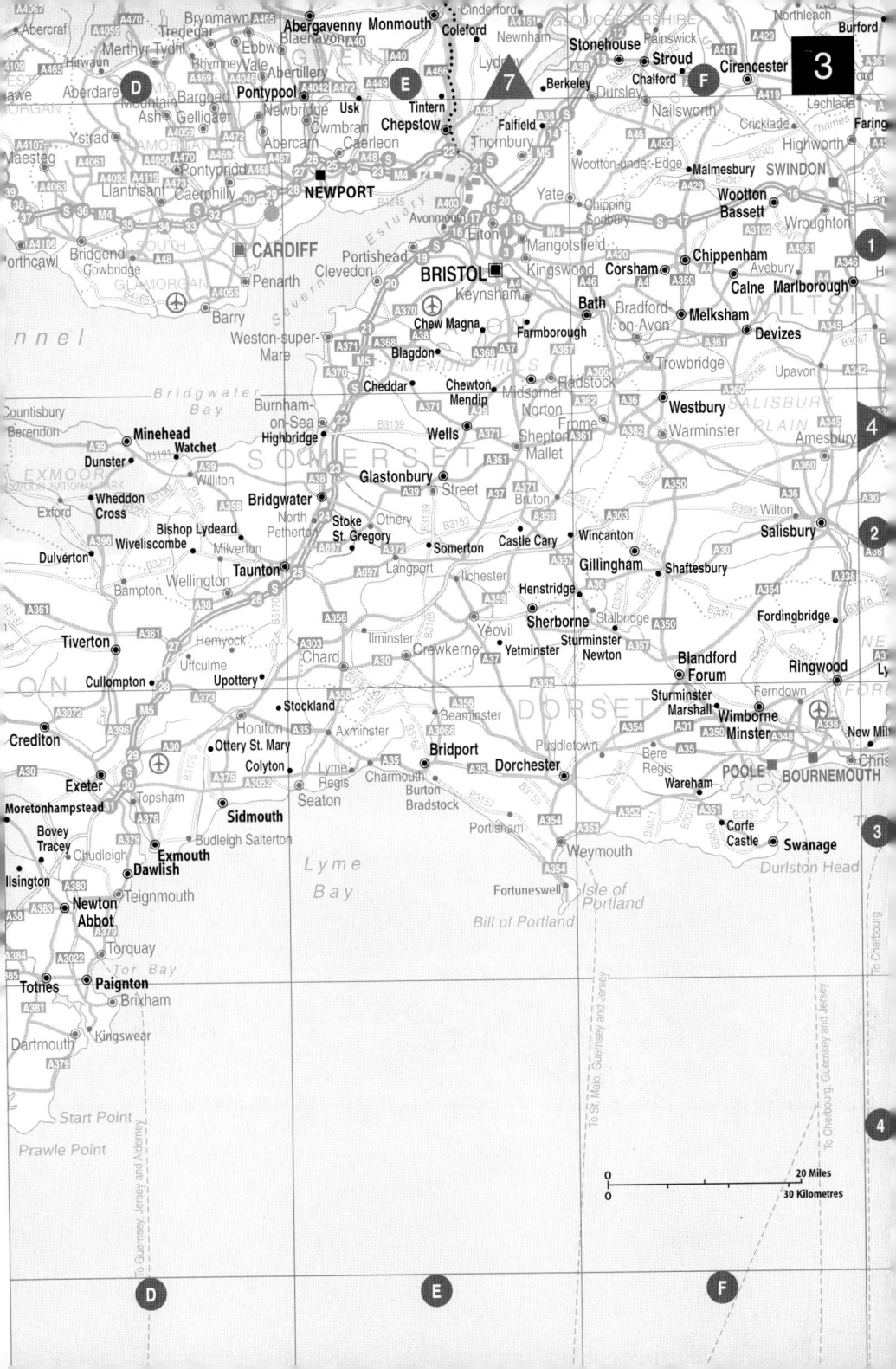

Abercraf
A4057
A470 Brynmawn A465
Tredegar
Merthyr Tydfil
A4059 Ebbw
Hirwaun
A4061
Rhymney Vale
Abertillery
Aberdare
A465
Gelligaer
Abercarn
D

Abergavenny Monmouth
Blaenavon A40
Usk
Cwmbran Caerleon
A449 Chepstow
E
Tintern
A466

Cinderford
Coleford
Newnham
Lydney
7
Berkeley
Falfield
Thornbury
Wootton-under-Edge

GLOUCESTERSHIRE
Northleach
Burford
Stonehouse Painswick A417 A429
Stroud
Chalford Cirencester
F
A419 Lechlade
Cricklade Highworth
Malmesbury SWINDON
A429 Faring
Thames

NEWPORT
CARDIFF
Penarth
Barry

Portishead
Clevedon
Avonmouth
BRISTOL
Keynsham
Chew Magna
Farmborough

Chipping Sodbury
Yate
Mangotsfield
Kingswood
A420 Corsham
Bath
Bradford-on-Avon
Melksham
Devizes

Wootton Bassett
Wroughton
Chippenham
Avebury
Calne Marlborough

Weston-super-Mare
Blagdon
A368
Cheddar
Chewton Mendip
Wells
Highbridge
Burnham-on-Sea

MENDIP HILLS
Radstock
Midsomer Norton
Frome
Shepton Mallet
Westbury
Warminster
Trowbridge
Upavon

SALISBURY PLAIN
Amesbury

Minehead
Watchet
Dunster
Wheddon Cross
Williton
Bridgwater
Glastonbury
Street
Bruton
Wilton
Salisbury

SOMERSET
EXMOOR

Exford
Bishop Lydeard
Wiveliscombe
Milverton
North Petherton
Stoke St. Gregory
Othery
Somerton
Castle Cary
Wincanton
Shaftesbury
Gillingham
Dulverton
Bampton
Wellington
Taunton
Langport
Ilchester
Henstridge
Sherborne
Stalbridge
Fordingbridge

Tiverton
Hemyock
Uffculme
Upottery
Ilminster
Chard
Crewkerne
Yeovil
Yetminster
Sturminster Newton
Blandford Forum
Ringwood
Cullompton

Crediton
Stockland
Honiton
Axminster
Beaminster
Bridport
Dorchester
Puddletown
Sturminster Marshall
Wimborne Minster
Ferndown
New Mil

Exeter
Ottery St. Mary
Colyton
Lyme Regis
Charmouth
Burton Bradstock
Bere Regis
Wareham
POOLE
BOURNEMOUTH
Chris
Moretonhampstead
Topsham
Seaton
Portisham

Sidmouth
Budleigh Salterton
Weymouth
Corfe Castle
Swanage

Bovey Tracey
Chudleigh
Exmouth
Dawlish
Teignmouth
Lyme Bay
Fortuneswell
Isle of Portland
Bill of Portland
Durlston Head

Ilsington
Newton Abbot
Torquay
DORSET

Totnes
Paignton
Brixham
Dartmouth
Kingswear
Tor Bay

Start Point
Prawle Point

To St. Malo, Guernsey and Jersey
To Guernsey, Jersey and Alderney
To Cherbourg, Guernsey and Jersey
To Cherbourg

0   20 Miles
0   30 Kilometres

D   E   F

D | E | 9 | F

St. Ives
Soham
Mildenhall
A143
Eye
Bramfield
A11
A1011
Ixworth
B1113
A140
A1120
A10
Cottenham
Burwell
A142
A14
Framlingham
Leiston
Histon
B1102
Newmarket
Wickham Market
Saxmundham
Thorpeness
Aldeburgh
A1049
Cambridge
A14
Bury St. Edmunds
Stowmarket
Needham Market
Claydon
A1152
Orford
Great Shelford
A143
A1141
A14
A1071
Woodbridge
Orford Ness
Melbourn
A505
Haverhill
Lavenham
IPSWICH
Hintlesham
A604
A1092
Hadleigh
Bawdsey
Royston
Saffron Walden
Sudbury
East Bergholt
A12
Shotley Gate
Felixstowe
Baldock
A131
A134
Nayland
Manningtree
Harwich
To Esbjerg
To Göteborg
To Hamburg
To Hoek van Holland
Buntingford
Halstead
Fordham
A604
Colchester
A120
Wix
The Naze
Stevenage
Stansted
Braintree
A120
Marks Tey
Wivenhoe
Walton on the Naze
Frinton-on-Sea
Puckeridge
Bishop's Stortford
Kelvedon
Witham
Brightlingsea
Holland-on-Sea
Welwyn Garden City
Ware
Margaret Roding
A12
Tiptree
West Mersea
Clacton-on-Sea
Mersea I.
Hertford
Harlow
Chelmsford
Maldon
Hatfield
Hoddesdon
Waltham Abbey
A414
A414
Cheshunt
Epping
Chipping Ongar
A130
Potters Bar
Loughton
Billericay
Burnham-on-Crouch
A128
Wickford
Brentwood
Rayleigh
SOUTHEND-ON-SEA
Foulness I.
BARNET
Basildon
Shoeburyness
A12
A127
Corynton
Canvey Island
Thames Estuary
LONDON
Grays
Tilbury
Grain
Sheerness
Isle of Sheppey
BARKING
M25
Gravesend
Rochester
Leysdown on Sea
Herne Bay
Margate
Cliftonville
BEXLEY
Dartford
Chatham
Whitstable
North Foreland
BROMLEY
Gillingham
Rainham
Sittingbourne
Faversham
Sarre
Broadstairs
CROYDON
Wrotham
A249
Canterbury
Ramsgate
Banstead
West Malling
Aylesford
A252
Sandwich
Caterham
Sevenoaks
Teston
Maldstone
Charing
Wye
Deal
Redhill
Edenbridge
Tonbridge
Sutton Valence
Hastingleigh
Walmer
Reigate
Lingfield
Markbeech
Southborough
Pluckley
Ashford
A256
Horley
Smallfield
Ashurst
Royal Tunbridge Wells
Marden
Dover
South Foreland
Crawley
East Grinstead
Hartfield
Cranbrook
Sissinghurst
Tenterden
Folkestone
Channel Tunnel
Cuckfield
Crowborough
Hawkhurst
Hythe
Strait of Dover
Haywards Heath
Burwash
Heathfield
Rother
New Romney
Burgess Hill
Uckfield
Sedlescombe
Rye
Lydd
Camber
Dungeness
Hurstpierpoint
Battle
Baldslow
Lewes
Hailsham
Hastings
Bexhill
Boulogne
Hove
BRIGHTON
Pevensey
Newhaven
Polegate
Eastbourne
Peacehaven
Seaford
Beachy Head
To Dieppe

0 ___ 20 Miles
0 ___ 30 Kilometres

D | E | F

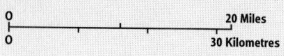

A B C

0 ____ 20 Miles
0 ____ 30 Kilometres

Carmel Head
Anglesey
Amlwch
A5025 Moelfre
Holyhead (Caergybi)
Llanerchymedd
B5109
Holy I.
Llangefni
A5
Rhosneigr
Menai Bridge
Llanfairpwllgwyngyll
A4080
Bangor
Beaumaris
Penmaenmawr
Conwy
Bethesda
Caernarfon
A5
Capel Curig
A487
A4085
A4086
B4418
A499
Caernarfon Bay
GWYNEDD
Blaenau Ffestiniog
Ffestiniog
Penrhyndeudraeth
A487
Porthmadog
Nefyn
B4354
A497
A497
Criccieth
Pwllheli
Harlech
A499
Aberdaron
Abersoch
Tremadog Bay
Barmouth
Dolgellau
Llwyngwril
A493
Abergynolwyn
A405
Tywyn
A493
Aberdyfi
Machynlleth
Borth
A487
Aberystwyth
A4120
A487
A485
Aberaeron
A482
New Quay
A486
Llangranog
B4342
Cemaes Head
Cardigan
B4570
PEMBROKESHIRE COAST
NATIONAL PARK
Strumble Head
Newport
Goodwick Fishguard
Newcastle Emlyn
Gwaun Valley
MYNYDD PRESELI
Croesgoch
St. David's
A487
Solva
A487
Haverfordwest
Whitland
St. Clears
Narberth
Laugharne
Broad Haven
A4076
A4075
Milford Haven
Dale
Neyland
A477
Saundersfoot
Pendine
Kidwelly
Pembroke
A
Pembroke Dock
A4139
Tenby
B
Burry Port
Llanelli
Carmarthen Bay
Caldey I.
PEMBROKESHIRE COAST NATIONAL PARK
St. Govan Head

Conwy
Great Ormes Head
Llandudno
Rhos-on-Sea
Colwyn Bay
Prestatyn
Rhyl
Rhuddlan
Abergele
St. Asaph
A548
B5381
B5382
A5
A470
Betws-y-coed
A498
Pentrefoelas
A5
Denbeigh
A543
A544
Bala
A4212
Trawsfynydd
SNOWDONIA NATIONAL PARK
A494
A4403
L. Vyrnwy
Dinas Mawddwy
Mallwyd
A45
A487
A489
A470
Caersws
A470
Llanidloes
A44
A444
Ponterwyd
Llangurig
Rhayader
A470
Tregaron
A482
Builth Wells
Lampeter
A475
Llanwrtyd Wells
Llandrindod Wells
POW
A483
Llandovery
A40
Llanwrda
Trecastle
A482
A40
Llandeilo
A4069
BRECON BEACONS NATIONAL PARK
Abercraf
A4067
A4215
Ammanford
A4068
Hirwaun
Merthyr Tydfil
A4109
A465
Pontardulais
Aberdare
Pontardawe
SWANSEA
A483
Maesteg
A4061
Ystrad
The Mumbles
Langland

DYFED
Tywi
WALES
CAMBRIAN
MOUNTAINS
Teifi

1

2

3

4

OLDHAM
MANCHESTER
Ashton-under-Lyne
Hyde
STOCKPORT
Chisworth
Glossop
Stocksbridge
Rawmar
Mexborough
A1(M)

Crosby
Kirkby
Atherton
Leigh
Salford
Sale
Cheadle
Marple
New Mills
Whaley Bridge
SHEFFIELD
Hathersage
Work

ST HELENS
WARRINGTON
Altrincham
Lymm
Cheadle
Bramhall
Dronfield
Staveley

BIRKENHEAD
LIVERPOOL
Widnes
Runcorn
Wilmslow
Knutsford
Alderley Edge
Macclesfield
Buxton
Bakewell
Chesterfield
Bolsover

Hoylake
Wallasey
Holywell
Neston
Ellesmere Port
Frodsham
Northwich
Marton
Congleton
Leek
Hartington
Ashover
Clay Cross
Matlock
MANSFIELD

Flint
Connah's Quay
Hawarden
Chester
Winsford
Middlewich
Sandbach
Alsager
Biddulph
Tunstall
Burslem
Hanley
Wirksworth
Matlock Bath
Alfreton
Ripley
Sutton

Mold
Buckley
Hope
Tarporley
Crewe
Kidsgrove
STOKE-ON-TRENT
Cauldon
Ashbourne
Ambergate
Belper
Kirk

Ruthin
Moss
Wrexham
Nantwich
Newcastle-under-Lyme
Keele
Longton
Oakamoor
Cheadle
Brailsford
DERBY
NOTTINGHA

Corwen
Llangollen
Chirk
Ellesmere
Whitchurch
Woore
Stone
Uttoxeter
Alkmonton
Mickleover
Castle Donington
Melbourne

Llanfyllin
Welshpool (Y Trallwng)
Oswestry
Whittington
Wem
Market Drayton
Hodnet
Eccleshall
Stafford
Sudbury
Burton upon Trent
Swadlincote
Ashby-de-la-Zouch
Shepshed
Loughborough

Llanfair Caereinion
Newport
Penkridge
Rugeley
Cannock
Lichfield
Coalville
LEICES

Montgomery (Trefaldwyn)
Shrewsbury
Wellington
Shifnal
TELFORD
Ironbridge
Brownhills
Aldridge
Tamworth
Atherstone
Hinckley
Nuneaton

Newtown (Y Drenewydd)
Lydham
Bishop's Castle
Church Stretton
Much Wenlock
WOLVERHAMPTON
WALSALL
SUTTON COLDFIELD
Coleshill
Bedworth

Clun
Craven Arms
Diddlebury
Bridgnorth
WEST BROMWICH
DUDLEY
Halesowen
BIRMINGHAM
COVENTRY
Lutterw

Knighton
Duslnall
Ludlow
Cleobury Mortimer
Bromfield
Bewdley
Stourbridge
Hagley
Kidderminster
Solihull
Kenilworth
Royal Leamington Spa

Presteigne
New Radnor
Leominster
Tenbury Wells
Woofferton
St Michael's
Abberley
Stourport-on-Severn
Bromsgrove
Redditch
Henley-in-Arden
WARWICK
Southam

Kington
Eardisley
Bromyard
Droitwich
Whitbourne
Worcester
Bidford-on-Avon
Alcester
Wellesbourne
STRATFORD-UPON-AVON
Kington
Ettington

Hay-on-Wye
Hereford
Preston Wynne
Great Malvern
Pershore
Dorsington
Oxhill
Shipston-on-Stour
Banbury
Deddington

Llyswen
Three Cocks
Ledbury
Malvern Wells
Upton-upon-Severn
Evesham
Broadway
Chipping Campden
Moreton-in-Marsh

Brecon
Llangorse
Portrilas
Dymock
Twyning
Tewkesbury
Winchcombe
Stow-on-the-Wold
Chipping Norton
Steeple Aston
Charlbury
Woodstock

Crickhowell
Ross-on-Wye
Newent
Huntley
Cheltenham
Bourton-on-the-Water
Northleach
Burford
Minster Lovell
Witney

Abergavenny
Brynmawr
Blaenavon
Monmouth
Mitcheldean
Minsterworth
GLOUCESTER
Andoversford
Cowley

Ebbw Vale
Abertillery
Coleford
Lydney
Blakeney
Stonehouse
Painswick
Cirencester
Fairford
OXFORD
Bampton

Rhymney
Newbr
Usk
Pontypool
Chepstow
Tintern
Falfield
Berkeley
Dursley
Stroud
Chalford
Lechlade
Highworth
Faringdon
Abingdon
Wantage

Brynmawr
Abercarn
Caerleon
Cwmbran
Thornbury
Wotton-under-Edge
Tetbury
Cricklade
SWINDON

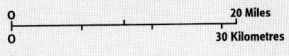

9

D   E   F

0   20 Miles
0   30 Kilometres

Withernsea
rington Easington
Spurn Head
Grimsby
Cleethorpes
Estuary

North
Somercotes

Louth
Mablethorpe
Sutton on Sea

Alford
Spilsby
Skegness
Wainfleet
All Saints
Gibraltar Point

Boston
The Wash
Hunstanton
Wells-next-the-Sea   Blakeney   Sheringham
Burnham Market
Holt
Cromer
Fakenham
North Walsham
Sandringham
Aylsham
Stalham
Holbeach
Long Sutton
King's Lynn
Reepham
Winterton-on-Sea
THE FEN
Wroxham
Acle
Caister-on-Sea
East Dereham
NORWICH
Great Yarmouth
Wisbech
Swaffham
Hopton
Downham Market
Corton
Thorney
Guyhirn
Stoke Ferry
Watton
Wymondham
Loddon
Lowestoft
March
Methwold
Attleborough
NORFOLK
Whittlesey
Mundford
Bungay
Beccles
Chatteris
Brandon
Harleston
Littleport
Thetford
Barnham
Diss
Halesworth
Ely
Thelnetham
Southwold
Soham
Mildenhall
Ixworth
Eye
Bramfield
St. Ives
Cottenham
Burwell
Mendlesham Green
Leiston
Histon
Newmarket
Framlingham
Thorpeness
Cambridge
Bury St. Edmunds
Stowmarket
Wickham Market
Aldeburgh
Great Shelford
Lavenham
Needham Market
Orford
Orford Ness
Melbourn
Haverhill
Hadleigh
IPSWICH
Woodbridge
Royston
Saffron Walden
Sudbury
Hintlesham
Bawdsey
Baldock
East Bergholt
Shotley Gate
Felixstowe
Buntingford
Nayland
Manningtree
Harwich
Stevenage
Halstead
Fordham
Wix
The Naze
HERTFORD SHIRE
Braintree
Colchester
Wivenhoe
Walton on the Naze
Welwyn Garden City
Great Dunmow
Kelvedon
Brightlingsea
Frinton-on-Sea
Ware
Bishop's Stortford
Tiptree
Witham
Clacton-on-Sea
Holland-on-Sea

To Rotterdam and Zeebrugge
To Esbjerg
To Göteborg
To Hamburg
To Hoek van Holland
To Zeebrugge

NORFOLK BROADS
SUFFOLK
ESSEX

To Esbjerg

20 Miles
30 Kilometres

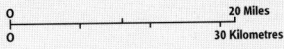

Newbiggin-by-the-Sea
Ashington
Blyth
Whitley Bay
Tynemouth
NEWCASTLE UPON TYNE
South Shields
Jarrow
Boldon
teshead
SUNDERLAND
Washington
Houghton le Spring
Seaham
hester-Street
Easington
Hetton-le-Hole
Horden
Peterlee
URHAM
Spennymoor
Hartlepool
Sedgefield
CLEVELAND
TEESSIDE
Jewton Aycliffe
Billingham
Redcar
Stockton-on-Tees
MIDDLESBOROUGH
Eston
Saltburn-by-the-Sea
Loftus
Darlington
Thornaby-on-Tees
Guisborough
Whitby
Stokesley
Great Ayton
Goathland
Robin Hood's Bay
Ravenscar
NORTH YORK MOORS
NORTH YORK MOORS NATIONAL PARK
Northallerton
Scalby
Bedale
Kirkbymoorside
Scarborough
Helmsley
NORTH
Masham
Thirsk
Pickering
Filey
Ampleforth
Nunnington
Hunmanby
Slingsby
YORKSHIRE
Ripon
Easingwold
Malton
Flamborough Head
Boroughbridge
Norton
Bridlington
Ripley
Fridaythorpe
Great Driffield
Bridlington Bay
Harrogate
Knaresborough
Stamford Bridge
THE WOLDS
Otley
Wetherby
YORK
Pocklington
Hornsea
Tadcaster
Market Weighton
udsey
LEEDS
Beverley
HUMBERSIDE
torley
Selby
North Cave
Rothwell
Howden
South Cave
HULL
Hedon
Castleford
Goole
Withernsea
Knottingley
Barton-upon-Humberside
New Holland
Patrington
Easington
Pontefract
Winterton
Immingham
Spurn Head
Wakefield
Thorne
Crowle
Scunthorpe
Grimsby
Cleethorpes
Adwick le Street
Estuary and Zeebrugge
To Rotterdam
BARNSLEY
Bentley
Hatfield
Brigg
Mexborough
Doncaster
Belton
Caistor
Rawmarsh
Conisbrough
Kirton-in-Lindsey
North Somercotes
ksbridge
Rotherham
Bawtry
Walkeringham
Maltby
Market Rasen
Louth
Mablethorpe
SHEFFIELD
Gainsborough
East Barkwith
Hathersage
Eckington
Sturton by Stow
Alford
Dronfield
East Retford
Worksop
Staveley
Horncastle
Lincoln

A B 14 C

Coll

Dervaig
Tobermory
Acharacle
Corran Onich
Kinlochleven
Kinloch Rannoch
Loch Rannoch

Glencoe
Lochaline
Portnacroish
Bridge of Orchy
Kerrera

Ulva
Salen
Craignure
Lismore
Connel
Loch Etive
Killin
Loch Tay

1

Iona
Fionnphod
Bunessan
Mull
Oban
Taynuilt
Lochawe
Clifton
Crianlarich
Lochearnhead
Comrie

Seil
Kilninver
Kilmelford
Ardlui
L. Katrine
Callander
Dunblane

20 Miles
30 Kilometres

Scarba
Kilmartin
Inverararay
Arrochar
Tarbet
Aberfoyle Port of Menteith
Doune

Colonsay
Furnace
Loch Lomond
CENTRAL
Kippen **Stirling**

Ardlussa
Lochgilphead
Luss
Garelochhead
Drymen
Balfron

2

Port Askaig
Feolin
Ferry
Craighouse
Tarbert
Coulport
Rhu
Gartocharn
Helensburgh
Alexandria
Kilsyth

Islay
Bridgend
Kennacraig
Tighnabruaich
Dunoon
Gourock
Greenock
Port Glasgow
Clydebank
Dumbarton
Milngavie
Kirkintilloch Cumbernauld
Bishopbriggs

rtnahaven
Clachan
Lochranza
Rothesay
Wemyss Bay
Kilbarchan
Johnstone Paisley
GLASGOW
Airdr

Gigha
Bute
Millport
Largs
Kilbirnie
Barrhead
Bothwell
East
Kilbride Hamilton
Mothe

Port Ellen
Mull of Oa
Arran
West Kilbride
Dalry
Beith
Stewarton
Strathaven

Glenbarr
Kilbrannan Sound
Brodick
Ardrossan
Saltcoats
Kilwinning
Stevenston
Irvine
Galston Darvel
Kilmarnock

Lamlash
Holy I.
Troon
Ayr
Mauchline
Muirkirk
Dou

Blackwaterfoot
Corriecravie
Prestwick
Holmston
Cumnock
New Cumnock

Campbeltown
Southend
Mull of Kintyre
Sanda
Maybole
Dalmellington

3

Rathlin
Fair Head
Ailsa Craig
Girvan
Carsphairn
Moniaive

Bushmills
Ballycastle
Ballantrae
Barrhill
Bargrennan
New
Galloway

raine
Glenariff
Garron Point
Milleur Point
Newton
Stewart
Castle
Douglas

Ballymoney
North Channel
To Cairnryan/Stranraer
Kirkcolm
Cairnryan
Glenluce
Creetown
Kirkcudbright

4

Portglenone
Ballymena
Larne
Island Magee
Stranraer
Wigtown
Kirkcudbright

Randalstown
Ballyclare
Ballycarry
Portpatrick
Sandhead
Port
William
Whithorn

Antrim
Carrickfergus
Whitehead
Luce Bay
Isle of
Whithorn

BELFAST
Newtownabbey
Bangor
Donaghadee
Sandhead
Drummore
Wigtown Bay
Burrow Head

Lisburn
Holywood
Newtownards
Comber
Mull of Galloway

17

A B C

20 Miles
30 Kilometres

15

D Blairgowrie E

SHETLAND

Blair Atholl
Kirkmichael
Pitlochry
Bridge of Cally
Aberfeldy
Dunkeld
Kinclaven
Amulree
Blairgowrie
Rattray
Alyth
Meigle
Coupar Angus
Glamis
Forfar
Kirriemuir
Brechin
Montrose
South Esk
Lunan Bay
Arbroath
Carnoustie
Buddon Ness
DUNDEE
Newport-on-Tay
Firth of Tay
Perth
Newburgh
Bridge of Earn
Cupar
St. Andrews
Auchtermuchty
Ladybank
Fife Ness
Auchterarder
Crail
Kilrenny
Upper Largo
Leslie
Markinch
Kinross
Glenrothes
Leven
Methil
Pittenweem
Buckhaven
Tillicoultry
Dollar
Cowdenbeath
Kirkcaldy
Alloa
Dunfermline
Burntisland
Firth of Forth
Grangemouth
Bo'ness
Inverkeithing
Queensferry
North Berwick
Dunbar
Linlithgow
Musselburgh
Tranent
Haddington
East Linton
Bathgate
Livingston
EDINBURGH
Dalkeith
Cockburnspath
Almadale
East Calder
Loanhead
Lasswade
Ayton
Whitburn
Penicuik
Duns
Berwick-upon-Tweed
Shotts
Carluke
Lauder
Stow
Greenlaw
Holy I.
Lanark
Carnwath
Galashiels
Earlston
Coldstream
Biggar
Peebles
Kelso
Belford
Bamburgh
Broughton
Innerleithen
Selkirk
Melrose
St Boswells
Wooler
Douglas
Abington
Hawick
Jedburgh
Alnwick
Moffat
Alnmouth
Beattock
Amble-by-the-Sea
Thornhill
Rothbury
Felton
Sanquhar
NORTHUMBERLAND
Kielder Water
Otterburn
Morpeth
Newbiggin-by-the-Sea
Newcastleton
Ashington
Langholm
Kirkwhelpington
Bedlington
Blyth
Lochmaben
Whitley Bay
Lockerbie
Ponteland
Gosforth
Tynemouth
Dumfries
Canonbie
Longtown
Haydon Bridge
Corbridge
NEWCASTLE UPON TYNE
South Shields
New Abbey
Gretna
Annan
Brampton
Haltwhistle
Hexham
Blaydon
Jarrow
Boldon
Dalbeattie
Prudhoe
Gateshead
SUNDERLAND
Carlisle
Allendale Town
Consett
Stanley
Washington
Silloth
Wigton
Thursby
Alston
Chester-le-Street
Houghton-le-Spring
Seaham
Aspatria
Caldbeck
Stanhope
DURHAM
Hetton-le-Hole
Easington
Maryport
Wearhead
Westgate
Wolsingham
Tow Law
Crook
Spennymoor
Peterlee
Cockermouth
Penrith
DURHAM
Sedgefield
Workington
Bishop Auckland
Newton Aycliffe
TEESSIDE
Whitehaven
Middleton in Teesdale
Stockton-on-Tees
Keswick
Appleby in Westmoreland
Barnard Castle
Darlington
St Bees Head
Cleator
CUMBRIA
MOUNTAINS
Shap
Stokesley

SHETLAND ISLANDS
Haroldswick
Gutcher
Mid Yell
Fetlar
Isbister
Yell
Ulsta
Hillswick
Toft
Sullom
St Magnus Bay
Muckle Roe
Papa Stour
Voe
Sandness
Mainland
Whalsay
Scalloway
Lerwick
Bressay
Easter Quarff
Sumburgh
Sumburgh Head

Solway Firth

D E 10 F

A B C

1

Cape Wrath
Dur

Butt of Lewis
Port Nis
A857

Gallan Head
Great Bernera
Carlabhagh
A857
Tiumpan Head
Port Nan Giuran
A866
A858
Stornoway

Point of Stoer

Laxford Bridge
A894
A838

En

Outer Hebrides

Lewis

Scarp

Kebock Head

Rubha Coigeach

Lochinver
A837
Inchnadamph

A894

Ledmore
A835
A837

Ovk

2

Tarasaigh
A859
Tarbert
Scalpay

Shiant Is.

The Minch

L. Broom
Ullapool

Pabbay
Bernera
A859
Roghadal
Renish Point
Harris

Sound of Harris

Rubha Hunish

A832

Poolewe

A835

HLANDS

L. Fannich
Gorstan
A832

North
A867
Lochmaddy

Vaternish Point

A855
Snizort
Staffin
Uig

Gairloch
A832

L. Maree

Kinlochewe
A890

Achnasheen
A890

Corrin

eatrafch
A865

3

Ronay

Dunvegan Head
A850
Dunvegan
A863
Bracadale
A850
Portree

Sound of Raasay

Rona
Inner Sound

L. Torridon
Shieldaig

Benbecula

Wiay
Creag

Skye

Raasay

WEST HIGHL

Farar
A831

Cannich
A831

South Uist

Sligachan
Scalpay
Plockton
A896

Kyle of Lochalsh
A87
A890

Invermoriston

Little Minch

Broadford
A851
A850

Lochboisdale

Soay

Shiel Bridge
A87

Sound of Sleat

Eriskay

Canna

Ardvasar
A851

L. Hourn

Fort Augustus
A887
A82

4

Rum

Mallaig

Invergarry
A87

L. Lochy
A82

Eigg

Arisaig
L. Morar

L. Arkaig

Spean Bridge
A86

Muck

Point of Ardnamurchan

Glenfinnan
A830
A861

Corpach

Caledonian Canal

Fort William
A82

Coll

Acharacle

Corran
A861

Onich

Kinlochleven
A82

Dervaig
Tobermory
A848
A884

Glencoe
A82

12

Lochaline
Salen

Portnacroish

Loch Linnhe
A828

Tiree

Bridge of Orchy

20 Miles
30 Kilometres

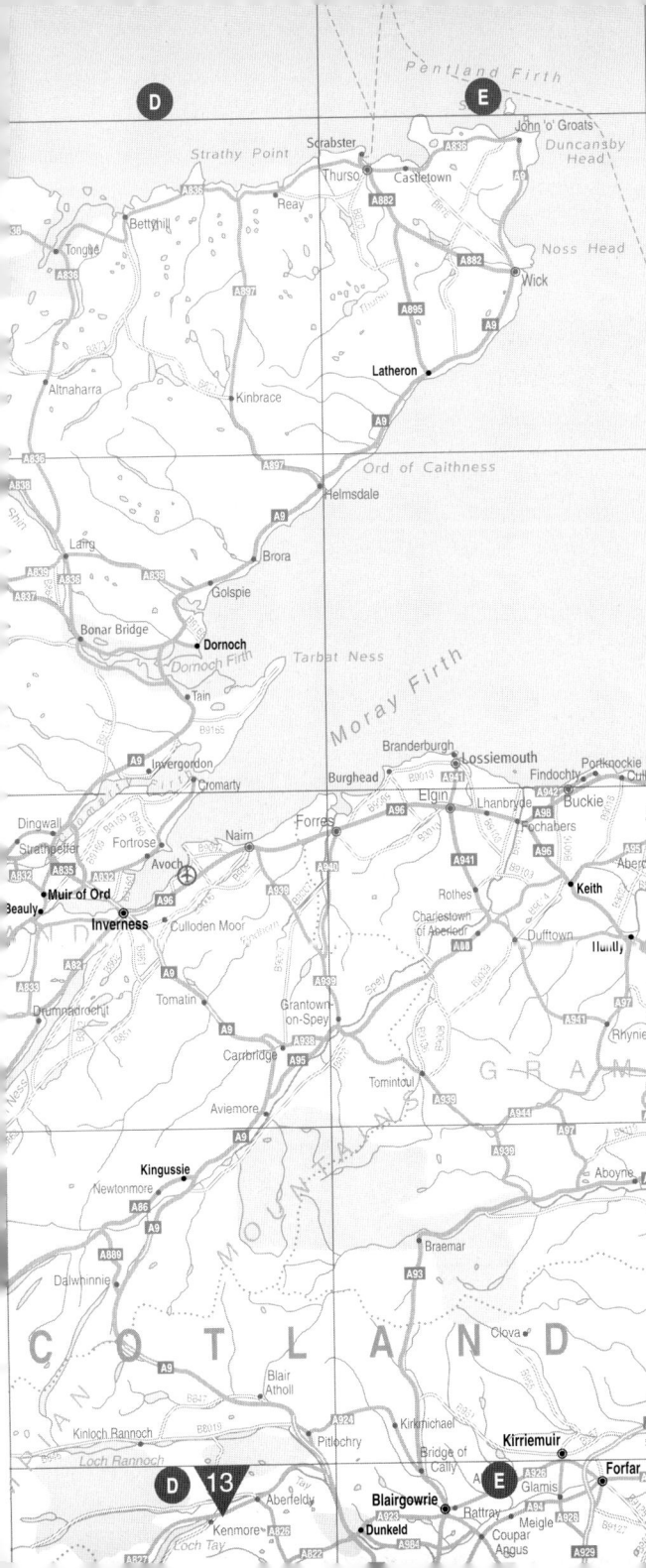

Pentland Firth

D
E
F

Strathy Point
Scrabster
John 'o' Groats
Duncansby
Head
Thurso
Castletown
Reay
A882
Bettyhill
A836
A9
Noss Head
A882
Tongue
A838
A836
Wick
A836
A895
Altnaharra
Kinbrace
A9
Latheron
A838
A836
Ord of Caithness
Lairg
A839
Helmsdale
A9
A837
Brora
A839
Golspie
Bonar Bridge
Dornoch Firth
Tarbat Ness
Dornoch
Tain
B9176
Moray Firth
Branderburgh
A9
Invergordon
Lossiemouth
Portknockie
Cromarty
Burghead
Findochty
Cullen
Portsoy
Macduff
Rosehearty
Fraserburgh
Dingwall
Elgin
Buckie
Banff
Strathpeffer
Forres
A96
Lhanbryde
A96
Fortrose
Nairn
Fochabers
Turriff
Mintlaw
Peter
Avoch
Aberchirder
Muir of Ord
A96
Rothes
A95
Keith
Cruden
Bay
Beauly
A96
Charlestown
of Aberlour
Dufftown
Huntly
A96
Ellon
Inverness
Culloden Moor
A88
A920
A92
Drumnadrochit
Tomatin
Insch
Old
Rayne
Oldmeldrum
A96
Dyce
A9
Grantown-
on-Spey
Rhynie
Inverurie
Kintore
ABERDEEN
Carrbridge
A95
Alford
A980
Girdle Ness
Aviemore
Tomintoul
Peterculter
Kingussie
Aboyne
A93
Banchory
Newtonmore
A86
Braemar
A957
Stonehaven
A889
A93
Dalwhinnie
Inverbervie
A94
Clova
Laurencekirk
Blair
Atholl
Kirriemuir
Brechin
A94
Montrose
Kinloch Rannoch
Pitlochry
Bridge
of Cally
Forfar
A92
Lunan
Bay
Loch Rannoch
D
13
Aberfeldy
E
Glamis
F
Blairgowrie
Rattray
Meigle
Kenmore
Dunkeld
Coupar Angus
Arbroath
Loch Tay

Orkney
Islands

Mull Head
North
Ronalds
Papa Westray
Westray
Westray Firth
Eday
Rousay
Stronsay
Sound
Shapinsay
Brough
Head
Birsay
ORKNEY
Stromness
Finstown
Kirkwall
Mainland
St. Mary's
Scapa Flow
Rose Ness
Rona
Head
Hoy
South
Ronaldsay
Burwick
Old Head
Pentland Firth
Stroma
Scrabster
John 'o' Groats
Duncansby
Head

Kinnairds Head

GRAMPIAN

MOUNTAINS

SCOTLAND

To Lerwick

To Lerwick and Stromness

A B C

0 20 Miles
0 30 Kilometres

1

Tory
Tory Sound
Tory
Bloody Foreland
Falcar
R257
Bunbeg
Gweedore
Aran
Dungloe
GLEN
N56
DERRYVEAGH
DO

Mass
R250
Glenties
Ardara

Rossan Point
Glencolumbkille

Carrick
R263

2

Donegal

Donegal Bay
Ballyshannon
Bundoran
Belleek
N15

Erris Head
Downpatrick Head
Sligo Bay
Sligo
N16
Manorhamilton

The Mullet
Belmullet
R314
Killala Bay
Dromore West
Knocknarea
R286
Gill
LE RIM

R313
Bangor Erris
R315
Ballisadare
N4

Blacksod Bay
Crossmolina
N59
Ballina
SLIGO
N17
Lough Allen
Lough

chill Head
Ballycroy
Lough Conn
Tubbercurry
Drumshanbo

3

Mulrany
Foxford
Charlestown
Boyle
Carrick-on-Shannon
Fenagh
Drumsna

Newport
N5
Swinford
Ballaghaderreen
N5
Frenchpark
N61

Clew Bay
Clare Bay
Castlebar
N60
N84
N60
Knock
N83
ROSCOMMON
Castlerea
Tulsk

Inishturk
Louisburgh
R335
Westport
Balla
Ballyhaunis
R325
Ballymoe
N5

Inishbofin
Killary Harbour
M A Y O
Partry
Claremorris
N17
R367

Aasleagh
N59
Lough Mask
Lough Carra
Ballinrobe
R332
Dunmore
N63
Roscommon
Lough Ree
RE

4

Letterfrack
CONNEMARA NATIONAL PARK
R345
Headford
Tuam
Athleague
N55

Clifden
N59
Recess
Maam Cross
Lough Corrib
N17
N63
Mount Bellew
Athlone
N62

ne Head
Oughterard
N59
N84
GALWAY
R346
Ballinasloe
IR

Gorumna Is.
Moycullen
Claregalway
N84
Galway
N6
Orangore
Athenry
R343

A
18
B
C

Aran
Galway Bay
Kilcolgan

Mull of Oa
Glenbarr
Campbeltown
Corriecravie
Blackw

Malin Head Ballyhillin
Fenad Head
Downings Ballyliffen Carndonagh
Carrickart
eeslough Milford Buncrana
Fahan
Bridge End Muff
Londonderry
Letterkenny
Lifford
Strabane Sion Mills
Stranorlar
Castlederg
Kesh
Dromore Fintona
Irvinestown
Enniskillen
Maguiresbridge
Lisnaskea
Monaghan
Clones Newbliss
Swanlinbar
Ballyconnell Belturbet
Butler's Bridge
Ballinamore Killeshandra
Cavan
Ballinagh
Bailieborough
Kingscourt
Granard
Longford
Edgeworthstown Castlepollard
Ballymahon
Mullingar Delvin
Moate Kinnegad
Rochfortbridge
Kilbeggan Edenderry
Tullamore Daingean

Moville
Portrush Bushmills Ballycastle
Portstewart
Coleraine
Limavady Ballymoney
Cushendall
Dungiven Garvagh Kilrea
Portglenone Ballymena
Maghera
Magherafelt Randalstown
Cookstown Moneymore
Omagh
Dungannon Coalisland
Aughnacloy Portadown
Clogher Armagh Tandragee
Markethill
Keady Belleek
Newtownhamilton Bessbrook
Ballybay Crossmaglen Newry
Castleblayney
Shercock
Carrickmacross Dundalk
Ardee
Dunleer
Collon
Slane Drogheda
Navan
Trim Balbriggan
Skerries
Dunshaughlin Ashbourne
Enfield Swords
Kilcock Clonee
Lucan DUBLIN
Lexlip

NORTHERN IRELAND
LONDONDERRY
TYRONE
FERMANAGH
MONAGHAN
CAVAN
MEATH
WEST MEATH
PUBLIC OF IRELAND

ANTRIM
Larne
Island Magee
Ballyclare
Antrim Carrickfergus Whitehead
Newtownabbey Belfast Lough
BELFAST Holywood Bangor Donaghadee
Lisburn Comber Newtownards
Lurgan Saintfield
Craigavon Dromore
Banbridge Ballynahinch Killyleagh
Portaferry
DOWN Strangford
Downpatrick
Rathfriland Castlewellan
Warrenpoint Newcastle St. John's Point
Kilkeel
Dundalk Bay
Castlebellingham
Dunany Point

IRISH SEA

Mull of Kintyre Fair Head Sanda
North Channel
Belfast Lough
Strangford Lough